To my favorite Cousin,
So great spending so great
times together. Hi to
the kids, Love Jeanie

THE WALK

THROUGH HELL

The Walk Through Hell

True Story of a WWII Courier

by "Mila"

as told to Jean C. Colp

Unlimited Publishing

Bloomington, Indiana

ACKNOWLEDGEMENTS

Thanks to Mike Cedic, who sat with me for so many hours, telling a story that had given him nightmares for years, and made me weep many times. His own sons had never before heard the details of his horror and sorrow, until he finally made them known through this book as a part of history.

Thanks to Richard West, the English author of the book *Tito*, who described in such detail the lay of the land and the political complications in the Balkans during the Second World War. His book helped many of us to better understand the religious complications and the many factions involved in that little known land.

Thanks to William Greenleaf, a gifted editor in Gilbert, Arizona, who helped me smooth out the rough edges and encouraged me.

—Jean C. Colp

FOREWORD

AMERICA, WAKE UP

To All People Worldwide

That's Mike Cedic's message: to spread the ideals of America, the only place on earth where people can speak out with real freedom. He wants peace, and knows from personal experience about killing.

Who are the people of the Balkans? Most of us have learned something about their politics, and who was fighting whom, in the 60 years since World War II. Few, however, learned much about the Balkans until the recent murders in Kosovo, with the people fighting each other. Who are these people, and who were they fighting in World War II?

Thanks to a recommendation from his lawyer, Mike Cedic came to me in 1999 to write this exciting story. For more than a year we met often, and this Serbian native told me of his true experience as a teenage courier in WWII. Amazed, I took down all the notes in shorthand while this book spawned in my thoughts, my heart, and my hands. Many times, he repeated the same buried adventures, bringing them to life. He and his wife, Dorothy, visited Serbia again during the year to verify the memories with living relatives.

Mike was born as Miodrag Cedic in Serbia in 1925. Mila (his Serbian familiar name) soon learned that his family came from well-known landowners who cared for their land, their families and the villagers who worked hard for them. His early life was one of love, especially from Baba, his devoted grandmother. She taught him history and dignity.

By the late 1930s, rumors, news of war and Hitler's grasp for power, increased by the day, until war came to the family's door. Fortunately, with family connections to save his life, he became a Serbian courier for General Draza Mihailovic, Minister of Defense of Yugoslavia. From then on, teenager Mila ran many dangerous missions alone, becoming part of the conflict in the Balkans. Mila's strength of character, daring attitude and determination carried him through.

Today, Mike (Mila) Cedic has a deep need to tell his message. Literacy and sophistication were rare in that country of hard working people, many of whom had no formal education, had never traveled more than a few miles from home, and never trusted anyone else. Who are these people? Reading this book will answer many questions. It will give us all a new understanding of the Balkans and other ethnic countries, rarely in the news until now, yet directly affecting our lives.

Family Members:

Miodrag Cedic: nickname, Mila (main character)

Paternal Grandfather: Cedomir Milonovic, hero in WWI, nickname Ceda. He married Milica, known to family as Baba (grandmother) to Mila. They had 10 children: two living daughters, Stenoslva and Milojka; and four sons, Svetislav, Svetolik, Svetomir, (Mila's uncles) and Sretein Milanovic, called Tata (father). Sretein is father of Mila. Selimka is the wife of Sretein and mother of Mila. She is called Majka, meaning mother. Sretein and Selimka also have two daughters, Drgica and Jelica, sisters of Mila. Mila's maternal Grandfather is Latiska Jovanovic, called Deda, father of Selimka and a son, Budimir, who became a senator.

PROLOGUE

The Walk Through Hell

Was that me? I clapped my hands over my mouth praying the guards didn't hear me. My own screams had awakened me. Sweat ran down my face despite the cold and I tried to catch my breath.

I looked around in the dim light. Somber, haunting eyes of the sick and starving prisoners looked my way. Used to disturbances, they fell back asleep.

The nightmare continued. Awake, I could still hear the whistling in the air and the explosion of shells and dirt all around me, sounds of death. I kept struggling to swallow with a paralyzed throat.

Hitler will go to hell. His cruelty and fanaticism must end. His maniacal need to conquer Europe has destroyed it. I've lost my freedom, my inheritance, my land and family, and maybe my life. Even if I get out of this rat hole, I can never go home to Serbia.

Should I try to sing softly, as my precious Baba taught me to do when I was afraid? Out of the question. I can hear her warnings that people must stop their mistrust and killing to ever find peace. Why am I still here when so many are dead? I'm young and I need to live. God help me.

I feel my tired eyes closing in the silence.

What happened to that innocent boy called "Mila?"

Chapter 1

"Miodrag, get up, get up." My Grandmother stood over me, lightly shaking my arm, her sweet voice a whisper so as not to wake the others.

"Oh, Baba, must I? It's so dark," I pleaded and pulled the warm covers up to my chin.

"You must get up and wash your face and hands. I cannot kiss you good morning unless you wash up. Miodrag, I'm going to teach you an amazing story of your people. It's time to start learning who you are. History is a wonderful adventure."

"It is?"

"It is, my darling. Go now. I put water in your basin for you. And comb out those messy curls after you dress. And wear a coat. It's so cold this morning."

I grumbled, crawled out of my cozy bed hating the icy floor hitting my warm bare feet. Reluctantly, I went to the bowl and washed my face and hands so Baba would let me kiss her hands, sometimes even her feet.

I followed her down the hall to her cozy quarters. She was slightly bent over from age but still elegant. She smelled sweetly and I loved to feel her long, beautiful dresses of silk. I was five years old and adored my Baba.

"Oh, you look so fine, a real little gentleman. Mila, you will achieve great things in your life." She kissed me on my forehead and my cheeks until my face felt hot with pleasure. She gently ran her hands through my tight, unruly curls and pinched my chubby cheeks. Before the sun slanted through the window, she started to talk to me beside her fireplace with the kindling just starting to throw out a little heat. Her eyes looked directly into my eyes and proceeded to tell me a confusing story.

"The first Serbs came to Europe with the Huns in the fourth century to a land they named White Serbia but encountered the Turks who tried to enslave them. Your ancestor, Simonovic, I think that was the name, later went back to Siberia when they heard of open land where they could be free. They stayed several years, but because the rocks and terribly cold climate was too hard for farming, they came back to settle in what is now Montenegro.

"A man named Petar and his son, Milan, left Montenegro to escape the Greeks who wanted to enslave them and their vicious enemy, the Turks who wanted to kill them. They were your father's people who came here to this beautiful country in 1617.

"Your great-grandfather, Milan settled in Kragavic. He formed two villages, named upper and lower Milanovac, peopled by pagans and farmers. This land was near Kosovo. Later they called it Gornjimelanovich. Even then, they were very stubborn and wouldn't listen to anybody outside their own tribe or state.

"Mila, listen to me. You don't get breakfast until I finish!" She took my chin roughly in her delicate hands and spoke into my face. "Those people always said, 'Don't tell us what to do,' and Mila, sometimes you are the same way, so stubborn! You don't always get to have your own way!"

My lower lip went out and my eyes focused on the carpet. I hated not to please my Baba.

"You come from a long line of strong people, my Mila," she went on.

"The Battle on the Plain of Kosovo was our greatest defeat by a very narrow margin in 1389. Imagine many hundreds of Serbian knights, whole armies dying along with our hopes for freedom on that legendary battlefield. Our Prince Lazar and the Turkish Sultan Amurath were both brutally killed. The deaths brought great revenge on both countries lasting for five centuries of Ottoman Turkish occupation. They forced their life styles on us all during the medieval period. Legend, poems and songs glorified our loss and built up our strengths. Oh, Mila, our history is filled with the strife and horror of politics. I pray we have learned for the future.

"We never forget our anniversary of St. Vitus' Day when we pray for the soul of Prince Lazar and the many heroes. Remember my son, on *Vidovdan*, no cuckoo sings and during the hours of darkness, the rivers run red with blood.

"Our Christian monasteries carried on our Orthodox religion rejecting the Muslim and Roman Catholic for the most part and became one of our focal points in our national culture just as today. These legends and struggles led to hope for the future and survival. That is an important part of your heritage, my boy, to be respected all your life. Now, we are finished today."

Baba and I stepped downstairs to the big, warm kitchen where she went about making my special breakfast as she did every morning. Our young kitchen girl helped the cook who stood at the stove humming to herself. Beside her stood Baba who never relied on the cook to make the eggs just right for me.

Baba separated the eggs into a bowl, using only the white part in my special dish. Carefully, she poured in the fresh milk, corn flour, and cinnamon just for my taste. Oh, how I loved the smell of the egg mixture striking the sizzling frying pan. I felt content as I sipped my cup of cocoa while I watched her finish dishing up my breakfast. How good she was to me, preparing whatever I asked for.

My pretty Aunt Milojka, her long, light brown hair swinging, scurried into the kitchen bringing more fresh eggs in from the chicken coop. She smiled at me, "Good morning, sweet child," and pinched my cheek but not too hard. I looked up as the rest of the family came downstairs for breakfast one by one.

Tata, my father, stacked logs on the fire. My Majka handed my baby sister over to Aunt Milojka while she checked on the cook. Our family gathered at the table, dishing up the food, everyone talking all at once about their business of the day.

Father then turned to me and asked, "Well, Miodrag, how did your first session of history go? I don't think five years old is too early to start learning.

"I love the study, Tata."

"You come from prominent people, rich people. You must pay attention at all times. Your world will extend way beyond our little village, Kamenica, or our neighbors in Kulina, or Aleksinac and Krusevac where your cousins, Vladislav and Zivadin live. Can you repeat the names of the villages?"

"Yes, Tata." I felt such love and respect for him. But I couldn't understand why Baba would tell me about all those old dead people and I didn't dare ask.

Aunt Milojka wrapped the blanket around the baby to keep her warm and smiled over at me "He's always been so curious and smart. He'll do just fine." Her voice sounded like music to me.

She turned to Majka, "Remember, Silimka, when Mila was a still a toddler, he asked so many questions that you said he must not even belong to us. But he couldn't have been switched at birth because we saw him born right here at home," her pleasant laughter made me laugh, too.

"With no doctor, don't forget." My majka's voice sounded pleasant, her dark eyes happy for a change. "And when he was born, being the first, you all wanted him named after yourselves and argued over it. And remember when his Baba was visiting in the next village last year, and Mila insisted he wanted to see her? I said, 'No' but he kept begging nicely and wouldn't give up. When I gave in and said I'd take him, his little voice cried out, 'Goody, I'm going to see my Baba!' And then you teased me, Milojka. You said I was too easy with him." Majka set her face on her sister-in-law. Her black eyebrows raised and her lips closed tight.

"Well, all I said was that he's so persuasive, he'll make a good politician like your brother," my Aunt Milojka said, "he is so good at getting his own way." She looked up at my Majka and smiled. Majka's eyebrows closed together and frowned. I looked from one woman to the other. Were they going to be mad at each other?

"I remember, Miss Milojka," she said sarcastically, " when Mila was two years old, how you challenged me because he was still being breast fed. He positively insisted, and I wanted to."

"But at least you finally started feeding him some solid food when he was a year old. No wonder he's so skinny." Milojka teased her, again. Majka firmly scowled at her. I couldn't figure out if they were friends or not. Tata and Baba didn't seem concerned about the two women in the slightest.

Aunt Milojka smiled at Majka sweetly, "Now you're going to have another baby. I'm excited for you, Silimka, really I am. Remember last year when Mila was four years old and found out a baby sister had been born? He threw a fit and said, "I'm the baby, I don't want anyone else." That brought a smile to all of them.

Aunt Milojka turned and said to me. "No, more, Mila. You're getting to be a big boy and you need to become a person in your own right because you will soon have another sister or brother. A girl will honor you and call you 'Bata,' a title of respect. If it's a boy, you'll have someone to play with besides your cousins."

I thought to myself, I'm used to the cousins. Vladislav was about three years older, a big, strong fellow, and Zivadin, was less than two years older. But I couldn't quite understand that I'd have to share with another child in my own house. Majka already put most of her attention on Drgica, my little sister, just learning to walk.

"Time to go to work, ladies," my Tata said quietly, scooting his chair away from the table. Baba never said a word to the two younger women while she cleared the table and sent me to fetch water from the pump on the back porch for the girl to wash dishes.

I set the pail of water down on the floor. I looked up at Baba's smiling face. "That's a good boy, Mila. You're getting better

about spilling the water. Such a big load for a such a little boy."
She bent over, and ran her hands through my curls.

"I'm not a baby, anymore, Baba, but I don't want another
baby. Will it be another sister?"

"We don't know, but you'll always be the responsible 'Bata' to
your little sister. Bata is a title of respect, Mila. That's why you
must learn the history of our people." I stared up into her face.
She looked beautiful to me. Her hair shined pure white, and her
bright eyes were soft and full of love.

I watched as Tata kissed Baba as he did every morning. The
man brought around his horse for my father to go supervise
his farms surrounding our property and the village. From the
living room window, I watched his big black horse carry him
out of sight.

The history lessons continued every day except Sundays. I
cheerfully jumped out of bed every morning before sunrise. The
servant brought up cold water in a basin for my early washing
up made tolerable by the comfort of Baba's kisses all over my
clean face. Because of my affection for her, I looked forward
to the lessons even though I couldn't always put the stories
together.

One morning during lessons my attention turned as I stared
out the window to see new leaves coming alive on the trees. A
silence brought my attention to alert. My eyes swung back to
her face from the window.

"Now listen, little Mila," her voice became so serious. "Our
land has always survived in turmoil and the end is not in sight.
Now all of Europe is suffering from famine and hard times.
Thousands and thousands died in the War. Many people have
died of starvation since the War but our families are fortunate as
we have our farms to live off of. Now the Germans are sneaking
up on our land once again. I fear war and death, Mila. Don't
be alarmed, but I hope I don't live to see another war like the
Great War. I would rather die first."

I felt the earth shake under me. I knew what death meant, or thought I did. I'd seen farm animals die. "No, Baba, don't ever say that. You mustn't ever leave me."

"That's why you must learn, my dear boy. I won't be here forever. I've seen so much cruelty and death in my time. When you get older, I'll show you. You must follow in your family footsteps and do what you can for your country. Do you promise?"

"I promise, Baba."

"Then we continue."

The history lessons became an adventure for me just as Baba promised. I awoke to wash and dress myself each day to go to her comfortable rooms. We sometimes sat at the table with the lace cloth, or I sat on a little stool staring up to her beautiful face sitting in front of her fire.

She told me how Christian forces tried to push the Turks out of the Balkans forcing the Serbs to rebel against their Turkish overlords. Many Serbs migrated to Austrian-ruled southern Hungary splitting them in half. I began to see different peoples in my mind and tell them apart from each other.

"The refugees founded new monasteries for the monks that brought Christianity to them. Austrian forces took Serbian regions from Turkey. But the Jesuits following the army persuaded the Serbs in the south to hate the Austrians as well as the Turks. The Serbs suffered attacks from soldiers on every side."

I awoke before dawn. I could see the village downhill still barely stirring to the new day with only a few lantern lights showing. I hurried to dress and wash up for my kisses. Baba would expect me by her fire shortly.

"I believe our rich soil and minerals prompted all our neighbors to covet this land. The Serbs in what was Southern Hungary prospered on their farms in the Morava River region north of where we are now but years later in the 1800s, the Turks took control again. As a people who stuck together, the Serbs did open schools and made some progress. Collections of Serbian folk songs, dances, and poems awoke pride in our history and traditions."

She made me study and answer questions. It was Baba who saw that I always said my prayers. And it was my Baba who taught me not just to obey people but to think for myself. She criticized the German people for being too obedient and not expressing themselves. She insisted I study God's laws about my precious soul and how it can guide me.

She pointed out the window, "See the sun, just one sun. Without it we would die. You only have one soul, Mila and without it, you will die." After the sun went down, I went down on my knees to say special prayers to God before I went to sleep.

Baba's soft voice sounded like music to me. Sometimes, she became emotional, pacing the floor waving her hands in the air. My eyes followed her every move.

"The tribe didn't want to pray in Roman or Greek, both early enemies, and refused to take on the Roman Catholic religion, so they wrote the New Testament of the Bible in Slovenic, the old language from the non-Christian days. The Serbian Orthodox Church was established. That brought religious knowledge to our people. They adopted new names, not the Greek or Italian names of their old hated conquerors."

"Your great grandfather was a relative to Karadjordje Petrovic, a notorious leader called 'Black George.' At that time, great grandfather changed the family name from Petrovic to 'Cedic' when they decided to become Orthodox Christians. Then the bishops decided each family would adopt a saint. Our family took 'John the Baptist'. When a family member wishes to marry, they must choose a person with a different saint's name. That's a church law and to this day marriages are based on that law."

She looked into my face so intently for several minutes, she made me squirm. Then she put her finger to her wrinkled cheek and continued, "Maybe it was to keep down marriages within families. I personally always thought the people just wanted to keep their dinars in the family," her beautiful smile turned into her soft laughter at her little joke.

She became serious again and grabbed my hands. "Oh, my darling boy, you must listen, study and learn. You know your mother's father; your Deda is also rich. He presented her as a good wife choice for your father even though she is six years older than he is. I know you don't like the old man very much, neither do I, but his big store runs at a nice profit and employs many people. Times have been hard with the depression and many people would have gone hungry if it weren't for your grandfather and your Tata helping men earn food for their families from our precious land. Do you understand?

"Oh, how I wish you could have known my husband, Ceda, your other grandfather." Her eyes looked up and her face became radiant.

"I can just picture him now, so tall and poised on his big, black stallion holding his riding crop. He was so handsome and is a well-known hero of the War twenty years later. Our family is the richest in the village, in the area, maybe even with the best in Nis. Our beautiful farms have belonged to us for generations. This is where I grew up and it was nearly completely destroyed by our enemies when I was just a little girl. My soul, my son, would you swear to God and to your Baba, promise to never to repeat such an offense?"

I didn't really understand but I did swear to God.

"My father built it back up with the biggest orchards and the best plum wine in the area. We exported our plum wine all over Europe, to some famous hotels and spas, just as your father does in the good times. You have responsibilities to carry on this tradition. They passed this land down to me, as I had no brothers. And, Mila, I'll pass it down to you and your own family when I die."

"To me?" I couldn't understand what that meant.

"Yes, to you. Your father is in charge but I never signed the land over to him. For years I thought your grandfather would come back to me."

"Where was he?"

"I will tell you in good time, my little Mila. You have so much to learn. Now listen. By that time, in the 18th century, the Serbians became more prosperous in this fertile valley watered by our precious Morava River. The monasteries trained scholars and writers who pulled our people even closer together, even though most peasants couldn't read. Russia helped fight battles along side the Serbs, then we got into a war with the Turks again, so the Serbs started their own militia to protect their frontier."

I turned six years old on May 5th. I watched my father proudly ride out that morning. Maybe someday I would sit so high and straight as the owner of all the land would. Now, I just couldn't wait for my party.

I asked Baba about our house. "Your father rebuilt the old house and moved another one beside it from the village. That was just two years before you were born, Mila. Then he had them converted into one big home for his little family including Milojka and me. He owns the house."

I explored our property with Baba, seeing it with different eyes for the first time. The old part of the house has food storage and cutting areas, the family kitchen, dining area, and sitting room all with fireplaces to heat them. Each big bedroom has its own fireplace upstairs. The newer part of the house is where we gather with the adults in the great room showing the best furniture for entertaining. A bigger kitchen took the burden of large dinners and groups.

The upstairs bedrooms in the newer house are where our Uncles and their families and other guests stayed. I loved to sneak up there with its big beds and beamed ceilings even though I wasn't supposed to be in there. A reddish-brown tiled roof covered both sections.

For my birthday, my older cousins and their parents from other villages gathered here for a party. I was so excited, I stood outside the huge double door of the company house. Everyone kissed hands of each other. I stared at gifts of chocolate or even dinars, the custom for a get-together.

My Majka scurried around ordering her servants to serve the special dishes on a long table with the finest cloths. Oh, it smelled so good. I could hardly wait to eat. All us boys sat separately from the adults and I proceeded to tell them some of our history I'd been learning. Vladislov, his thick hair falling in his face, and Zivadin just looked at me as if I was a strange creature. Baba took me aside later and explained I was "showing off" and it wasn't necessary to share the stories unless someone asked to know.

That night, sleepy from all the excitement, I thought, Why learn all that history if I couldn't tell it to anyone?

⌐

Baba's stories became the highlight of my day. I began to understand these were my people, my history. I decided I really wanted to be a warrior and protect my land.

The weather proved too sunny to stay in so I started playing in the yard. I spied the perfect long, limb broken off from a tree, and pretended it was a sword. I transformed into the fierce warrior, hearing sounds of war, winging and stabbing the shining sword into the invisible enemy.

My Majka appeared in the doorway of the main house, broke into my violent play world, and yelled at me "Miodrag, come in the house this minute."

Slowly, I trudged into the great room. Her voice sounded angry. My head went down when I saw she held a switch up. She dragged me down the corridor into the smaller family room, "I don't want you in battle, or even playing at war. You will be a lawyer and senator like my brother Budimir. You will make peace for us."

She started on my backside with the switch, only to meet head on with an angry grandmother. Baba grabbed me away.

"Silimka, you will not touch that boy again with the switch. He has his own mind and we will guide him, not punish him. I will guide him myself."

I'd never heard her voice so harsh. My Majka stopped, turned pale, and backed off from Baba's unexpected wrath. Baba's voice was icy cold. "He doesn't need pain now. He may feel pain in war someday. Now Selimka, go lay down."

"Is Majka sick?" I asked Baba.

"No, she's not sick. You know she's going to have another baby brother or sister for you, my little Mila, and she's not feeling so well. You mustn't upset her. She'll feel better in a couple of months."

The next morning after our private time by the fireplace we went downstairs for breakfast. I asked Baba, "Will I still be the Prince in our house?

She looked right into my eyes and said, "My precious boy, you will always be first. You are the leader, the Bata. You will help take care of your new sibling. It will be fun."

She went right on with stirring up my white eggs with the milk, flour and my favorite cinnamon as she did every morning.

My Majka slowly spooned food into my baby sister's mouth. "Let her start feeding herself, Selimka. She's two years old," suggested Baba. Drgcia was just learning to say a few words. Sometimes, I talked and played with her and enjoyed her laughing at my antics.

One day, I became intrigued with her hands so tiny and perfect. I asked Baba, "Why does she have perfect fingers and one of my fingers is so crooked?"

"You have one special finger that no one else has, Mila. A bone is missing at the top of your index finger. Someday you will realize that finger makes you unique, different from other people on earth."

I watched my Tata leave every morning until finally he lifted me up to let me ride with him. We rode into the countryside filled with orchards, wide fields, livestock, the vineyards, hills, and water. I became more aware of the land. Tata told me it had a richer soil than Switzerland or Austria, with the richest forests in Europe in Bosnia. Within two to three miles, many kinds of fruit grew wild in the hills and forests. I learned the Balkans has four seasons and pleasant climate.

The history lessons continued. "A rebel leader named Milos Obrenovic set up the murder of Karadjordje Petrovic, 'Black George' and sent his head to the Turkish sultan as part of his takeover. He turned out to be strong even though he had to overcome the bloody rivalry between the Karadjordjevic and Obrenovic clans. He did eventually bring trade and helped the peasants improve their farms. But Turkey wouldn't let him rule freely, and he quit in 1838.

"Prince Mihajlo Obrenovic, the son of Milos, took over our government in 1860. He was Western-educated and won the withdrawal of Turkish garrisons in 1867. He started industrial development even though 80 percent of Serbia's million people were still illiterate peasants. Serbia gained more freedom and began to raise scholars. Now, remember these names, Mila. Obradovic and Karadzic. My grandfather knew these people. They promoted translations and songs and poems to spread to the people. Their efforts greatly helped the people recognize their nationhood with their own language, religion, and regions.

"Karadzic translated the New Testament again in the language of the people. He started a regular army to win the rest of the lands from the Turks, but eventually he too, was assassinated. I hate to say this, my Mila, but our whole history has been one of crimes, ignorance, and misfortunes. His cousin, Milan became Prince in 1868, and became the first king of modern Serbia in 1882, but his politics made him unpopular and he quit in 1889. His teenage son Aleksandar, carried on his father's unpopular wishes to align Serbia with pro-Austro-Hungarian policies.

"Because of the scandals he brought, and strict and sometimes foolish rule, Aleksandar's military officers murdered him and his wife in 1903. Europeans were horrified at the killings, but the people in Belgrade celebrated. So then King Petar Karadjordjevic, remember that name, Mila from before the Obrenovics? Anyway, he came back from exile to take over the throne and helped restore the constitution.

"He improved the finances, the trade, and education, and he succeeded to turn Serbia away from the Austria-Hungary hold and turned toward Russia. He made an agreement with Bulgaria to export goods to break the Austria-Hungary monopoly. Vienna put a tariff on livestock, Serbia's most important export. As a result, King Petar worked hard to find new trade routes and a shipping port."

Baba had a way of bringing out exciting adventures to help me understand, and she showed me old, crude maps so I could follow the countries with my fingers and imagine the huge world around us.

My Majka's father, Deda, came to our house for occasional Sunday visits. Majka told me her mother had died many years ago. One Sunday, dressed in my best suit, I had to stay in until he arrived. His fat body waddled up the walk as his driver helped him into the great room. I dreaded his entrance because he pinched my cheeks so hard that they hurt and were red for hours, it seemed. I kissed his hands as I was formally taught, but wrinkled my nose as Deda smelled bad to me.

While the grownups sat in the great room to visit, I hid behind the open door to peak through the crack and listen. Deda's bushy, gray, beard bounced up and down as his booming voice took command. I had to clap my hands over my mouth to keep back a giggle. He always took over all conversation while Tata politely sat quietly.

Even his own daughter, Selimka, my Majka seemed nervous around him. She tried to set quietly and never spoke to him after greetings except to ask if he needed something. He always wanted to eat, so she would signal the maid to bring in specially prepared pastries and coffee. He bragged over his big store in Kulina with crumbs spilling out of his full mouth. He always repeated how hard he worked and how rich he was. Crumbs and coffee drops stuck on his beard and fell in his lap and his coffee cup threatened to spill any second. And he bragged about his son, Budimer, the senator and the influence he brought for the family all the time.

My Tata nodded politely and would try to answer a direct question but got interrupted every time. Poor Tata looked so uncomfortable.

"I have my contacts in Germany," Deda went on. "France shouldn't have pulled out after the War even though they ruined the economy before they left. They should have held a firmer rule over Germany. Now a new Furher, Adolf Hitler, a fervent Nazi, has taken over the government, and I hear he's a fanatic. He practically started the Nazi party, but his only talent is to give great speeches believing the average person is as stupid as he is. He's convincing them the Jews are evil and deliberately brought about Germany's defeat in the World War. He builds a colossal lie for the people and sticks to it."

He never spoke to me again after his arrival. Deda never gave anyone including his own sons or my Tata a chance to answer back. I didn't believe him or trust him at all. As I wasn't allowed to sit at their dinner table, Majka waved me out of the room, and I went upstairs to Baba's parlor bedroom.

I knocked on her door and found her in front of her huge fireplace comfortably tatting lace with the cat curled up beside her. She kissed my face and smiled at me.

"Aren't you happy you don't have to eat with that loud, boring man? I shouldn't say that as he is your grandfather and you must respect him, but that doesn't mean we have to like him."

Her crinkled face broke into a big smile and her tinkling laughter warmed my heart. The servant laid out our dinner on the table now set out in a formal manner with a lace tablecloth and candlesticks. I felt content once again.

I wondered what Deda had been like when he was young. "Baba, was this Grandfather ever in the War like Grandfather Ceda?

"Yes, dear, he spent his time stealing and securing food for the troops. He never went to the front or was in any battles like Ceda who was a great hero." She set down her fork and looked up at the ceiling.

"Deda Jovanovic's last wishes before he left the village for a dangerous post in the mountains was that his daughter, Selimka marry our third son, Svetomir, the ambitious one. But after they returned from the War, things had changed. In the village, another girl from a nice family had taken Svetomir's eye. He asked for her hand in marriage, but her father said NO, that she was too young. She had to be 17 by law. Those two were in love and promised to each other. Her father was killed in the fighting and because she had no brothers, she inherited their farm. So Svetomir married her and they still live on that farm, as you know. She's been a good wife and mother to Valdislav and Zivadin and has helped Svetimir earn respect in his area.

"So Selimka Jovanovic's father was angry and declared he'd formerly arranged with Ceda before the war that since Svetomir didn't marry Selimka, then Svetomir's younger brother, Sretein, your Tata, must marry his daughter even though she is several years older than he is. We never knew if Ceda actually made that promise or not, but sweet, loving Sretein agreed. Now we're stuck with that silly father of hers. That marriage did bring me my precious Mila." She reached over and pulled me to her for a big hug.

Chapter 2

One morning, Baba took me out of the house just as the sun spread beams of light and shadows around our yard. She looked excited. Her smile, so happy, "You have a new baby sister, dear Mila, her name will be Jelica. You may see her later when your Majka feels better. You know Mila, your Majka's only sister died during childbirth and so she loves these little girls as much as she loves you, but not as much as your Baba loves you."

"Is my Majka going to die?" I ask her. I'd heard the whispers before of her sister dying when she had a new baby. The whole thought was very scary. Baba assured me both of them were fine and took me to see the "beautiful baby." My Majka lying in bed, tried to smile at me, her face pale.

The nurse carefully pulled back the silk wrap, and I gasped when I saw the baby. It was red and ugly! Baba pinched me so I wouldn't say anything. Drgica, less than two years old, was pulling at the covers on Majka's bed, whining for some attention. Majka patted her head, then brought the new baby up to her breast. The unexpected sight made me feel sick and Baba had to drag me out of the room.

It took me a long time to put up with the crying from another little girl baby and all the attention Baby Jelica received. As soon as I could, I checked her fingers to make sure she didn't have a special finger like mine. She didn't, and I felt better. But I did eventually learn to like her as she felt so soft. Her little face filled out and became much prettier. Sometimes Majka let me feed her with the dropper. Sister Drgica thought Baby Jelica must be one of her dolls and became very possessive of her.

Baba stirred my breakfast while I was holding Baby Jelica one morning and I wondered, "Baba, where do babies come from?"

"From heaven, from God. You must always remember. Your sisters, Drgica and Jelica have a soul just like you. Your soul comes from God. Let your soul guide your heart and your brains. I learned that most important lesson from my own parents and grandparents."

The history lessons continued throughout the year, sometimes repeated many times. Aunt Milojka. who grew up listening to my Baba teaching her brothers their history lessons, questioned me and praised me when I could answer correctly.

I loved to kiss Aunt Milojka's face and run my hands through her dark hair. She was so pretty, I could just sit and stare at her. She helped my Majka with my little sisters all she could and never complained. I began to notice how she played dolls with Drgica and laughed with her when setting up her toys to play. Drgica was growing into a quiet little girl with light colored hair not quite as light red as Tata's, but she had his beautiful blue eyes. I could accept her more now that she began to look up to me and address me respectfully as Bata.

"Baba, why isn't Aunt Milojka married?

"Well, your Aunt Milojka is special and she must wait until your father or his brothers find a suitable husband for her. Don't you worry. She's young and happy here. Just enjoy her as long as she's with us."

My chores eventually broadened from just hauling in the water to gathering the eggs from the noisy hens. I hated those chickens, always trying to peck me, but I loved the dish Baba made for me from the eggs every morning. Even Majka praised me when I managed to bring them in unbroken.

Finally after much pleading, Tata allowed me to ride out on his big work wagon further out on our farm than I've ever been. My father sat straight and tall holding the reins guiding the huge, bulky horses with his foreman, Milan.

Since my earliest memories, I admired Milan like a member of the family and trusted him totally. He was bigger than Tata with showy muscles, always a twinkle in his eyes, and a big black mustache. I listened to these men and learned.

Acres of orchards in straight rows grew fruits, and long rows of colorful vegetables thrived in the dark soil. "Tata, does everyone have so much land?"

"No, son, our orchards are one of the largest that Serbians own anywhere. There are some German, Austrian and Hungarian families who own great estates and run them like the feudal lands of old. They helped Serbia get out from under the Turks but slowly took over as much as they could."

"Tata, when can I ride the horses by myself?"

"When you are older and we teach you." He explained the sharecroppers system from Roman times to me; how people lent their land to others to work and then took most of the profits. The Yugoslav government tried to change that situation, but gave the peasants plots to own too small to support their families. The peasants remained poor.

"We provide work for many men and women in our villages, and we treat them well. I'll teach you and you'll understand when you're older, my son. After the War, we couldn't get enough dinars for our seed crops and couldn't borrow anywhere. Without these workers who sometimes have to work just for food, we could not raise our vegetables, take care of the animals, harvest the grain, and pick the fruit and nuts from our trees."

I loved the old stories but Tata talking to me made our farm seem important and real today, a business that would be mine in the future although I didn't really want to be a farmer. I knew I had a lot to learn.

"Are we really the richest family in the area?" I asked him.

"We are all the same family in your Baba's eyes, but actually my older brother, your Uncle Svetomir is the richest man in the area, even richer than me. He's a landowner and helps his people keep within the limits of the law. He's very important to the King. My parents choose a good wife for me, and your Majka's brothers are very rich, too. Now Milodrag, remember, we do not discuss dinar matters with anyone outside this house, not even your cousins, do you hear?"

My cousin Vladislav bragged to me how he could read books in school just to make me feel bad. I desperately wanted to go to school and begged Tata who replied, "Your cousins are older. You will wait to go to school for another year, Miodrag, when you are seven. Now you will learn from your Baba." He thought a moment. "You may ask cousin Vladislav to teach you to read."

With his permission, I pestered the cousins every chance I got. Vladislav proudly showed me his schoolbooks. He taught me the alphabet, and helped me with the simple words. Reading seemed a magical work to me.

Baba gave me some tattered cloth children books she'd saved from my father's childhood. My head hung over the little books trying to remember the words. One morning Father asked me to read a few pages to the family as we were finishing breakfast. Pleased with the attention, I stumbled through, peeking up to see if they were listening. Their eyes were riveted on me in interest. I felt a thrill up my spine. Then a strange word appeared and I got stuck. I turned to Baba, "Baba, what is this word, I can't get it."

"Oh, dear boy, I don't know. I never learned to read. I can't help you with reading the words, only the meaning."

I stared at her, my mouth open. Could that be true? My Baba can't read?

"Most girls didn't learn to read then and only a few now. I learned the history from memory taught to me by my Tata."

My father looked at her proudly. "And she is more educated that many people who read and don't comprehend the words."

He turned back to me, smiling, "Your Baba is smarter than all of us. Remember that, my boy. We all have the greatest respect for her. She's the family historian and you must carry on for her. Do you understand?"

I shyly looked over at Baba standing by the fire and nodded my head. I stared at her. She looked beautiful to me with her shiny white hair, her striking blue eyes and still pretty face. She was tall for a woman, taller than my Majka, but not as tall as my father. Her smile shined down at me, her eyes full of love. From that moment, I understood and respected my beloved Baba all the more. I also felt important learning the history of our country. Oh how I loved my Baba!

When my father dressed in riding clothes, formally introduced me to our two best riding horses, my heart pounded in my chest. My seventh birthday was coming up and appearing brave to my father was important.

I stood staring at Vidian and Dana, the most awesome, scary riding horses in our stable. I'd always been warned to stay distanced from these elegant horses, but now I could actually feel their breath and smell their shiny coats.

"Look Mila," Tata introduced them. "This black stallion is Vidian, from a famous line of Thoroughbred horses in our family for a hundred years and our great breeder. Dana, the beautiful brown mare is of the same breed."

The stallion Vidian, tall and shiny, featured a big star on his forehead. His eyes staring right in my face grew big and he snorted threatening me raising a pang of fear. He was truly stubborn, stamping his feet, spitting into the air, and throwing his massive head back in defiance. He scared me silly.

Dana, smaller and friendlier than the imposing Vidian, soon nuzzled me when I petted her nose. Tata obviously choose Dana for me, boosted me up on her back and start teaching me. He gently showed me how to hold and handle the reins. I had ridden some of the calmer workhorses bareback before but now felt a swell of pride mounted such a beautiful animal.

After many lessons with Tata and Milan, I was on my own. Dana's stirrups often were too high, so I would lead her over beside a fence and climb up a couple of rungs to get my foot in the stirrup and swing over. When no fence was near, that sensitive animal on her own, bent her front legs nearly to the ground so I could reach the stirrup and swing my leg over her easily.

Milan continued the riding lessons with me until I was flying over the grounds and fields ignoring warnings from everyone except Baba. She came out to watch me, clapping her hands in glee.

"Oh, my Mila. You ride just like Ceda. He would be so proud. He taught all his boys to ride."

She shook hands with the tall, rugged Milan, my Tata's trusted foreman. "I trust you Milan, to take good care of my reckless boy." I listened and learned from the patient Milan to make my father proud of me.

My red haired father was known all over the country for his beautiful singing voice. Baba told me when dinars were tight after the War, he went to Belgrade and was hired to sing on the radio. And what really got me excited to hear was that he had been invited to the United States to sing but he gave in to his new bride, as she was too afraid for him to go.

He was always in demand, and when I was old enough to be invited to go with him, I felt very grown up. He often sang at our family gatherings as well. He knew all the old traditional melodies from Macedonia and Bosnia and the admiration from everyone made me very proud of him. Little by little, I realized I couldn't carry a tune at all and more embarrassing, I couldn't get the hang of the traditional dances, either. A sense of rhythm was never given to me.

⤶

My history lessons with Baba were often repeated over and over to help me memorize it all. "Our King Petar respected and communicated with Austria. He restored the constitution, put Serbian finances in order, and made changes in trade and education. The Cedic family owned land in Austria and over the years helped build a theological school and churches. Then King Petar attempted to pull away from the growing hold Austria had over Serbia and looked toward Russia."

"Oh, my dear boy, you'll learn later in your studies what a turmoil this whole area was in. After 1875, both Austria-Hungary and Russia were trying to take over the dying Ottoman Empire. Russia wanted all the Orthodox nations like our Serbia, Montenegro, Greece, Bulgaria and Romania." She pointed the countries out on newer maps introducing me to an even wider world.

"The Orthodox refugees told of such cruelty and horrors, that Serbia and Montenegro went to war with Turkey again but were driven back after the deaths of about 12,000 Orthodox Christians. Then the Russians offered to fight along side the Serbians. Women in long lines were hauling ammunition up from the coast to use in twelve-and-a-half-pounder guns. For all the people's strength and loyalty, the Austrians still treated us like an inferior race.

"Oh, my son, so much of our history shows the important role religion plays. You must observe this as you go. And the warlike Croatians who think they are so pure, have nearly the same language as the Serbs. It's mostly just a difference in political tendencies and religion rather than blood. We don't give service to the Roman Pope as they do. I cannot teach you why we don't all get along. You must observe and learn for yourself."

"From 1804, a Serbian Orthodox Monastery named Siremska in the city of Mitrovica in Serbia had been under Turk rule. In 1912, Austrians helped Serbs to win that territory back so the Siremsja Monastery would be ours again. My fourth son, your father, was just 12 years old when I wanted him to go into the church. But the country was in turmoil. People worried Austria had gained too much authority, stolen a monopoly on our exports, and was taking over entirely." That could not happen.

Chapter 3

1932-1933

When I was seven, my family finally made arrangements for me to enter grade school in Kulina, a bumpy wagon ride two miles from our village Kamenica. It looked huge to me. My eyes bulged out in new excitement. My Tata pointed out to me the building was made out of bricks covered with plaster. We had to climb many steps to get in the front door. Our two Slatojes, a man and wife teacher team were very nice, but strict. We addressed them both as "Sir Teacher Slatoje." School commenced in September and ended about June 20th.

Baba said to me one morning, "My darling boy, my Mila. I've been thinking. You are going to school now. No more lessons from me. From now on, you must learn and obey your Sir Teacher Slatojes." She held my head, looked at me, then kissed me on the forehead.

"But now, come. One final lesson, the most important of all. I have to show you something. My dear, my son, you must promise to your Baba." She looked so nervous; her face white.

"You must always remember for all times." she said. I stood there baffled but managed to promise her.

My skin prickled. What was so terrible to bring this look on her pale face, her voice quivering? I feared for myself and for her.

"You must come with me," and she took me by the hand, leading me quite far out on the farm to foundations left from of old buildings. On the way, she talked, "When I was a small girl almost seven years old in 1878, the Turks came again, this time right into our area. My father was in the mountains fighting for our freedom. My grandparents stood fast against the hated Turks and refused to be shoved off their land.

"But my majka grabbed me and everything she could carry in our wagon. We raced into Krusevac, the capitol at the time and lived with relatives for two or three months. Finally, Napoleon leading French troops passed through our area on his retreat from southern Russia and pushed the Turks out."

Her hands gripped me tightly. She continued, "My mother took me back home when she thought it was safe. I'll never forget the horrible sight of ruined homes and dead cows. Most of the Kamenica smelled of smoke and smoldering thatch. Thirty families were burned out, and many were dead or disappeared. On this property our house had been destroyed.

"She hunted for my grandparents, crying out their names, searching through many of the other burned buildings and ruins. We found no sign of them so just the two of us had to live in a crude, little building, still standing where my parents had kept their wagons and firewood."

Her voice went up almost like a young girl. I could plainly see her as a child like Drgica. She swallowed and continued her tale. I felt paralyzed looking up at her stricken face forcing the story out.

"It was August so we lived off the fruit orchards and gardens. One day soon after, while she was working in the kitchen vegetable garden, she called to me to go to an old wooden barrel and roll it closer to the shed to put in the new cabbages. I skipped over to two barrels. One already had pumpkins in it, so I opened the top of the other barrel and saw long, white strips and thought it was snakes. I dropped the lid and jumped backwards. I was shivering but nothing moved in the barrel. So I got up my nerve and peered in again and saw skull and bones. I started to scream and cry.

"My Mama dropped her spade and ran over. The bones showed from two sets of arms and hands each holding each other over two heads with the rest of their bodies stuffed below. My terrified Majka ran to me and started screaming, squeezing me way too tightly, crying to God and keening into the sky. It turned out to be my grandmother and grandfather cut into pieces."

Baba and I stood there crying out loud, imagining the bones of our own people as if they were in front of us.

"Mila, my son, You must always remember this for all times. You must take an oath to God and yourself. You must swear you will always remember and convey to your children and grandchildren. This murder shall always be remembered as long as the sun is shining," her voice broke again. "Promise to continue with God. Never let this horror of man killing man be forgotten for all generations."

We fell to the ground crying together, my head in her lap. Without words, we rose and she took my hand walking me slowly back to our house.

How could such terrible things happen? Baba tucked me into her bed talking softly, assuring me the incident was in the past, always to be remembered, but nevertheless in the past. She kissed me softly and tiptoed out of the room.

I pulled up the covers and tried to think of my new toy truck. A vision merged into bones rising out of the barrel, arm bones floated over me coming down on my face cutting off my air. I woke up screaming until I realized the bones were gone and my parents and Baba were standing over me, trying to calm me down.

After my Baba told me this terrible story, my innocent childhood seemed to slowly disappear. Up to now, the worst thing that ever happened to me was carelessly losing my favorite toy truck. Nightmares plagued me for months over that vision of the barrel of bones. Grisly images just clung to my mind and I dreaded sleep. But I began to understand how Baba could stand up to the thought of war. She had seen death. Would I have to see that?

⤺

The excitement of attending school at last helped wave some of the horror and sorrow away. I began to love school, my Sir

Teacher Slatojes, and the other students including my cousins. When weather permitted, the other boys and I preferred to walk and fool around together. With my head start of already knowing how to read and write, I became an excellent student in history, geography and was asked to stand and recite poems Baba had taught me.

One late Sunday afternoon after I turned eight years old, my father was visiting with all three brothers around our dining room table. I hid behind the door to listen to what they were saying. Tata's voice rose. "I just learned from my associate on the trip to Austria that the economy is somewhat better and finally we are getting more than a pittance for our crops. But politics are looming up again. A big German industrial group agreed to finance Hitler and his 800,000 Nazis. What are they thinking, dealing with that maniac?"

I couldn't hold back my curiosity and peaked around the door.

"Could he be so terrible, Sretein?" asked Uncle Svetolik, lifting his huge flask of Sipovitz to his lips. "The people and the economy seem to be in better shape. They say the Furher is a great orator and maybe he's a genius."

Svetomir teased his older brother. "Come on now, Svetolik. You've had too much of the vine. Those Nazis are ruthless and hateful."

Svetislav, the elder and wisest Uncle jumped in, his voice raising, "That Hitler is crazy, I'm telling you. I heard Hitler put on a big show in front of his Reichstag. They had a loudspeaker mounted on a statue. He stood up there and sounded like a fanatical preacher, shouting in his screechy voice. And the giant crowd of people seems devoted to him. That's a man we have to watch."

The others were all staring at him as he rarely expressed himself so strongly. They put their heads together until I couldn't hear anymore but remembered the name "Hitler."

I even mimicked Hitler at school the next day, standing on the steps and shouting in a high voice to make the boys laugh. Sir Teacher Slatoje jerked me back inside and bawled me out and told me not to mention the name Hitler again. I figured Hitler must be someone important.

Baba heard about the incident and asked my father to teach me about the beginning of the Great War as his father had taught him. I overheard Tata ask Baba if she thought I was old enough to hear it, and she said, "Yes, he's heard worse."

Tata sat me down at the family table one evening after dinner and told me this story, "Your Grandfather witnessed the circumstances and here's what he told me.

"Young Archduke Franz Ferdinand, heir apparent to the Austro-Hungarian Empire, intended to make radical reforms to save the empire, but his plans didn't set well with those with vested interests in the existing structure. The factions became even more divided.

"Then in 1908, Austria-Hungary formally annexed Bosnia and Herzegovina, Slavic provinces that Serbia wanted to keep together to be part of a Serbian led pan-Slav state. That aggressive move upset some European governments and inflamed many of the Serbian people. The Serbs mobilized but under German pressure Russia persuaded Belgrade to cease its protests. The Serbs tried to maintain its relations with Vienna, but we did prepare for a war to liberate the Serbs still living under the Turkish yoke in Kosovo, Macedonia and other regions who had been forced to become Muslims."

He stood up waving his arms.

"The upper classes were ardent patriots. They appreciated the Austro-Hungarian Empire who helped rescue and defend them against the Turkish Muslims. But they all knew deep down, it was built by conquest, intrigues, and treacheries. Along with the lower classes, the upper classes shared hatred of the oppression of the Austrians.

"King Petar invited your Grandfather Ceda, to come to Sarajevo in June 1914, to discuss the issues with him. He was told Archduke Franz Ferdinand, heir to the Hapsburg throne, now as Inspector General of the Army, had accepted an invitation to visit to inspect army maneuvers and would be in Sarajevo at the same time." Tata sat back down and lowered his voice.

"On June 28, St. Vitus' Day, the anniversary of The Battle of Kosovo, Ceda anxiously awaited with government people for the arrival of the Archduke and his retinue driving from the railroad station to the town hall. They suspected terrorists might be planning something and had placed all their police force out front and instructed the cars to drive fast past the crowds on the street.

"They arrived safely, but had survived a thrown grenade hitting the side of the car. Francis Ferdinand told how he threw himself back along with Archduchess Sofia and neither was injured. Several officers riding in the car were hurt. The cars continued to speed to the town hall.

"After the reception, General Potiorek, the Austrian Commander, pleaded with Duke Ferdinand to leave the dangerously rebellious city. They were shown the shortest way out of the city and raced along. The road to the maneuvers was shaped like the letter V, making a sharp turn to cross the River Nilgacka forcing the car to slow down.

"There, one of the conspirators took his stand. He moved toward the car from the curb, raised his automatic pistol and fired two shots. The first bullet struck Sofia in the abdomen and she died instantly. The second bullet struck the Duke close of the heart. He uttered one word, 'Sofia.' His head fell back and he died. They found later Sofia was expecting a child."

I watched Tata lower his head into both hands, his voice silent. I looked over at Baba with tears in her eyes and slowly began to realize the importance of this terrible tragedy.

"What happened then, Tata?"

He finally looked up and cleared his throat.

"The officers immediately grabbed Gavrilo Princip, the shooter, beating him over the head with the flat of their swords. The shocked observers said the officers kicked him then scraped the skin from his neck with the edges of their swords, tortured him and nearly killed him. The authorities verified who was responsible. Most of the young men were members of 'Young Bosnia' but Borijove Jevic, one of the leaders of the Noradna Odbrana, or Black Hand who helped in the plan was also arrested within minutes after the assassination. Jevic related the details immediately.

"His story was that someone sent them a clipping from a newspaper announcing that on June 28th, Archduke Ferdinand would be in Sarajevo. The conspirators saw their opportunity to protest against Austria's takeover. They carefully planned the assassination aided by dinars and guns from the Black Hand. All twenty-two men had lined up about five hundred yards apart over the whole route, armed and ready. At first, he said, the cars were traveling too fast, and concluded throwing a grenade would have killed many innocent people.

"One did try to throw a grenade and when he failed, the rest did not interfere until Princip had a second chance on the trip out. Jevic told how he went to prison with Princip who was in chains until his death. At his mock trial, Princip said he was actually aiming at the Governor of Bosnia when he accidentally hit the Archduchess Sophie.

"Sarajevo is mainly a Muslim city with a large Croatian population who hate the Serbians. Ceda heard a bishop of the Roman Catholic Church call to the crowd to hang the Serbs, that 'hundreds of hangings would not pay for the death of Ferdinand and his wife.' The bishop incensed a mob to attack the Serb owned Europa Hotel where Ceda was staying, but the King protected him. In the next few days, Serbs were attacked at random, assaulted, and even hanged."

My father had tears in his eyes. He pulled himself up and started to leave the room. Baba's voice was shaking, but she spoke directly to me, "Stop crying, Mila."

Baba said, "Ceda told me that they were going to move the assassin Princip to another prison but he made an appeal to the prison governor. Princip said, 'There is no need to carry me to another prison. My life is already ebbing away. I suggest you nail me to a cross and burn me alive. My flaming body will be a torch to light my people on their path to freedom.' "

Then her voice rose addressing her son. "Sretein, come back in here. If your son can hear this, you can, too." Tata immediately reappeared, slowly sat down with his head bowed and never said another word.

Baba continued, "Immediately, the assassination quickly prompted Austria to threaten Serbia with war unless Vienna could join in the murder investigation and suppress secret societies. Ceda knew that King Petar or the Serbian government had conspired to the assassination. He felt certain another group was behind it all. He told me the terrorists couldn't have pulled it off without help and the King ordered a very confidential investigation."

"In the city of Paracin, a Croatian named Kleficsa owned the largest poultry factory in Europe that buys the biggest turkeys and chickens to sell all over Europe. He was very rich and powerful.

"Kleficsa didn't know that King Petar wanted to do business directly in Austria without the 'greedy Kleficsa' until he invited the Bosnia Prince to visit Paracin to observe his huge business empire. During the visit, Kleficsa learned his giant monopoly may be threatened, and he desperately wanted no competition. So he contacted the Black Hand, a secret society in Belgrade and offered them large amounts of dinars to kill King Petar. Apparently, instead, the terrorists decided on their own to make their mark on their 'real' enemy, the Archduke.

"They probably were young men, Orthodox, Roman Catholic

and Muslim radicals trying to build a new Yugoslavia. Princip never admitted to being a Serb at his trial.

"Serbia tried to cooperate but wouldn't give in to Austria's demands. Austria sent gunboats down the Danube and fired on Belgrade, and War was declared, treaties were signed with our allies, and the killing began.

"The most tragic part was the Central Powers, Germany, Austria-Hungary, and Turkey going to war against the Triple Entente, France, Britain, and Russia. Then the Croats, Slovenes, and many Serbs in Austria-Hungary split and went to war against Serbia and Montenegro. The conflict spread through the alliances all over Europe. Then Germany invaded Belgium to outflank France, invaded then occupied Yugoslavia hoping for help. That win for Germany forced Britain into the war. The rich and the poor people in every country felt patriotic. Next thing we knew, Europe was filled with trenches, machine guns, and dead soldiers."

I watched Baba in awe as her eyes glazed over and she seemed to have drifted away to another time. Her voice sounded remote.

"You know that our families had arranged for us to marry when I was 15 years old. Ceda was seven years older and such a handsome man, and I just worshipped him. We had the ten children. I lost one baby boy and three little girls at birth or in infancy," she paused and her mouth went down and she closed her eyes for a moment.

She took a deep breath and continued, "Your grandfather, Cedomir Milanovic joined in the Resistance in 1914. Ceda was very loyal to his country, a favorite of King Petar and an important leader in the Radical Party right from the beginning of the war. He became a great leader of the Resistance. He was like a General.

"Mila, your father, Sretein, was only a boy about twelve years old so I kept him home with me and the girls, but his three brothers were all older and had to go off to fight. I lived every moment in fear for Ceda, terrified my sons would be killed.

"These very brave Serbian resistance guerrilla fighters cleared the land twice of the invaders. Then Italy joined our side, but Bulgaria joined Austria and they attacked Serbia again in 1915. By then, many of our men in the mountains had typhus from the bad conditions and lice and they tried to escape through Montenegro and Albania right in the middle of the winter and so many died. French ships took the survivors to Corfu. Then the Austria-Hungary and Bulgarian troops rushed in and occupied Serbia.

"The rest of us were just barely surviving eating off our land sharing with our neighbors. War and death was all around us. Then one day, I saw a Bulgarian officer approaching our doorstep backed up by men with machine guns in the yard. I ordered the children to hide in the root cellar before I opened the door. The officer wanted to know where Ceda was. I told them over and over that I didn't know. Finally, they said if I did not tell them, they would execute all three of my older sons who had been captured and were in prison, and all their families would also be killed. I cried and begged them not to. But they said I must find Ceda soon and convince him to turn himself in to them. I knew they would keep to their threats. What could I do?

"I left the little children with relatives and went up into the mountains, a scarf on my head disguised as a peasant. I trudged and begged rides and finally found someone I could trust and who could take me to Ceda. I only had an hour with him as they were in the middle of fighting and in immense danger. I forced myself to give the message to Ceda that he must surrender to the savage Bulgarians or they would kill his three sons and all their families. The escort finally pulled me off of him. I was in such anguish and pain, wondering if we'd ever see each other again."

"My Ceda made the supreme sacrifice. I heard later, he did surrender, not only for his sons, but to save his soldiers as well.

He was taken to prison in Bulgaria. I heard nothing more of him or my three sons and prayed we would all be safe."

Baba's weak voice continued. "We hid in our cellar while other farms were being ravaged, villages burned and people murdered. Sometimes we couldn't even sleep there as the soldiers were so close, and we sneaked to hide under hay in the barn. Sretein and I tried to keep to our history lessons and his studies but the times were hideous, full of terror and destruction.

"Our Army finally recovered and helped the French and British capture Bitola in 1916, but it wasn't until 1918 that our troops routed the vicious Bulgarians out along with the Austrians and Germans, drove them clear into Hungary and later the war finally ended.

"They ruined our country, and we found out later that 850 million people, a quarter of our population were killed and half of our resources were destroyed. Oh, my dear boy, I hope you never see such war, the hunger and destruction."

Her voice faded and she forced out the words, her voice shaking, "When the war ended, my three boys came home from filthy prisons in Bulgaria, sick and disillusioned, I asked them why they weren't released after I told the Bulgarians where Ceda was. It was then I realized my sons never knew their father had sacrificed his freedom to save their lives. I had been deceived. At least, the boys weren't dead. When they heard the real story about their father's sacrifice, they were devastated, and we all tried to find out what happened to Ceda.

Her voice raised, and a look of rage crossed her face. "A few months later, I found out from two returning prisoners. They stopped to tell me my precious Ceda had been murdered. They finally admitted to me he was cut up piece by piece and roasted on a spit by those savages who enjoyed the meat. I could never quite believe it."

My Baba looked at me with the most forlorn look, then she curled up into a ball, her hands holding her face, and made little mewing noises like one of the cats. She started rocking back and forth just as Aunt Milojka stepped in the room and motioned me out.

She glanced at my horrified face and told me, "Miodrag, take little Drgica for a walk outside. Show her the new batch of kittens in the small barn, please."

I felt relieved to be excused as I couldn't bear to see my Baba and my Tata so miserable and I had to take time to think about the horrible stories she'd told me while I watched my serene little sister playing with the kittens. History teaching was one thing as it happened long ago, but so much had actually involved my own family, I could never get it out of my mind. Could stories like that actually happen to me? My heart jumped at the thought.

∽

After dinner, Baba kissed my hand and emphasized, "Now Sretein, help me keep this straight. After the War, the Austro-Hungarian, Russian, German and Ottoman empires broke up and independent states of Finland, Estonia, Latvia, Lithuania, Poland, Austria, Hungary, Czechoslovakia and our land of the Kingdom of Serbia changed to Kingdom of South or 'Yugo Slavia.' Isn't that right?"

Tata smiled and nodded to her and she continued, "We became known as the losing side of the "Versailles states" because the Germans thought we were just created by the victors of the War. With all our problems, Yugoslavia, called that since 1929, was not just invented by foreigners. Our country has existed many hundreds of years. We have plenty of food and wine. We have minerals. We should all live in peace."

I thought, maybe so, but seems to me from all the history I'd learned, our land never had been calm or peaceful for long. I wondered if it ever would be. The pleasant, admiring look that Tata gave Baba for her extensive knowledge set my fears at ease at least for the time being.

I asked my Tata why some of the boys at school thought we were different from other families around us. My father told me, "My brothers were able to be educated in France after the war. I was schooled here as far as I could go. Most of our people don't travel away from home ever, Miodrag, and they distrust all other people because they don't understand them. They isolate themselves and work very hard for their families, but don't realize they are considered the wildest people on Earth."

Tata would point to peasants shouting and swearing in the village of Kulina and warned me never to act that way. Even though our family were all born farmers, we were taught good manners with good discipline and a better living style than most of our neighbors.

Everyone knew my grandfather Ceda was a major hero in the War fighting against the Croats and Slovenes who had fought for the Germans. Sir Teacher Slatoje taught about him. They said our casualties had been huge and the Serbs wanted the major share of victory. Feelings still ran strong between the states. The Croats had been ruled and patronized by the more sophisticated Germans, Hungarians and Italians and thought they belong to "western" Europe and were superior to us "primitive" Serbs.

I started to explore beyond my play yard, the animals, the barns, and our orchards farther out where I'd been riding. I looked around my school, and my Deda's big, bustling store in the little village of Kamenica. Us boys loved to drop in and see if we could talk him out of some candy. I learned my way around the countryside. I studied geography and all our maps. I wanted to see it all.

Chapter 4

1934-35

I was nine years old, still the youngest boy cousin about to be included in a fine journey. Our destination was a huge cathedral where we would celebrate our name-day feast, a three-day festival. The women were all dressed up in their best silk dresses. I was so excited as my Majka and Baba plus my two little sisters and their nursemaid climbed into our big carriage. It had three seats in front and three in back and pulled by four of our biggest harness horses. I sat up on the front bench between my father and Milan who was driving.

I looked up to Tata, scanning the countryside proudly. He commented to Milan, "The depression is still so bad, we have to find some new markets to sell our corn and brandy, the exports that won't rot. I believe this terrible depression helped that illiterate Hitler rise in Germany. What a serious threat to all of us! That fanatic man rules with his 'insipid intellectualism' and the advice of ruthless characters surrounding him. And the destruction of the Jews is horrible. I can't understand some of our own leaders looking towards communism with Stalin the way he's pricing goods and seizing farms."

His voice sounded strained and agitated and almost whining now. "Oh, I'm sorry. I didn't mean to get carried away," he added.

Milan smiled at him, used to his political views but rarely giving his own opinions. He said, "Trading with those countries will not prevent the possibilities for conflict, Sretein. Neville Chamberlain thinks his policies of appeasement with Hitler's Nazis would keep them as friends. It won't."

My father looked at him in amazement. He depended on Milan, a gentle, nice, clean, handsome man. I wondered about his background. No family seemed to live around here although he'd been here as long as I could remember. Unlike most peasants, he could read, and often discussed school topics with me.

Tata turned to me and said, "Serbia has the best agricultural products in all Europe. Just a few miles away in Bosnia, Miodrag, the climate is a little different and they'll raise even more fruits and vegetables to export than we do when the economy improves. Of course, we have the best fruit, the best vegetables and the best wine in good times. Pay attention Miodrag. Someday, this will be your responsibility." Would it?

The sun broke through clouds, shining down on all of us brightening the day. A strange feeling came over me as I took in the countryside filled with ripe fruit orchards surrounded by the mountains on both sides of the valley. I felt a peaceful God. For once, I'd pushed the awful stories Baba told of the war out of my mind as we turned towards Nis about 30 kilos southeast. I always wanted to see Nis but knew we'd stop before we reached the big city.

As we approached, the Church loomed up, the biggest I'd ever seen. Its very tall spires representing our faith in God. Outside woman and chefs scurried around preparing food for the *Slava*.

Inside, the sanctuary took away my breath. To me the ceiling seemed to reach several stories high to the sky with stained glass windows all around. I stood there with my eyes sending emotions to my heart until Tata finally pulled my arm to catch up with the family. We joined other relatives to take part in a graduation ceremony for my group of boys.

The boys gathered in the private room pushing each other trying to find the right size of white smocks, and my nerves calmed down. Pushing and shoving always does that for me. I tried to concentrate on all the different garments to keep my excitement from exploding.

We boys were led out to meet the attending priests in their black robes and hats. The Bishop met us dressed in a scarlet robe held by a circular gold brooch. Beautiful colors and gold braids hung off it and his garments were topped with a huge, high cap on his head. His person struck me as so impressive and powerful. We boys lined up trying to act civil.

When my turn came to be introduced, a little shiver of nerves came over me. I glanced out to the audience to find my family in the second row. To my surprise, there was short, fat, immaculately dressed Senator Budimer sitting next to his sister, Selimka, my Majka.

From her seat, she sternly gestured for me to kiss the Bishop's hand. My family, especially Baba with a big smile on her face, looked proud of me as I bent to kiss the outstretched hands as tradition dictated. I said "Good Day" and announced my name in a firm voice as I'd practiced with Baba. Pride swelled up in me from the Bishop's compliments and I held my head high as I walked off the dais.

After the short ceremony, the boys shed their tunics along with their patience and good behavior, and poured outside into the sunny courtyard. Steaming dishes of food filled the tables under the trees. The cousins and other boys playfully started running around noisily letting off some pent up steam.

After the enormous on-going dinner, I stopped with curiosity at the table where my father and Uncle Budimir were sitting with the Bishop. Sprawled out in a big chair, Uncle's buttons were bursting on his vest and his cigar ashes were falling on them. His hair was thinning, and he was short like my Majka but his eyes were always totally alert. The Bishop was speaking in French with them.

"This is Serbia, speak Serbian, not French," I blurted out to them. Majka was sitting aside, her face red. She grabbed my arm, and started to stop me. The Bishop turned to her, laughing, stood up and walked my way. To my astonishment he grabbed my face and kissed me on the forehead.

"Oh, Miodrag, you are so loyal like your family and so right. But, my boy, you must also learn to speak French, and German fluently. You will travel around Europe someday and you must know the languages and what our friends and enemies are saying at all times. You must learn five languages before you leave this country. I know you want to travel and you will."

"Yes, Holy Bishop, I will learn 20 languages!" I proudly bowed to the smiling adults, and ran to join the boys.

"You must think you're the big cheese, Mila," yelled Vladislav pushing me around.

His mother grabbed him and said loud enough for me to hear, "Vladislav, don't you tease your cousin, you're much taller and stronger that he is and you must help him. One day he may become King! Now behave yourself or I'll call your father!"

I ignored the other boys making fun of me because I had a plan and not just to be King. I wanted to be a Czar!

After feeding ourselves to the point of realizing my Majka's warning of getting sick, we sat on the grass to watch the brightly colored Slava dancers performing our native dances in their round caps, embroidered waistcoats, knee breeches and sandals with curled-back toes. My head was reeling from the whirling, and fast paces of the musicians and the dancers pouring their hearts out. I loved to watch but never could learn how to dance.

The next morning I awoke to strange sounds, sat up surprised to discover I was not in my own bed, but in a tent near the Church celebration. I rubbed my eyes, looked up to see Baba bringing me my favorite dish just like at home.

"Oh, my sweet boy, you're awake," she said. "Look what I have for you. Now just swing your legs over and eat your breakfast."

I said "thank you," but looked long and hard at her pale face with a little knot in my stomach.

"Baba, are you feeling well? Has the trip and all the excitement been too much for you?"

She tried to reassure me, but her face was so white compared to her beautiful, bright dress and cape. I prayed she wasn't ill.

The day became one I'd never forget. Suddenly, the noise stopped. I looked around to see the entourage of King Aleksandar arriving. The way the King greeted my Uncles left me in awe. For all his majesty, he greeted them as friends, kissing their foreheads. My cousins and I stood aside silently watching the procession pay homage to the Bishop. Later the boys mingled around waiting for the King to introduce us to the young Prince Petar.

My Tata instructed me, "Miodrag, I want you to treat the Prince and his two brothers just like one of us to make them feel comfortable except you must address him as Prince Petar. Understand?"

His security guard hovered around the 11-year-old Prince with soldiers watching all three royal sons and the chosen companions. I stared at the Prince, kind of a skinny kid, plain and looking rather scared. Didn't look like a Prince to me, but then I'd only ever seen one in pictures.

We all stood around staring at each other until Vladislav and Zivadin who couldn't stand still any longer, started hollering and ran over to a few goats grazing by the fence. Vladislav jumped on one and started riding it around. Zivadin followed and motioned the middle brother of the Prince who suddenly broke away, ran over and held the horns until he could straddle the frantic goat jumping around. The little brother tried to follow. I was bent over laughing and we all laughed until the Prince finally started to giggle, too.

"Go ahead and try it!" I shouted to him.

"Oh, no, I couldn't. Let them do it." The Prince looked pathetic and I tried to cheer him up but he just stood there, clinging to his security guard. I stayed with the Prince and tried to start a conversation with him. "What's it like to live in a castle?"

He looked at me sullenly and said, "We move around often."

I looked up to see my cousins and the Prince's brothers hobble back after being thrown off the goats and threatened with the horns. I'd much rather be with them, I thought.

"Where do you go?"

"I don't know." Petar said.

I stared at him and looked around to see where my parents were. They'd moved to shade and settled in chairs under the trees visiting with friends and politicians. I turned back to the Prince. I wish I didn't have to stay with this guy. What a dud! Then the Prince asked me if I was from Belgrade and I started to laugh.

"No, I'm from the country. We own large farms. I've never even been to Belgrade. Do you know where Belgrade is? Point the direction."

"I live there in a palace but I don't know where it is. They just take me places," he said quietly.

"Do you know where Austria is? Can you read a map?"

"No, why would I do that?" Now the other boys started to gather around and started to giggle. "You don't even know where Austria is? And you want to be my king? You don't even know your geography!" That brought a smothered laugh from the Prince's brothers and my cousins who started to egg me on.

"You don't even know where you are? Do you know where your head is and where your ass is?" The Prince threw his hands to his face, but even his security guard was laughing along with the boisterous boys pushing and shoving each other teasing the Prince.

"Touch your head and your ass!" I shouted at him. All the boys including me were jumping around, pushing each other, laughing and slapping their knees. I turned just in time to see my Majka coming at me like a storm. I started to run away with her trying to catch me. Even the solemn Prince started giggling, then laughing, too. Out of the corner of my eye, I saw Uncle Svetomir run up with Majka and catch her arm.

"Stop, Selimka. They are just playing and now the Prince is laughing. You just don't know who you brought into this world. That Miodrag is not afraid of anything or anybody. He'll go places."

On the way home, Baba hugged me close to her and whispered, "You should have respect for people, my precious boy, and mind your manners. But I'll tell you, I believe in the future there will be no more royalty in this country. Aleksandar named a Serb, General Petar Zivkovic as premier Now we're called Yugoslavia. I hate the Communists and the Nazis but we must find a better form of government that is fair to all."

I thought about the young Prince on our way home. How could he run a country of different opinions and languages? He seemed like such a weakling, I felt sorry for him. Maybe Baba was right that our country would manage better as a democracy someday.

The Bishop's advice about languages stuck in my mind. Before I went back to class, I rehearsed a little speech to persuade my Sir Teacher Slatoje into loaning me a German language book. To Baba's delight, I began to study constantly. I knew I did not want to be just a farmer. I would study, travel, and perhaps go to university to become a senator like my Uncle Budimir, my Majka's brother. Maybe someday, I would pull this country together myself.

After a family dinner in the formal dining room was cleared, I stood back and watched my other three Uncles linger there for privacy from the women. The servants served drinks then the uncles lit up their cigars with my Tata.

Uncle Svetislav, thin and gray, was the elder and obviously the wisest. He was tall like Ceda. He'd never recovered from his horrible time as a prisoner of war. All three uncles had old wounds from the War and prison camp. Svetolik, the second son was often whispered about for his heavy drinking problem. His face sagged and his eyes always looked watery. Svetimir, third son, looked very much like my Tata, Sretein with darker red hair, a handsome, kind face and just a little taller.

My Tata became aware I was still in the room and politely asked me to go play with the cousins.

I avoided my cousins and hid under the open window where the Uncles gathered. I could barely hear the first part of their conversation but heard my father's voice rise and the word "leaders."

Then, I moved as close as I dared. I was surprised to hear Baba's voice, "No, the king's men employ tactics and methods leading us up the wrong path and hold back important information, Svetomir and Sretein. The word "Confidential" should be formed with barbed wire. Tyranny happens wherever that word is formed. Human beings are betrayed by ignorance, then tortured physically and mentally for their behavior. In the history of the world, planet Earth has never seen how human beings are misled as in this so-called advanced civilization. Humans are employing and exploiting other human minds to destroy the human brain."

"My majka, you are so right and so wise, thank you," I heard my father say to her. She must have left then. I ducked down behind the bushes until I was sure she was in the family side of the house.

"Sretein." Svetomir continued, "I saw it with my own eyes on my trip to Germany. She's right. The Third Reich is a real threat. They think we are bad? Hah! That Hitler is a maniac. You should have seen him. He put on a big show in front of his Reichstag, an old Opera House with 230 seats, now his headquarters. He had loudspeakers mounted on a statue."

"What was he like, Svetomir?" Tata looked up to him.

"Hitler sounded like a fanatical preacher capable of holding the audience to believe anything. And Goebbel, an evil man close to him called Catholics enemies of the state! He called them reactionary and Communist! Can you imagine? The madman thinks he's 'Ruler of the World' and can pull that army together to conquer England, Russia, all of us." He paused for a drink of our homegrown Sipovitz.

"And all the 'Heil Hitlers' and that awful Horst Wessel song they sing. And I hear the man who wrote that stupid song may have been a storm trooper but ended up a petty criminal killed in some street fight, Hitler is gaining power by threatening disaster from the Reds. Now he's making every organ of German life his personal business; professions, trades, the law, even the

Lutheran Church are under the control of the Nazis. You all wait and see! They are liable to start another war just like the last. Hitler wants to be king of the world! We should all read his *Mein Kampf.* He cannot be ignored. He's determined to be a dictator and he's building gigantic army!"

Svetomir paused, thoughtfully. "Do you think he'll invade Yugoslavia?"

"I doubt it," Tata replied. His voice raised in anger. "He doesn't even respect us as a country. I hear from my business associate, Drazek Kodlj, that Hitler and his henchmen have been stashing great amounts of money most likely for a war. I could kill that maniac! Other countries are not paying enough attention to him."

I'd never heard my mild mannered Tata or Uncle Svetomir so upset, and the reason rattled my peace of mind.

"We're surrounded. Italy on the south is full of Fascists. King Aleksandar made an offer to Mussolini for a Balkan alliance again. I don't quite know where France stands. I think they want to make a deal with Italy and want us to do the same. Of course, Bulgaria won't join the pact with us. Nor will Romania, Greece, or Turkey for our mutual defense, and now I'm afraid Yugoslavia will turn to Germany to avoid a real threat from Italy."

The complications sounded overwhelming to me. I got another taste of politics when we traveled to Aleksinac, our district seat for a local election. We stayed at the Hotel Balkan on the main street, bigger than my school, the only large building I'd ever seen, and I felt terribly grown up as I was the only youngster present.

Tata explained that every three years, an election was held to decide on the senators and my Uncle Budimer was running again. Majka was dressed in her best but plain dress, her black hair curled around her face. She smiled with pride at her impressive older brother whom she addressed as Bata.

She had spent days hustling the servants in making special pastries along with cheese and white bread to bring for the elite group of politicians on both sides. Rivals and bureaucrats all sat around together in a huge upstairs room playing cards, and entertaining prominent supporters. Occasionally, they discussed the problems and people who were in power.

I heard dancing girls performed in the evening but of course, I was kept from the fun and banished to our quarters alone. I lay on the bed reading quietly when I heard noise of people in the street below growing nasty. Suddenly, gunshots rang out. I leaped off the bed, turned out the light and rushed out on the narrow balcony hanging over the railing to look down.

Astonishment turned to excitement as I tried to figure out who was shooting whom. It never occurred to me I could be in danger. These men on the street were dressed like minors and factory workers, unlike the elite inside. The light from the dim streetlight caught the glint of real knives held up for slashing at each other. My feet froze to the spot.

Flashes of guns discharging cut through the darkness and sharp cracks punctured the roar of the crowd. This was no forbidden book. This was real.

The street filled with more men ready for battle, shouting rough words of anger but almost like they were having a good time. The noise grew and I couldn't believe no one from the Hotel came out to stop them. Are my parents safe in the protected second floor meeting room? Were they just watching the dancing girls entertaining them, unaware of the free-for-all in the street?

I couldn't take my eyes off the scene below. Suddenly sirens announced the police. They spilled out of their vehicles barging into the crowd, kicking fallen men, hitting them with clubs, and dragging people off ignored by the other fighters. I stood mesmerized on the balcony until the end of the riot, and afterwards could barely get to sleep.

The next day I heard from my parents; the men in the streets were Communist-led Partisans trying to illegally force their representatives into the election fighting against the democrats.

I tried to explain why I'd been seen hanging off the balcony, but Majka shook me and angrily wailed, "Hide under the bed if you hear shooting again. You could be killed, you foolish boy!"

I'd never felt really afraid.

∽

Home again, I bragged to the boys about the excitement of the riot. Then I had to settle down to study. We were preparing for a school play and I wrote a battle scene for us. I, of course, acted as the captain and chose four boys to act as two horses. I knew exactly how it should go insisting on having my way at every detail including our crude costumes. At our dress rehearsal, I held the reins tied to the boy horses, and really got carried away. I snapped the whip above their heads and drove them out into the schoolyard. Everyone was shouting and laughing, and I drove them right into a neighbor's vegetable garden ruining most of the new plants.

My Majka found out when she received a fine for destruction. When I saw her grab the paddle, I ran outside with her chasing me around the back yard. I just kept running and yelled back, "You can't catch me, you're a Turk and I can outrun you."

My father really came down hard on me for that one with a long lecture on treating my dear mother with some respect. But even though I tried to feel contrite, I saw a glint of humor in his eyes.

Now, Drgica had shyly started school sitting in front of the class with the few other girls. She spoke softly but outperformed even the students ahead of her. I looked at her in a different way. While I teased her at home, I protected her on the playground, and surprised myself when I came to admire my smart sister. Too bad she wasn't a boy.

My history lessons continued except now the information became real and seemed to be repeating itself in this day.

Awareness set in as I began to realize the information could possibly affect my life.

About that time, a new feeling entered my heart. A sweet, pretty little girl named Vera caught my attention and brought out feelings never experienced before. I burned with need of attention from her and tried everything to gain it.

Finally, I couldn't stand it any longer. In the absolute stillness before dawn, gazing at my favorite star, an inspiration came to write another poem; this one a most serious love poem to Vera. I sneaked into the classroom during recess and hid it in the book on her desk.

I sweat blood waiting for her to find, read it, and give me her beautiful smile so I could speak to her. Instead, later in the day, she returned my heart wrapped in that piece of paper. Rejected and overwhelmed, my heart turned to powder. I couldn't face anyone. Alone, my feet barely shuffled me all the way home feeling real depression.

The next day, a very tall girl named Radmila Krstic approached me on the playground. To my intense embarrassment, she told me Vera had let her read her most private poem from me. I just stared at her.

She explained, "Mila, I was so moved by your beautiful feelings for Vera but she doesn't love you, and I do and want you to be my lover. I would like you to write me beautiful love poems."

I stood there in the hot sun, paralyzed, the blood leaving my face. For once in my life I could think of no clever remarks, no comebacks, no nothing. My only choice seemed to run away.

I ran most of the way home that afternoon, again avoiding the other boys, feeling sick. I dumped my books on the kitchen table, changed clothes, and went out to my private grassy place by the small barn to stare at the clouds.

A great knowledge came upon me. I could not just turn on and off that weird intense feeling between boys and girls. Somehow it just had to come without any prompting from me,

I guess. I knew the feeling I had for Vera was not the same as the caring I had for any family member, even Baba. I knew no one could explain this sensation for me. So I sunk down in the dumps and stayed there for at least two days.

Neither Vera nor Radmila ever spoke to me again, just ignored me. I'd experienced the pain of rejection and months passed before it dawned on me that Radmila must have felt the same pain.

At a family gathering at home, Uncle Svetislav's wife's grandmother took her off into the house. I went outside and stood under an open window to hear what she was going to tell them. It seems that Uncle's oldest son wanted to marry a nice Croatian.

Majka and Aunt Milojka thought it could possibly be acceptable but the other grandmother agreed with Baba who said, "No, No, I don't care if the girl is the prettiest and the best cook, he must marry one of his own even if she's blind or deaf! She must be Serbian!"

That firm announcement from the grandmothers stopped the marriage and made me swear I'd never marry a girl who wasn't Serbian.

Chapter 5

1936-38

On a beautiful spring day my father took me along in the wagon with Milan to drive around the farms and through some of the glorious blooming orchards.

Milan patiently explained the process of harvesting the plum crop to me. "The best plums are used to produce our famous plum wine known as Slivovitz, or boiled down to make into jam. The rest of the crop is fed to the pigs. Many of our pigs are exported to other countries to make dinars for us. Not even the farmers in Hungary can compete with us for our delicious plum-flavored pork."

Tata, promoted by my interest, explained, "Agriculture is now all we have. Now, the richest gold mines and oil in Europe are in Bulgaria and Romania, but we have copper and chrome mostly in Bosnia that the Germans badly want. You have learned that the Balkans are made up of people who speak different dialects, and radically different in song and dance traditions. We practice the Orthodox religion, similar to the Bosnians and Croatians, except they are mostly Roman Catholics submitting to the Pope in Rome.

Maybe we will travel together someday, my son. The Muslims are scattered everywhere left over from the time the Turks conquered us. Many Muslims look and talk just like us, some are darker with a different language and religion. Now, my son, you must pay attention to learn how these farms are managed."

I felt very grown-up and tried to pay attention. I still could not imagine myself as a farmer.

I'd rather listen to the Uncles and friends who often talked politics; of lack of trust of Mussolini in Italy, Stalin in Russia, and Furher Hitler in Germany. From behind the door, I often heard them say, "Hitler is crazy." Besides intense loyalty to our King, the men only admired Leon Blum now Chancellor of France. Blum backed the French Popular Front, passed social reforms for the people, and hated the Germans. The Uncles knew him during their education in France and followed his career carefully.

I got the creepy impression our position was changing rapidly and I should pay attention. I tried to talk to Baba about it, but she looked so distressed that I didn't want to upset her further. So I begged Tata to teach me French and help with my German. Every chance I got, I continued to study my German books.

On a still gray day, I brought Baba down stairs for dinner, feeling very important with her arm in mine. When we were all seated and served, Tata excitedly announced, "I'm planning a trip to Switzerland for business and I want to take Miodrag with me. I think he's old enough and he deserves a trip as his accomplishments at school are superior."

Majka jumped clear out of her chair. "NO! He's too young. I can't let him go."

Baba, startled by her outburst stared at her, her mouth open. Aunt Milojka raised her eyebrows, her fork halted midway to her face, and tried to hold back a startled smile. A sinking feeling settled in my stomach at the shocked look on my Tata's face.

I prayed silently. "Oh, God, I want to travel so much. I pray they'll let me go. Please God." I remembered hearing how my mother's fear stopped Tata cold in his tracks when he was invited to the United States to sing. They had just married and Tata cancelled the trip of a lifetime so she wouldn't be hurt.

He said, "Do you think he's not ready, Silimka? There's no danger in Switzerland. They remain quite neutral."

"It's too far, too many mountains. And it's winter. And you'll spend too much dinars. The Nazi's may be hiding there. Please don't take him, Sretein. Take him to Nis or even Belgrade, but not all the way to Switzerland, please." Her voice pleaded with him and to my distress, he gave in. My deep disappointment took over and I jumped up without excusing myself and ran into the horse barn, threw myself in the hay, pounding on the bales, and cried my eyes out.

As a compromise, a few days later, Tata announced he was taking me to Nis, the largest city in Yugoslavia. I stood looking at him struck silent, as a hot ball started in my stomach and rose up to my face.

"Oh, Tata, I can travel with you?" I threw my arms around him, in bright affection while Aunt Milojka gathered up Drgica and Jelica laughing and began dancing around us. I didn't remember ever being so excited. The plans began.

Tata took me to his tailor in Jakovlje to fit me for a new suit for the occasion. I felt so grown up and important.

Then Aunt Milojka invited me to join her for coffee in the kitchen. "Oh, Mila, you are in for a wonderful adventure. I like Nis even better than Belgrade. It's so lively and gay. Of course, I was younger and the food was scarcer then but your Baba bought me some lovely silk clothes. Oh, you'll have a wonderful time with your father, Mila. Someday I hope to find a nice husband so I can go again." She winked at Tata and I wondered why. Her eyes turned back as she bent to kiss me, "Bless you darling, and have a wonderful time for me, too."

No stories from others could have made the impact on me that driving into Nis did. Our big carriage was entering the largest city in Yugoslavia. From the village on the outskirts, the dirt roads turned into paved streets, many real automobiles and buildings of many floors. Our luxurious hotel loomed much larger than the Aleksinac hotel and appeared as elegant as a castle. I couldn't believe people actually slept here acting so casually. Milan took the carriage away and a boy in a funny uniform took our valises to carry inside the huge, elegant, lobby. No pictures had prepared me for this only to be continually overwhelmed with new sights and experiences.

Tata took me to a musical concert in a giant hall with an elaborate ceiling. Drowsiness came awake hearing a loud sniffle from Tata. He actually had tears running down his cheeks. I stared at him, then became aware his heart was spilling over from the professional orchestra, and the choir singing such beautiful music.

On the streets, the noise seemed deafening but highly charged. Milan, now my chaperone, dressed in a suit, took me for long walks to see the sights while my Tata was engaging in business. Milan pointed out stores on the wide streets and told me stories of the people. We visited beautiful parks, and ate in elegant cafés. Cars zoomed by sometimes honking. I thought they were honking at me but Milan explained they were honking at each other to stay clear out of their way and I had better watch where I was going also.

In a large plaza, we noticed peasant women sitting on the sidewalk on blankets with their farm produce spread out for sale. I went over to speak to them as I often did at home in our village. Suddenly, several big, young fellows started to act up. One big, rough guy reached out and kicked at the vegetables and fruit arranged on the blankets. The other two joined them in the fray scattering the fresh vegetables all over the street and laughing like fools.

The peasant women jumped up screaming and started to cry, begging them to stop. One city boy started yelling, "You peasants are the same as goats, and pigs."

Another chimed in, "Like donkeys, asses, worse than animals. Go home! Go back to your pig sty!"

I pulled away from Milan, trying to pull me back and ran toward a policeman, dragging him back to catch the mean boys. By then, the beautiful produce was scattered all over the streets with people grabbing up the vegetables and fruit. The boys scattered and ran off chased by the police. I was watching them when a couple of the women came up to me, one even kissed my forehead and mentioned how brave I was for standing up and trying to stop the hooligans. Later, when my father heard about the incident from Milan, he was upset.

"Miodrag, you could have been hurt or even killed. Those young men are probably Ustasha or Communists and are dangerous people here. Promise me you won't leave the side of Milan and get into any more trouble. These boys are much rougher and more dangerous than you know."

"Yes, Tata." I tried to be serious and contrite to him, but I couldn't wait to tell my cousins at home. I felt sure that incident would be the highlight of my visit to the City of Nis, even better than seeing a moving picture for the first time.

As a surprise, Tata invited me to attend a business dinner with him. He warned me not to speak unless I was spoken to which was very hard for me as I had so many questions to ask. We entered a most beautiful restaurant with high copper ceilings, and white tablecloths and flowers on the tables. The maitre d'hôtel, seated us, and waiters in fancy black and white suits bustled around taking orders and carrying steaming trays of food. He introduced his business associate and guest as Drazak Kadlj. I knew he was important in business but I thought him a rather a small man compared to my Tata with lots of wrinkles up and down his face. We shook hands and I did try hard to behave like a gentleman.

During dessert and coffee, Drazak Kadlj who frequently traveled to Germany and Austria, finally stopped talking about crops and exports and more intently starting talking quietly about Hitler. I started to listen. His craggy face became more animated as he announced he'd attended the 1936 Olympics in Berlin.

"Jesse Owens took away much of the thunder from the Germans and Hitler was furious. You should have heard him, never a moment of calm. And the German athletes saluted their ugly Furher like he was a god."

Tata answered, "He swears he's not a dictator even though they print the exact same stories written by Nazis in every newspaper in the country. For the life of me, I don't understand why, but Hitler seems to be popular with many Germans and his very young officers are so loyal. He's just not a man to be trusted. Then I hear he's raising an army and has been censored from the League of Nations, and now he's turning against Russia. Surely they wouldn't start another war!"

"Sretein, this man is no thinker. No Schiller, Gotthe, Kant or Neitzche books left in that country! You know what he said?" He cupped his hand so I wouldn't hear, but I was very experienced at eavesdropping.

"He thinks the Jews should all be exterminated. He accuses them of hoarding all the marks and for starting the War and even believes they brought syphilis into the country! He wants to exterminate all of them! God forbid that should happen."

They both wondered why France and Britain ignored Hitler's efforts to rearm Germany, a situation those two nations had agreed upon with the United States to never happen again. Then the United States just withdrew from the politics of Europe and adopted "isolationism."

"What were they thinking?" Tata said, "And Hitler and Stalin are both trying to swindle the other. Those two dictators smiling at each other with their fingers crossed, made the Nazi-Soviet Pack. I think the Red Terror is worse than Germany, although Hitler's speeches sound identical with Stalin's from listening to the BBC. Bolshevists or National Socialist— both the same! Men possessed by becoming dictators always bring misery and death to the people."

I pretended to be interested only in the fancy dessert, and I think they forgot I was even there but I listened to every word.

Tata's guest, Drazak said, "Nobody trusts the Kremlin. I've heard they are re-arming along with France and Britain. I don't think either one has the heart for another fight, but they better pay attention to keep Hitler in check. Hitler has clout and has the people hating the Jews, blaming the depression and every other thing on them. Hitler shouts like a drunk, crazy peasant. You should hear him! People are going around saying 'Heil Hitler' everywhere."

When we arrived back home, I talked incessantly about the trip maybe inventing just a little more excitement just to amuse everyone. I didn't mention the bad boys on the street because Tata did not wish to tell Majka about my run-in with the hooligans. But he did talk it over with Baba who took me aside and shook her finger at me.

"Those hooligans could have turned on you. You know what I've taught you about fighting, Mila. You must try to talk yourself out of it and if you do fight, you'd better have a good reason and be prepared to be injured."

Baba pointed out the differences in our people, "Near us are people who urinate off the curbs in Kamenica and Kulina. You are to ignore those people who don't know any better. And don't cause trouble on the street and call attention to yourself, Mila. Even though our family members were all born in the country, I came to appreciate as a child how we were all taught good manners with good discipline and a better living style than most of our neighbors. You must live up to that responsibility!"

She emphasized, "Our family is invited to important events because of our status connected to the Royalty and our high social level of Serbians. You must never embarrass us."

～

One evening in October after the sisters were in bed, Tata was listening to the Yugoslavian Radio when he jumped up and started yelling. "Oh my God! Oh, my God! " We all ran to him in panic.

"They've murdered King Aleksandar in Marseilles! Listen!"

The broadcast message said he was on a state visit to France, and a Ustashe gang member living in Italy plotted and killed him. My Baba fell back into a chair and fainted. Majka fanned her, while Aunt Milojka lifted her head up for her to try a sip of water. When Baba came to, she was white and shaking. My Tata paced the floor nearly in tears himself.

"This is the end," she cried, "This is horrible! We are all part of the Kingdom of Serbs including our enemies, the Croats, and Slovenes. And the Ustasha group is being supported by Germany, Bulgaria and Hungary. War is coming, I can feel it."

My father ignored my presence and his voice raised until he was shouting, "Yes, and our Balkan Entente is supported by Britain and France and they don't want to fight!"

Baba cried out, "Only twenty years since Sarajevo and now we'll have another War! I know it. This is the end!" Her distress brought the family to our knees. She always seemed to have a special sense when it came to history and its fate.

I thought of Prince Petar. That poor kid, losing his father in such a brutal way. Everyone was crying. I sat with my father and watched Baba's face quietly as she reclined on a couch on the other side of the room sipping a glass of slivovitz. Majka, my two little sisters, and Aunt Milojka continued to sit around her keeping watch. The house servants huddled in the doorway, wringing their hands with deep concern on their faces, some weeping.

For days I watched the household and the village people mourn. Quietly sitting by the fire, Baba sat in repose. Her vital energy slowly flowed out of her from that day on.

Later, we learned Aleksandar's brother; Prince Paul was appointed Regent to the young King Petar. I felt better knowing someone besides that kid who didn't even know his geography would be running the government.

The boys at school, my cousins, and family all grieved over the assassination and worried about the future. We heard the Croatian separatists clashed with the police and Croatian militia organizations formed. Communist student activists started marches in Belgrade. The government took a position of moderation even though they were the aggrieved party.

When Tata and the Uncles met as usual, I hid behind the door threatening sister Jelica who threatened to tell on me. She stuck her tongue out at me and left just as I heard my Tata say, "Of course, Italy is to blame for supporting those Croatian Ustashe killers, and now France and Britain may refuse to back a League of Nations censure of Italy."

Svetomir represented our family at the State funeral in Belgrade. "The most amazing thing happened," he later told the uncles. "Reichsmarschall Hermann Goering attended representing Germany. Really, I actually met him in person. He said he was flattered by our reception considering our countries had been such enemies during the War. I must say I was impressed but I didn't believe a word of his insincere rhetoric."

I peaked around the door. The Uncles frowned, wrung their hands, and sounded worried. Tata said, "Our country needs some respect; we were not 'created' by the Treaty of Versailles. Yugoslavia was created by our own leadership, such as it is, and now we are in the middle of a tug of war. We have enemies on all sides it seems. And it may be that our Roman Catholic neighbors, the Croatians may become the worst."

"But we've been peaceful compared to most of Europe," Uncle Svetomir said loudly. His voice often was loud unlike my Tata even though they looked very much alike with their reddish hair.

"Everyone around us has suffered dictatorships worse than our Kings. The English and the Irish are more vicious with each other than our battles with the Croats. Oh, I know we have to deal with the Communists and the Ustasha, and yes, I know we have a long way to go with all our complications."

Tata held up his hand for attention, "Do you think we can fend off a civil war, much less a European War?"

"Sretein, you are too naïve. Right now, the Austrians have some kind of a civil war with heavy fighting in Vienna. They are leaving themselves open to be overthrown. They should be looking over the border to the Nazis who want the whole world. Will we do the same?"

Their conversations were scary, but I listened to the adults every chance I got.

Svetislav, his hair already white, said, "Chancellor Dollfuss has forbidden political parties except his own. Of course, the maniac Hitler appointed him. Chancellor Dollfuss also is determined to keep Austria preserved as a Catholic country and has outlawed the Socialist Party."

"I think our Majka is right," Uncle said, "Germany is headed for another World War. All the signs point to it. Hitler is determined to conquer the world and I heard he's starting compulsory military service! Just what we've feared all along."

"And Russia is just coming out of depression, extermination of their own people, and dealing with serious famine," replied Tata. "Now Stalin wants to show how Communism can raise crops and support the country but in my opinion, they are creating slaves. Communism has become vile and is spreading into Germany and our country as well. Without our King, how can our government cope with all these pressures?"

The questions and speculations went on. Baba took the worry off when she appeared happy at dinner and wanted to surprise the family. She made an announcement.

"I've decided to go to the St. Stevon Monastery at Adravac Gornji." Tata stared at her, a puzzled look on his face. Despite her smile, her eyes revealed she was very serious. He suspected she was not just thinking of a vacation. He knew right away there was no point in trying to talk her out of it. She obviously had a mission.

"My Majka, are you well enough for such a trip?" he asked her even though the Monastery was only about five kilometers away. She appeared frail to all of us.

"I heard the old Bishop is ill and I must see him before we both die. I intend to take Miodrag with me. He is my strength. Will you give him permission? And, I must borrow Milan and one other protector. I want to go there in two days. We will only be gone one day."

Her voice sounded steady and determined.

"I will make the arrangements, my dear Majka." Tata said.

My heart swelled. I couldn't wait to see the legendary St. Stevon Monastery. I knew the history. Turks and Serbians once fought over this ancient place. Baba enjoyed talking to me about our planned excursion and I loved hearing the history again.

On the way, Baba seemed to renew her energy. "Did you know, my son, that St. John the Baptist was beheaded at St. Stevon?"

My head swirled to see her face. What? St. John the Baptist?

She shook her finger at me. "Yes, St. John the Baptist!" And she proceeded to tell me the story.

"Pontius Pilatus, the Roman procurator ordered John's imprisonment. He escaped up here to the old church to hide out. Then Salome, daughter of King Herod's wife, demanded John's head as punishment for an insult to her mother, and the soldier's found him and beheaded him. He left a note requesting to have his body taken to Lebanon to be buried. They built a chapel over the site where St. John is buried." When you are 20 years old, you must promise me that you'll go there and visit his body.

"Then in 1876, Russians pushed the Turks out when they liberated the Serbians. An important Russian Commander under the Czar was wounded at the same spot by the Turks and died as a hero. They buried him there. The Serbs set aside 12 to 15 acres and built this Monastery in his honor. Every year there is a festival on that land in honor of the battle. Monks keep up the place and farm the land. No services, marriages or baptisms are held there."

When we arrived, I jumped down from the carriage and cast my eyes around at a peaceful wonderland of green grass and full green trees. Milan raised his hand to Baba in respect, then lifted her down from the carriage. She stood in awe at the scene. I kept my voice low so I wouldn't interrupt the birds singing in this peaceful place on the edge of the forest.

A robed Monk silently appeared beside us to my surprise and led Baba and I inside to see the Bishop. This surreal icon appeared in shadow in the gloomy room and seemed to be expecting us as he slowly rose to his feet. When my eyes adjusted, I could see how tall he stood, much older than Baba, but extremely pale with sad sagging eyes.

His face lit up when he saw her up close, and he grabbed both her hands. "My dear, dear Milica. I never thought I'd lay these poor old eyes on your beautiful face again."

Baba knelt at his feet and kissed his robes. I stood back in the shadows until Baba was ready to introduce me. The monk helped her up and she turned to me proudly,

"This is my grandson and escort, Miodrag, the son of my youngest son, Sretein."

Another monk stood in the dark by the door watching, quiet as a stone. I felt a little nervous but bowed and kissed the Bishop's hand. We were invited to sit down and the Bishop began to talk about Ceda as if he were still here.

"Ah, I wish we could visit again. If ever there was a great man and a gentleman, Ceda was that man. A god-loving family man and protector of the peasants. He saved so many people during the war. How is he?"

Baba stared at him, her pale face went white and I started to reach for her in case she fainted. The monk motioned me to stay in the background, and stepped in beside her, never uttering a word. She seemed to recover her composure as I listened to her grasping for breath. My own heart started thumping heavily in an eerie silence.

Her voice sounded strange; "My Ceda is dead. I killed him."

What was she saying? My body went weak and I feared I'd fall off the chair. Somehow I managed to stay upright while Baba continued. She told him how she was threatened and forced by the enemy Bulgarians to go into the mountains searching for Ceda, how she begged him to surrender to the hateful Bulgarians who reneged on their promise to release her sons.

The Bishop listened intently, his mouth open, and his old eyes blurry with tears.

Her voice staggered, "I begged him to give himself up. But the bastards never released my sons until the end of the War, and they murdered Ceda, chopped his body to pieces. I killed him! I killed him." She let out a wailing, piercing, scream. I jumped to her side, held her hands, tears running down my face. The monk ran to the Bishop to bring water and fan him.

"Forgive me. Forgive me" Baba kept repeating holding onto me with a death grip. I clung to her struggling with all my might to give her courage.

"God please release her!" I prayed hard as I had ever done. Somehow, peace came over me and as I held her, she stopped shaking and finally looked over at the stunned Bishop.

Her eyes were glazed but her voice became strong. "Your Highness, I have more to confess. Svetomir, my third living son wanted to marry a suitable Serbian girl he loved. I talked to her first. In our conversation, I found out she'd promised to wait for Svetomir to come back from the war to get married and then, God forgive me, she broke down and told me that she had been raped and brutalized by the Bulgarians soldiers. I must tell you.

"She was captured by the Bulgarians, tortured, stretched out naked on a table to be ravished by several soldiers. She passed out and they left her for dead. She woke up later, escaped and very slowly she recovered. Later, I told Svetomir about the tragedy so he could decide to help her or leave her. He declared he loved her and wanted to marry her. Since his father was dead, I struggled with the situation. Could she bare children? But they loved each other and I gave my permission." She stopped to catch her breath.

"I need your forgiveness, Your Highness. Since Svetimir was betrothed to Selimka, according to her father, I convinced Sretein to marry a woman he didn't love. You must forgive me. You must forgive me."

I held her and rocked her while the monk helped her to kneel beside her chair while the Bishop gave her absolution and the release she yearned for. She kissed the hem of the Bishop's robe, rose and seemed to feel calm. In fact, through her tears, she smiled, held both his hands while he kissed her forehead and then she began to relax.

The monk slowly walked us out and guided us to the graves of the first Serbian Bishop, and the first Serbian King educated by Romans who coronated himself long before the Monastery was built. I walked along with Baba holding her up until she seemed strong enough to take the trip home. I was filled with her courage and elegance. She was still taller than I was but she'd become very thin.

Milan picked her up and set her in the carriage. His face expressed his deep concern. His helper settled us in the carriage and we started toward home. Soon he drove off the road, pulling up to lead the horses to drink. We all ate our picnic lunch in this beautiful meadow near the Morava River Bridge outside Adravac. We talked softly about the weather and simple things.

"Miodrag Cedic," she used my whole name so I knew something serious was coming. "We will have War again. Now listen to me. You are very young, to young to go into the Army, I hope. And you look like such a young man. Your face is so smooth, not a whisker, just like your father. And look at those chubby cheeks!" She rubbed her soft hands over my face and pinched me softly.

"Oh, Mila, And that curly hair, not as red as your father's, but so thick. Your precious smile with your good little teeth, and that mischievous twinkle in your eyes. You're growing up to be handsome like my Ceda and Sretein. Oh, Mila, don't be unhappy because you look so young. Take advantage of your looks. If you get into a sticky situation, pretend you cannot hear or talk like a deaf mute. You must prepare yourself to survive. You must find a job with the military but not as a soldier. Your Uncles can help you as they have influence. You must not kill unless you have to, and you must live through the disaster to come, as you are destined for bigger things. Do you promise?"

"I promise anything to you, Baba. I love you so much."

"Now, sing to me, my Mila."

I tried to sing the same song about the River and the town that my father sang so beautifully, but I could never match his voice and it came out funny and off-key. Milan and his helper started laughing, but I was rewarded by Baba's sorrowful smile.

"Oh my son, my beloved Mila," and she kissed my hands. "Your heart is ahead of your singing voice but your intentions are what counts."

She bent towards me so the men could not hear. "We will never mention our conversation with the Bishop to the family. Is that understood?"

I promised. Tears trickled down my cheek. The future she'd just predicted loomed in front of my eyes.

"My son, my soul. When you start to cry, stop and sing. Be grateful for all you have. Listen to my words for all time and let your soul and your heart lead you, then your brains."

↞

In the days following, Baba took to her room. Tata begged her to come downstairs, but most days she did not come down even for dinner and had to be served in her room. She encouraged me to come in, sit and talk to her. She seemed like my Baba and other times she seemed lost in her dreamland. I sat quietly with her long hours and held her hand and sometimes she would smile at me, her eyes alert to let me know she was still there. Her beautiful face gradually faded to gray. I felt she was leaving me and I begged her to stay.

Within a few weeks, she seemed to crumble into an old, old woman. She began drinking our wine on the weekends and crying in that soft mewing way. Gradually, her beautiful hair and robes became disheveled. Milojka tried to brush her hair and bathe her. Baba's skin sagged and she faded more each day. My heart hurt. I felt sick and couldn't concentrate on my studies. Life could mean nothing without her. One morning when I went in, she didn't respond. She'd given up at age 65 with a broken heart.

⌇

I cried with my family. I couldn't help it. My Baba, my life was gone forever. My Aunt Milojka hugged and rocked me, cried with me, her sorrow for her precious mother was as deep as mine. Drgica and Jelica hung on me, recognizing the terrible loss of Baba but bewildered at my extreme behavior. I couldn't pull it together. My Baba was gone and life would never be the same. I wanted to go with her.

The day she would be buried, my breath threatened not to continue. I just wanted to die. I begged Tata to be buried with her. Then I threatened to jump in the grave with her. My tender Tata, crying himself, held me and tried to console me in his soft voice. The pain was unbearable.

The funeral was to be held at our Orthodox Church in Kulina with all the relatives and people paying deep respects from villages all around. I heard later that many people came to our house. Someone gave me a powder so I remembered very little for of the rest of the day. Tata told me later, I was so distraught, he was afraid I'd keep my threat of diving into the grave after her. I vaguely remember seeing Milojka's visiting sister, Stanoslva grieving for her mother, but the day floated by into nothing.

I felt my Baba was the only one who truly understood me besides my busy Tata. I wanted to be dead with her. She taught me manners to be accepted in any class of people. What good would that do now? Who would make my special breakfast, just the right dash of cinnamon on my whites-only eggs? New tears came at the thought. I knew at almost 11 years old, I was too old to cry but I couldn't help it. I hoped the cousins didn't see me.

Our household continued in mourning. I really thought I couldn't live. My Baba was gone. How come I was alive? My sisters and Aunt Milojka made me drawings and brought my favorite foods although none could measure up to the breakfast Baba always made just for me. My sisters even decided to be nice to me and played music trying to release me from pain. I appreciated their caring, but couldn't seem to pull out of it.

My cousins and friends took turns visiting me trying to cheer me up. I could barely talk to them, concentrate on my studies or even eat. The pain was like being thrown from a horse into a stone wall. I felt woozy most of the time.

About three weeks later, I lay in the grass outside of the chicken pen. The air was still and the only sound was the chickens clucking at each other. I stared at the sky. Images of animals I always enjoyed roamed in the moving clouds. Suddenly, a large cloud floated by and in it I could clearly see my Baba's face, her white hair, and white silk dress, smiling at me. It brought soft tears to my eyes.

I heard her say as clear as if she were beside me, "When you're ready to cry, begin to sing! Remember? Promise you'll remember."

Her words came clean and clear. The clouds moved on, the bright sun continued to shine, and the chickens continued to cluck at each other in the background. I got up and walked into the house feeling much better.

Tata talked to me often trying to assure me that my Baba was with my Grandfather Ceda, her beloved husband in a better place, in Heaven. I listened. I prayed. I tried to make sense of her absence and to bide by her words, "When you're ready to cry, begin to sing!"

Eventually, Tata saw to it I went back to our tutor and tried to focus on catching up all the schoolwork so I could graduate. But it took months to recover from the awful pain in my heart, the nightmares of jumping in her grave. I felt alone without my Baba. My life would never be quite the same.

Chapter 6

1939-1940

News was hard to come by. The winter wind blew hard at a high pitch threatening to take part of our roof off. As a result of the bad weather, limited access to news on the new radio frustrated our family. We couldn't tune into the BBS and scratchy, noisy broadcasts from Germany were only from the Nazi version. Free speech ceased to exist. When Hitler himself was speaking, the exaggerated language of the Third Reich was frantic in his continued effort to influence the people. He talked of "the way to eternity."

Tata called the distortion of the facts, "Hitler's clumsy lying." He pointed out Hitler's need to constantly be defending himself, praising himself, never broadcasting with any straightforward news. "They are liars!"

Closer to home, we all prayed we wouldn't loose our roofs from the high winds.

Our limited Belgrade radio announced, "The Reich declared if Chancellor Von Schuschinigg restored the Hapsburg monarchy in Austria, Germany would be forced to enter Austria and take over with acts of violence."

Von Schuschinigg did resign and more than ninety percent of the Austrians voted "yes" to union with Germany. They took it without a shot.

Aunt Milojka seemed to have a glow about her helping Majka and teaching my sisters to embroidery. At least they were quiet when they cuddled up to my beautiful aunt taking in her every word. Woman seemed a curiosity to me. I liked them but they did seem silly sometimes. And I did miss Aunt Milojka when she went away on visits and wondered vaguely where she was going.

Hitler's fear of England and France sounded diabolic, too. The news from Hitler's own broadcast announced that France surrendered and he insisted that England had been invaded and was defenseless. How could we know the extent of his lies? Who would back down? Had war been declared? At every opportunity, we sat around the radio, straining to hear through the static trying to gather some true facts and learn our fate.

Later in April, against the calm beauty of full apple blossoms in the orchards, we listened as the Nazis occupied Czechoslovakia with no blood flowing. Would we be next? Nearly every day after my chores, I saddled and rode the high spirited Dana. That beautiful, patient mare flew me across fields, down the rough roads, around the farm buildings, and over small creeks. My green, fruitful world blurred out reality. When we stopped to cool down, I walked her and brushed her beautiful coat talking in our special language. Her big brown eyes penetrated into me diverting my anxiety about what would happen to my education, my family, and our land.

Just before my 14th birthday in May, the Uncles sat around the table discussing the situation. I hid behind the door to listen as usual. I had just settled down in my corner when the room became quiet. I looked up just in time to see my father appear over me.

"I, I huh, was just—."

"Don't worry, son. I know how curious you are and how you've been sneaking around here trying to listen. It is time to join the men. You must understand how complicated our situation is for your own future."

Tata actually formally introduced me as a man into the group. For once I was speechless and felt self-conscious as I sat quietly to listen.

Uncle Svetomir turned to me, "We are trying to pull ourselves together after centuries of fighting as you know from your history lessons, Miodrag."

Tata spoke, "Hitler declared that England and France are 'castrated minor states.' We hope he's wrong. Now Mussolini has marched into Albania and we have threats from all sides. What do you think England will do, Svetomir? Will they declare war?" Silence.

"Who could know? We're starting to hear about German U-boats' success in the North Sea."

Uncle Budimir told us how the Nazis had begun to court the Balkans. He said it was because they needed to command the Adriatic Sea coast so the Allies could not land there, but their word could not be trusted.

"Prince Paul is fearful that Germany may try to invade us next. He has been working on an agreement hoping to unite Yugoslavia by giving Croatia more autonomy to remove the threat of their Ustasha terrorists. He's using the *Sporazum* and an earlier agreement with the Vatican."

At that moment, our servant girl knocked on the door and summoned us to dinner. Walking into the dining room with the Uncles as one of them, and the questioning look on my sister's faces made me feel so proud everyone accepted me as a mature person.

⤷

On one clear Spring night, Chamberlain's words came though clearly on the BBC radio, "There is no peace after Hitler's government invading Poland and a five week battle without a chance to bargain."

He went on to tell us how they attacked with tanks and march-ing troops reeking havoc and killing. Up to now, Chamberlain could not conceive Germany would move so radically.

The Nazis bombed Poland's cities and countryside heavily sparing nothing including people's homes. The nerve of them to try to make it appear the Poles had started the fighting. I looked around at our nice big home and tried to imagine losing all the memories and our beautiful furniture lovingly passed down for years within our family.

⌐

All summer the brave Poles attempted to defend their land. We received few details and often long after the fact.

When Germany refused to pull back, Poland finally surrendered the end of September, their country in complete devastation. Chamberlain acknowledged the breach of the Treaty of Versailles and the bombing and terror it generated.

Britain declared war with Germany on September 3, 1939, "from their bad faith, oppression, and injustice."

As a result, the Nazis retrieved all the land in Poland taken from Germany in 1918, with about half going back to Russia under an old pact agreement.

Tata despaired, "Germany's been bombing London from that first day of war, every night sometimes. I don't know how much England can take. All we can do is stay loyal and go along with Prince Paul. Most Yugoslavians seem sympathetic to Britain and we have kept the Axis powers at bay somehow."

Uncle Budimir brought more news. "Now we have a looming conflict with the Communists growing in this country. A man named Josep Broz from Croatia; they call him 'Tito,' a common nickname in the district of Zagorje where I think he came from. He has been officially appointed general secretary of the Communist Party and they are working diligently to build up the Party again."

At dinner when the conversation turned to farming, I lost interest and silently remembered when Sir Teacher Slatoje at school had mentioned Tito. He'd been a prominent soldier and sounded like an exciting person to me. Prison in Russia after the War pressured him into becoming a communist. Our Sir Teacher Slatoje suggested Tito had found a way to get to the top through that political tactic. He was becoming known as a strong leader but we didn't like his politics.

None of boys I knew or their families believed in Communism after learning of Yugoslav workers in Russia being exiled to Siberia prisons for no apparent reason. We heard of atrocities worse than Hitler's. Stalin sounded like a monster. The boys at school made fun of Hitler as "little mustache," and Stalin as "big mustache."

"Surprise!" I jumped and my mouth fell open. Majka stood behind the two girls holding up a big cake, all smiling and giggling at my astonishment.

A birthday cake! "For me?" I sounded so stupid even to myself. Tata handed me a wrapped small gift. It felt hard. The paper fell to the floor as I stared. A real pocketknife, silver and brown with two folding blades. My heart beat hard as everyone stared at me, my fingers running over it as if I was blind. I'd been begging Tata for one for at least two years. Feeling myself growing bigger, I could no longer act like a child. I owned a knife. And I sat at the table with the men. I'd have to take responsibility now and stop teasing my sisters. I'll never forget this day, if only Baba could have been here. Never again would I cry. I had my own knife.

Uncle Budimir's close relationship with Prince Paul and the government brought constant stress on him. His close relationship with his brothers-in-law made them all nervous about the possibility of Serbia becoming isolated or worse, the Germans invading us. Hitler's sounded more like a real maniac all the time, declaring himself invincible and eternal, making exceedingly dangerous sounds. The Serbs recognized they'd once again been caught in the middle of Europe's war and faced a difficult decision on which side to align.

Then we heard about Serbian prisoners in Austria being traded like farm equipment and the frightening possibility of the Nazis landing in our back yard. The Yugoslavian Army was small and unprepared. The reality was that no one else except Russia and maybe Poland seemed to have a real Army to even begin to match Germany. Their leaders expected to conquer all of Europe and probably the World.

Returning from another business trip, Tata related that his business associate, Drazak Kadlj told him that on November 8, Hitler attended a meeting at the Burgerbraukeller in Munich and made a violent anti-British speech. He left the building at 9:15 P.M. with all his important Nazi chiefs. Twenty minutes later a bomb, concealed in one of the supporting pillars shattered the building bringing down the ceiling to collapse on the large assembly. Many of his earliest supporters were still there and nine people were killed. Naturally, Tata said Hitler blamed it on British Secret Service but the rumor was even worse, that he may have set the bomb up himself for a publicity stunt to increase his popularity.

By December, the British and all her colonies, had risen up against the Germans and the Italians. Rumors of sea battles and ships being sunk on both sides came through in bits and pieces when we could get radio contact. The British showed much more sturdiness than we ever gave them credit for and they wouldn't give up.

1940

During the winter of 1939-40, the schools were closed, and no one knew when they would open again. We seemed to be living in limbo. Already holding Croatia, Hitler demanded the rest of Yugoslavia to align with them while his army marched through Europe

From pieces of information, we learned Hitler's troops had invaded Finland in March, Norway and Denmark in April, bombing heavily and pushing the British out of their bases. The British were fighting the Germans on land, air, and sea battles. I cringed again to think again about people just like us experiencing the terror of the bombing, losing everything they owned. Germany Nazis bragged of flying their symbol swastika flag over those countries. We felt generally uniformed and helpless.

On May 10, 1940, just after by 15th birthday, Tata read us the news that Sir Winston Churchill had taken over as Prime Minister in England. Tata said, "He'll valiantly try to keep up the spirits of the people. I believed in him even when he was completely isolated and deemed a pariah. He has a strong will."

A few days later, Nazi Panzer divisions rolled through the low countries, their monster tanks in advance of dive bombers clearing away many of their obstacles but causing indiscriminate destruction to homes, hospitals, and churches in France and Holland.

Nazis continued the nightly bombing of England, on London, too, destroying many of their famous churches and starting fires everywhere with people running for bomb shelters, tasting death from the skies. British bombers, many sent from America, bravely attacked the Germans who often forced them back.

The war became worse. Belgium, Holland, Denmark and Norway had been invaded and Nazis troopers broke through the Maiginot Line on the ground in France. Then they continued bombing France finally reaching the Channel. France collapsed and surrendered in June crushing any hopes of support for us.

Imagine, those rotten Nazis in France! I do believe my Uncles intense love of France hurt them most of all so far. On the big table where we usually met, maps were spread with us leaning over trying to follow the giant push the Germans were making.

The British attempt to break through to the South to join the French became hopeless. From every side and from the skies, the Germans forced them back. On May 14, the Germans hurled their armored divisions against defenses near Sedan and drove a rapidly enlarged bulge into the French lines. My mind rolled again to that spot I tried losing: visions of German tanks pushing into our village.

Belgium surrendered leaving the British front unsupported. Despite the valiant effort, the Allies decided to retreat on a fighting march from Luxembourg all the way towards Dunkirk to evacuate by sea. They fell back forced by the Germans who had reached the channel at Boulongne and Calais. This information came from the BBC coming in clear as we huddled over the radio every night, taking in all the action we could.

During the whole long wait, German planes bombed them and made machine gun attacks. Courageously, the soldiers stood ground on the beach while British fighters and anti-aircraft batteries fought the enemy overhead. Every type of boat and ship came under fire to rescue the British. We later learned over 300,000 English soldiers including English and French wounded, waited on the beach, then waded to the rescue vessels.

On the BBC, the British Admiralty called the amazing rescue, "The most extensive and difficult combined operation in British naval history."

From May 27 on, during the day some one of us stayed by the radio to report on the progress. On June 3, Paris was bombed after an air raid during the noon hour. Over 1,000 bombs were dropped directly hitting a hospital and five schools inflicting many casualties with more than 250 deaths. The French tried to fight back, but Paris watched the Nazis enter Paris to fly their swastikas over the French capital. Churchill promised support to the French but once Paris fell, France asked for armistice terms.

On June 18, once again the British troops crossed back over the Channel returning home. Many French soldiers escaped into Switzerland. The Uncles mourned for their French friends, dead and alive.

Just a few days later, the R.A.F. started nightly bombing military and industrial centers on the Ruhr and Rhineland in north Germany. Marshal Goering's Air Force bombed all over England but the R.A.F. fighters used anti-aircraft guns bringing down many Nazi raiders. Then we found out a young General, Charles de Gaulle, brought a growing army of free Frenchmen to England to fight side by side with the British. That piece of news made the Uncles feel a little better.

In July, Sir Winston Churchill told the Nazis, "We seek no terms and ask no mercy." Englishmen grew even tougher, determined to push forward with all their might.

Here at home, Milan and Tata worked the men and I often worked right along side of them. Our farms brought in a record crop that summer keeping us busy and everyone fed, thank God.

Hitler needed Yugoslavia now that he had Rumania, Bulgaria and Hungary safely enrolled under their banner. Only Yugoslavia and Greece remained to be taken, and a British expeditionary force bolstered Greece. We stood isolated and vulnerable.

Chapter 7

1941

In February, Uncle Budimir returned from Germany with our Premier and Foreign Minister after an important summons from Hitler, himself. Uncle was amazed at Hitler's charm, bullying, and threats that convinced Yugoslavia, Romania and Bulgaria to sign a Tripartite Pact on March 25. He tried to be fair and explained Prince Paul himself and most Yugoslavians were sympathetic to Britain. But the Nazis with their Axis powers demanded common sense and caution and self-preservation.

The Belgrade radio announced, "Our representatives have been assured Germany will respect our sovereignty. The Nazis will not ask for our military assistance for their free passage through our country or move its army into our land. We think the Pact will keep us out of their war."

All the Uncles recognized that most Serbian peasants or working class never held characteristics of common sense or caution. They responded to the Germans in rude defiance.

A few days later, on March 27, shocking news came over Belgrade radio. The family listened horrified. In Belgrade Prince Paul, as acting Regent had been deposed by a group of young military officers in a coup d'état. They overthrew our Cvetkovic-Macek cabinet and kept demanding the cancellation of the Tripartite Pact much to the new government's fear of our perilous position. The news kept coming that they had placed the sixteen-year old King Petar II into position and formed a new cabinet under General Dusan Simovic.

Huge crowds gathered in Belgrade and demonstrated their favor of Britain and their extreme hated of Germany by smashing windows in the new Gestapo headquarters and tearing up the swastika flag. Oh, how I wished I could be there in all the action.

Our family toasted to the Serbians standing up to the Nazis. Tata and most of our family never wanted to side with Germany, especially the Nazis and never had or would trust them. But we were alarmed realizing without the Tripartite Pact, we could be surrounded by enemies.

On the BBC, Sir Winston Churchill, Prime Minister announced: "Today, Yugoslavia has found its soul."

Germany's anger at the coup d'état spoiled their plans to be aided by us through Yugoslavia in their advance to Russia and the interruption drove them to a fever pitch. The German press accused Yugoslavia of "atrocities" against German residents in Yugoslavia, and German consular officials were called home.

Nine days later, on Palm Sunday, April 6, we turned on the radio after coming in from church. The music stopped and an excited announcer announced Nazi Luftwaffe bombers crossed the Danube without warning and combed the military airport. Within the hour, Stukas dived down to the rooftops of Belgrade, releasing their bombs wiping out blocks of houses, hospitals, churches and schools. The small Yugoslav air force gallantly attacked the superior Luftwaffe but barely made a dent.

The first account estimated about 200 people killed. Once again, our family and servants were stunned beyond belief. This invasion was real and close to home. Our women wept. The men's faces showed great anxiety, too, but valiantly tried to hide it from the women.

A few days later, after dinner my father told us. "I just learned that a friend, our new Prime Minister, General Dusan Simovic is among the dead. His daughter's wedding party gathered and just about to take their places in the Church of the Assumption in Belgrade when the second barrage of bombs started to hit the City. The wedding party and all the guests ran for the shelter, but no one lived." His facial veins stuck out as he tried to keep his anger from showing as our mouths fell open.

"Belgrade was supposed to be an open city but they bombed us anyway! We are in terrible danger again, my dear family." Tata's brown eyes filled with tears of sorrow.

I looked over to my Majka. Her dark skin had turned almost white, her eyes widened in horror. Drgica and Jelica, dressed in their pretty silk dresses, ran to cling to her side. My little sister's apprehension felt her terror radiate through them and cried, "What shall we do? What will happen to us?"

"We'll get down on our knees and pray." We all got down on our knees. Aunt Milojka put her arms around the girls holding them tightly, "Dear God, give us strength to face the horror in front of us. Spare these children to have a future and help us all to understand how people can kill people," she prayed, her brave, soft voice quavering. Drgica and Jelica looked into her face with comprehension.

Their age of innocence was over.

King Petar immediately wrote a sorrowful message about the tragedy of hundreds of people dead in the bombing published in the newspaper; "innocent children asleep in their beds dying, planes flying low and machine-gunning mothers and children running from the bombs."

In Zagreb, Croatia, the same newspaper that carried the article added, "Croatia is also resurrect; all that is right and true as Christianity stands on the side of the Germans."

We became divided.

Belgrade radio went off the air temporarily, but occasional, clear newscasts came in from England, Radio Moscow, even the *Voice of America*. The second attack to Belgrade appeared far more violent than the first. Later, we heard gypsies came in from the country, broke into stores, to steal food, and furs. A few days later, the Nis paper came out with a full article including accounts of a bomb that hit the zoological gardens, causing wild animals to wander around the burning city. I could see the whole scene in my mind.

Figures finally came in of thousands of people killed in the bombings by Axis forces invading us with no warning or declaration of war. Apparently, there had been no preparations against attack. After the bombing, the Nazi Panzer division moved in. Yugoslavia's roads were quickly overrun with tanks pushing aside our traps, causing general destruction. All 30 divisions of the Royal Yugoslav Army collapsed against 52 invading Axis combined forces.

On April 9, British airmen made the heaviest attack on Berlin with heavy high-explosive bombs killing more than 2000 civilians. We all knew that a win for the Allies would be of no help for us.

Hungary had signed a pact of eternal friendship with us in February. Hungarian and Yugoslavian foreign ministers had marched together through Budapest in celebration. Then, on April 11, Hungarian troops invaded the Banet, a Hungarian territory in Yugoslavia before 1918.

On April 16, the Germans captured Sarajevo. Our outdated weapons floundered against the new superior equipment of the Nazis. Britain and America promised aid and we expected it to come in from the Adriatic shores.

"Tata, you must let me join the army. I want to be a soldier!" The fever ran through me at a high pitch.

Tata put me down quickly, "Son, you are too young and besides we don't really have an army for you to join, I'm afraid."

He was right. The next day April 17, Yugoslavia's remaining formal army forces surrendered unconditionally. The family just looked at each other in exasperation without wasting any words at all.

Another week later we heard from one of Tata's business friends, our boy King Petar and his Cabinet members had driven into Bosnia and then on to Montenegro where they boarded a plane to Jerusalem. Tata's friend told us that just like Petar's father, King Alexander had done years before, they took off after helping themselves to our country's money. The men around the new King Petar were seen loading ten cases of gold stolen from the National Bank onto the overhead racks of the plane. Supposedly, as they were flying over Greece, they got caught in a storm and a case of gold fell on one of the ministers and killed him.

A major distraction came when Tata made a big announcement over dinner. "Selimka and I have set a date for the most exciting family gathering. We are planning a wedding for Aunt Milojka."

"What?" I nearly yelled, nearly tipping my chair over. "How could I not know about this?"

The family laughed. Tata said, "Settle down, my son. A wonderful man introduced to her by Budimir has courted Milojka. His name is Radojako. He lives a few towns away and of course, he is Serbian. That's where she's been on many chaperoned trips away from us. She preferred to keep it her business until she made a decision, didn't you Milojka? You'll meet him soon," Tata nodded at Drgica, Jelica, and me.

I resented not knowing Milojka even had a serious beau before now. Why was I left out? I looked around but everyone was smiling including the housekeeping servants, so I smiled and kissed my sweet Aunt Milojka's face as soon as I got the chance. Once I got over my left out feeling, I felt truly happy for her.

Milojka explained, "My fiancé, Radojako fears the war will separate us, my precious boy, so we've decided to be married right away. Lord knows, I've waited long enough to find the right man. I hope you approve, Mila." She held me and looked deeply into my eyes with that sweet smile.

Our household all joined in the preparations for the marriage. We sent announcements, arranged for the church service and the entertainment, brought in supplies, cleaned, and cooked.

On the same weekend in May, I celebrated my sixteenth birthday. My extended family surrounded me but I accepted the fact, they were really there for Aunt Milojka's wedding. My first sight of the groom encouraged me. They seemed to match in height, personalities, and attraction. She had chosen our Orthodox Church in Kulina, the family church for several generations. The choir sang the ceremonial songs, and our old priest presented a solemn ceremony chosen without frills in respect of the war.

Radojako's clean face seemed to shine at the sight of his beautiful partner coming up the aisle. Aunt Milojka looked radiant in her simple but stylish dress, even more beautiful than usual.

After the ceremony, most of the villagers and all the visitors trudged happily up to our house. Squeeze boxes and hammer music provided by a village Gypsy band played many hours on the lawn and could be heard clear down the valley. All the people breathed in the perfect soft air of spring, happy in the present trying to put off the fears of the future.

My family served succulent lamb from the big spit with all the traditional dishes and kegs of our wine. After filling with food, several people presented toasts to the newlyweds, and the guests joined in the kola dance led by the bride and groom. Their arms touched on each other's shoulders, straight-backed with heads held high, they bounced around the circle with their feet moving through the intricate steps.

I clapped happily on the sidelines beside my Majka who usually stood out of the limelight and continually worried about keeping the table full. Neither one of us could dance, but that didn't stop most of the others. Even the quiet Milan, very handsome in his best clothes, caught the eye of several young unmarried women from the villages and danced for hours to my amazement. My lively little sisters danced with the others, swinging and laughing under the vivid blue sky. Everyone soaked up the joy and our love for our beloved Aunt Milojka whom we'd miss so much.

Even relatives I'd rarely seen like Aunt Stenoslava, Milojka's older widowed sister, joined our wedding group. I vaguely remember meeting her at Baba's funeral but memories blurred from that time. Now, I could talk to her as an adult and discovered she taught school including French she'd learned as a child from the Uncles. She was not as pretty as Aunt Milojka, but had the same speech and grace as Baba. And I admired her courage when she told me how she had traveled with an armed chaperone on a very long and dangerous distance for this happy event.

Her young daughter, about the same age as Jelica had accompanied her and looked so much like Jelica. Everyone commented on it. The girls giggled together and let the boys chase them around until Majka caught them and ordered them to "settle down and act like young ladies."

I kept by my cousins. Zivadin, much less impressive in looks and talk than his brother, wouldn't even comment on this pretty cousin. He and Vladislav were both worried about joining the guerrillas just the same. We talked about the war where the adults couldn't hear us. Vladislav was waving his fists and roaring that he was ready to fight a battle. I bragged to them that I sat in on the Uncles' meetings regularly now and learned a lot of what was going on behind the scenes in the other countries, and tried to persuade them to learn more. They still didn't take me very seriously.

In respect for the bride and groom, all our guests tried to keep the visiting light-hearted even though the war loomed foremost on everyone's mind. To me, the highlight of the celebration was the beautiful singing voice of my Tata bringing tears of joy and sadness to the guests. His voice touched our souls and expressed all we felt on that emotional day, maybe the last gathering we'd all share together.

Late into the evening Aunts and Uncles and their children stayed up kissing each other and sharing the gossip and news, then crowded into our guestrooms to sleep.

Aunt Milojka's and her new husband, Radojako stayed on a few days in the nicest, and most private suite not much changed since Baba occupied it for many years. When they dined with us, I decided he seemed all right when he talked directly to me. Actually, I came to like him. He was her age, humorous, and well educated. Of course, he was a determined, stubborn Serbian still loyal to our absent King. But I felt jealous of him for some reason I didn't understand. I did know I hated the fact Aunt Milojka was moving away and felt another loss in my chest.

Vladislav, and Zivadin finally took up an interest and sat in on a family meeting. I looked at them and suddenly realized skinny Vladislav had grown several inches taller. I'd never catch up.

That night by candlelight I looked into a clouded mirror in the kitchen trying to see any sign of whiskers. Surely at 16, I should have some. None showed and none could be felt. Envy attacked me because Vladislav's face proved he used a razor, and he could actually grow a beard! Even the quieter Zivadin, showed some fuzz. I stared at the reflection of a very young boy and deeply wished for facial hair and the growth spurt my Majka kept assuring me would happen. I told myself I was just trying to take my mind off the disastrous situation placed in our country and all of Europe and how it would affect our lives.

The reality and consequences started to hit me. Our men actually would have to fight. We couldn't just sit here like the Austrians and Cheks who just rolled over. Would Vladislav have to go to war? Would the rest of us? Who would die? But the excitement of battle, of being a hero caused a thrill right through me just thinking of it.

Apparently, the Nazis considered the destruction of Belgrade as a conquest. The Third Reich incorporated northern Slovenia and started to divide up Yugoslavia with other would-be Axis countries as a political move. Our area along with Macedonia, was placed under the Wehrmacht High Command clear to the border of territory the hated Bulgarians claimed.

In the weeks following, the proud Nazis continued to pour into Yugoslavia expressing enormous prestige. The SS bragged of certain victory and Nazi planes continued to bomb England. Serbs were hauled off against their wishes to work in armament factories in Germany and Austria.

We heard that on May 29, Germany suffered when their most modern battleship, the "Bismarck" was sunk. It was irreplaceable. Even so, Hitler bragged about winning "the greatest air battle," "greatest bombardment," "greatest battle of enrichment and attrition in world history."

Yet, Tata found out the German people were suffering real starvation and gasoline shortages as their war effort was using everything the Nazis had built up for years. No promised aid came from the Allies, but we prayed it would come soon.

More bad news followed in bits and pieces. Italy aligned with Germany, won Montenegro and much of Dalmatia on the southern part of the Adriatic Sea coast. Italy's puppet State of Albania was given the providence of Kosovo. They annexed northern Slovenia and tried to steal farms sending peasant families on the road pathetically trying to haul some belongings with them. Bosnia-Herzegovina and Croatia, caught in the middle, became recognized as the Independent State of Croatia or NDH under the Ustasha leader, Ante Pavelic, organized by Adolf Hitler and the Nazis.

Tata, the Uncles, Vladislav and Zivadin gathered around the table trying to figure out how the Ustasha would affect the war. Svetomir yelled in fury over the division. He even pounded on the table so hard, the coffee leaped out of the cups. The Nazi decision seemed to verify the Croatians as serious enemies to us when my family felt they should be on the same side with us.

The Uncles' agitation made listening difficult, and my eyes flew from one to the other trying to understand their intense anger. Svetomir stood up knocking his chair over, his eyes burning in anger.

"Obviously, the Croats have gone over to the Germans, just as we'd heard. Those traitors! They've never considered us

Serbs as kinsmen and have been set on killing all of us as Orthodox Christians. What's more, the majority of Roman Catholics in Croatia have the support of the Church and the Pope in Italy."

"Why?" I started to ask a question and all heads turned towards me, as it was the first time I'd spoken at these now secret meetings of the men.

Uncle's voice became even louder. "Because they resent our Serbian Orthodox Church for not recognizing their Pope, and we never, never will acknowledge the Pope over Christ!"

"That's history now." Tata spoke harshly. "We should focus on the fact that Croats have been ruled and patronized by the more sophisticated Germans, Hungarians and Italians. For centuries they've assumed they belonged to 'Western Europe' and were superior to us 'eastern' primitive Serbs. They are more ambitious than Mussolini's Italian troops and more violent than Hitler's Reich. Ustasha, means uprising, and the Ustasha Croats are dangerous killers and hate all of us Serbs. What did our father Ceda die for? Why did you, my brothers spend years of your life suffering in prison?"

Tata's voiced choked, "Now our neighbors are still our enemies! We must support the royalist's detachments now. They were strong fighters the last three years of the first World War, and now will fight for our King and our democratic government or what's left of it."

His voice softened, "From now on, the military is in charge. We will support our General Draza Mihailovic. He is gathering up the remnants of the Army who would have refused to surrender and volunteered to be guerrillas. They're trying to build a secret base in the mountains and are maintaining lines of supply to Greece and the Allies."

Tata's voice came loud and clear. "We don't want the Nazis or the Communists to rule us. As a country, we will fight them until we die." He brought his fist down so hard on the table, the glasses all jumped at once.

The brothers clapped and stomped their feet at his emotional speech.

"Tata," I impulsively asked. "Who is this Mihailovic?"

"I'll answer that," said Uncle Budimir. "Your grandfather Ceda knew him personally in the first World War fighting in the mountains. He was a young Colonel in the regular Army then, and recently he has acted as the leader of the Chetniks, a club for veterans of the Turkish and Austrian wars. Now I hear our government in exile in London has appointed him a General and our Minister of Defense.

"The British are greatly cheered to have someone here capable at the helm. Our only resistance is guerrilla warfare and Mihailovic has studied that. He's is an intelligent and intense man. Most of the men fighting for him are older, local people concerned for their families and often peasants right off the farms. I know he'll hate leaving his farm and return to fighting, but what can we do? And I mean all of us."

"Mihailovic is a good capable leader," replied Uncle Svetislav, the eldest and closest son of Ceda. "I knew him personally through our father. We are in dire jeopardy. Our family must keep a low profile. Our connections must be kept secret. That goes for all of our workers and house servants. We are their protectors, but do not speak of our position in the war in front of anyone but this group. All of us must watch every word we say and stay close to home except for absolutely necessary business trips."

"Brothers, I agree." Tata said, "We must be very careful not to speak of any political news beyond this table. Now, our business is working hard so the fields will grow food and grain, and these precious orchards will provide fruit for us and all the villages around here."

Svetomir agreed, "We'll join with Svetislav to keep quiet and concentrate on our farming. I'm planning to put in more wheat and I hope the rest of you will join in a co-op group. We must be able to feed our people plus aid the guerrillas and all people who need us, even a stray enemy. Does everyone agree?" All agreed.

New terror centered from within the Balkans. From the beautiful old town of Zagreb, 30 priests were murdered in the Ustasha massacres in April, 1941. Those murderers kept killing, some victims forced to dig graves to be buried alive. In one small town, the Ustasha butchered 1,000 Serb men, women and children inside an Orthodox Church after setting it on fire. The killing went on and on. Murders of that scale did not seem real.

Hard work on all our farms kept us so busy we didn't have much time for complaint. The crops had to be planted, animals fed and cared for, people organized, and water kept pure. Even my sisters at home helped care for the chickens and geese, checked eggs and boxed them up to sell through Deda's store.

Coming in from checking orchards one day, I reined up Dana to a halt behind some trees, and stared at my sisters spreading corn for the chickens. At ten years old, Jelica had big, dark, serious eyes like Majka. She secretly envied Drgica who was fourteen, as tall as me with red-blond hair, and blue eyes like our Tata. The fiery little Jelica often harassed the shy, studious Drgica who just ignored her much of the time. I had helped teach both of them to read. And in spite of her limited four years of schooling, Jelica insisted she would become a teacher. I looked at both of the blossoming young girls carrying buckets of eggs, and teasing a rambunctious rooster. War seemed very far away.

But not for long.

Everyone talked about German convoys and troops marching through northern Yugoslavia to the oil fields of Romania in May and the heavy bombing in London destroying so many churches. The bravery of the English surprised us and gave us faith.

Apparently, "Tito" using a false name, came out of hiding in Zagreb. Uncle Svetislav knew Tito had built the Communists up to over 10,000 full party members and three times that many members of the youth organization underground. We heard of possible military help from Tito's group, formerly the Communist Party of Yugoslavia, later called "Partisans."

Many of these motivated, younger men came from Belgrade University and the artisan class. They played a part in the demonstrations in Belgrade but many of my friends out here in the country forgot or didn't recognize that group had previously worked for the breakup of Yugoslavia.

Many peasants fell for the "Death to Fascism, Freedom to the People" slogan. It appeared better than having the Nazi foreigners in our midst.

Mihailovic and Tito, both World War veterans, met a few times but General Mihailovic later told Uncle Budimir that he could not tolerate Tito's ultimate goal to use the war to establish Yugoslavia as a Communist state and become its president.

We felt quite isolated from the tyranny of war and the killing but thankful that for now we were not being overrun by one enemy or another. All of us, family, servants, and farm workers from all our farms continued to pull together and concentrate on producing as much as possible for our own storage and market preparation for others.

The railroad lines along our Sava and Morava River valleys were confiscated by the Nazis. The guerrillas set up tank traps, but the Germans' huge tanks just pushed them right over. Our guerrillas began tearing up and destroying those railroad tracks to prevent the Germans from using any part of it on their way to Greece.

So we just used our wagons for transportation on the back roads as far as we dared to travel.

Even my old, fat grandfather, Deda bragged how busy he was at the store. Majka complained that somehow her father was making lots of dinars, and suspected he was selling food to German troops. We wouldn't put it past him, and hoped he put poison in it.

We continued to huddle over the radio after dinner every night hoping to tune into in the BBC or reach Moscow. News had nearly stopped from other parts of Europe. We did hear nasty rumors about many Yugoslavian people, especially Jews taken hostage by the thousands and imprisoned. Our hearts sunk.

In June, just as we were tending the first tiny sprouts poking up through the rich dirt, and the new chicks, calves, piglets, and other farm animals, more news came. On St. Vitus' Day June 28, the Ustasha started another round of atrocities to Orthodox people first in Croatia and then Bosnia and Herzegovina near the Adriatic coast.

It was learned the Germans did not approved of the barbaric killings but weren't much help as they were being pulled out to participate in the Russian launching called "Operation Barbarossa."

The radio announced German troops had actually invaded Russia.

That news excited those who were not Communist members. Many people thought the Russians would stomp the Germans. That angry segment of the war should keep both enemies busy for a while. But the wisest of the Uncles, Uncle Svetislav was not at all confident and predicted a bloody, drawn out war.

The very thought of Baba filled me with courage to conquer fear of whatever was to come. At 16, I thought I was a man even though to my annoyance, I still looked like a young boy. What would be my destiny?

The fall harvest of our fruits, wheat, vegetables kept us all busy and filled our stomachs. The profits filled our purses to pass on to the workers. Tata and I spent hours going over the books in his grimy, but comfortable office adjacent to the tack room. Banking the dinars was impossible with any banks still in commission were located too far away. So dinars had to be hidden. All the money from the plum wine sold was traded for gold coins. And the gold was buried in bags in a secret place near our house. No one but Tata knew the location.

The brothers Cedic still met at our house for family meetings including Uncle Budimir who traveled to meet other politicians in secret places, and then joined us when he could. I usually sat in also. As we suspected, Deda was selling bulk food mostly vegetables, fruit and wine, to the Germans military through his store just as he'd done for our own troops in World War I.

Budimir confirmed the peasants were split on whether to fight the Germans soldiers in their area or not. Some, especially those following Tito's Partisans considered themselves guerrillas and ached to kill Nazis.

"Which is worse; sitting still afraid of retaliation, or fight as best we could? Our people are born fighters," Svetolik said.

Budimir told us later the controversy exploded when General Mihailovic, fearing guerrilla reprisals would turn into a Serbian holocaust and ordered his troops not to openly fight the Germans.

Mihailovic also swore Tito had recognized his own advantage of the horror to the peasants. With information eventually verified, peasants in fear came running to join the Partisans Communists for protection. Tito's long range plan appeared to be aimed at winning personal power in Yugoslavia rather than focus on damaging the Axis war effort.

The Uncles believed Tito ordered attacks on our Cetnici to coincide with German action against them. They also had reason to believe Tito guilty of arranging for local politicians to be killed to hide his Partisan plans when necessary.

The peasants were generally leery of the Partisans being "outsiders." But the rough, trusted Cheknik guerrillas tried to protect their people and began sniping German troops taking over towns. They never ceased their activities of sabotage and open armed combat every day.

In reprisal, the Germans sent a shocking message that for every one German soldier the resistance killed, 500 Serbs would be killed in retaliation.

They were serious. After dinner one stormy fall evening, Milan knocked loudly on the back door, dripping wet and urgently asked to speak to my father. I called Tata down and stood by as Milan, hat in hand, with his head bowed, and voice shaking, told us terrible news.

"In Kragajevac, a Partisan official stirred up the peasants against Germans troops who were taking the peasants food. They killed ten Germans and wounded twenty-six in a tough fight. Then, then—," Milan mumbled his words, "I heard the entire male population of the town and the farms were rounded up and 7,000 men including schoolboys were shot. Then, over a thousand more were executed in Valjevo."

Tata flared up in anger and grabbed Milan's face with both hands forcing him to repeat the unbelievable disaster just a few miles away.

Milan's pale face showed tears spilling down as he mumbled out the ghastly news again. He turned and ran back down the path leaving Tata and me standing frozen in the doorway.

"Oh, dear God, God help those families. I'll try to send food. Oh, dear God!" Tata stumbled back into the kitchen area and plunked himself down in a chair. He held his head in his hands.

Majka came slowly into the room. Her eyes held my eyes as she took my hands.

"My son, I heard." Her voice sounded shaky and on the edge of tears just like Baba's did when she told me about the deaths of her grandparents so many years ago. Disaster cuts us in half.

Late that night, I went to my room and sat on the edge of my bed feeling so confused. I lay down with my arms under my head and stared at the ceiling. Shadows from the trees blowing in the wind threw moving shadows across it. My life seemed to run across with the shapes and forms. It dawned on me how protected I'd been, how incredibly fortunate I'd been for God to have placed me into such a good, caring family. I wondered how long it could last.

A few nights later, aware of loud voices outside, I sat straight up in bed, alarmed. Tata had left that morning to meet a buyer from Nis and wouldn't be back until tomorrow. I looked down over the sill and saw several soldiers in uniform on the ground level, one or two banging on the front door. The scene turned my heart to ice. Oh God, I have to handle this myself.

I heard Majka running to Drgica and Jelica's rooms, frantically ordering them out of bed. I threw on my pants and shoes and grabbed a lantern, my coat, and ran into the women in the hall. The girls' eyes held terror as they clung to each other while being pulled along by Majka.

"Come with me!" a ferocious looking Majka ordered. She pushed the frightened girls down the stairs towards the hidden root cellar door. I nodded but rushed towards the front door before the soldiers could knock it down and start shooting.

I steeled myself and threw open the door to face guns in my chest. I expected to hear German instead heard these young men speaking Bulgarian mixed with a few words of Serbian that I could just barely understand.

"Bring out everyone in the house!" one ordered as he barged into me.

I turned quickly trying to block the soldiers out. They yelled the orders back into the house, "Leave the house or be killed!"

Our housekeeper, her husband, and the other younger servants came running out of their separate quarters with only coats hugging their nightwear. The soldiers must have assumed they were family and never looked further. As scared as I was, and dark as it was, I noticed many of the soldiers were not much older than me. They clumsily lined up our household and ordered us down the road to the Kamenica village square at gunpoint.

I squinted my eyes in disbelief recognizing every villager I ever knew lining up in the dark road. The silence of the night was pierced by cries and pleading from the woman, swearing from the men, and soldiers yelling orders back at them. The commotion threw the dogs into frenzy barking. I prayed no one would miss my mother and sisters.

The soldiers pushed us to line up with other terrified villagers. "Women on one side and men on the other side." For a few seconds, the scene melted into a vision of the ruffians in the Nis plaza shoving around the peasant women. I swallowed my fear and tried to stay in the present. The so-called soldiers' Nazi odd uniforms were well worn, and their boots old and broken down. But this was no joke. Woman, shaking and wailing, lined up on one side with men on the other as ordered.

The Corporal stepped forward screaming questions at us in his broken Serbian. "Who is resisting? Who left to the mountains? Who is supporting the enemy? Who is supplying the enemy?"

We shivered from the cold and fright trying to respond to the officer's intense questioning. Most of the people didn't know anything. Most didn't even read or own a radio. I cringed as a soldier punched the butt end of his rifle into the shoulder of one old veteran who spit in his face.

After about two harrowing hours, the Bulgarians were getting nowhere. You could just see frustration on their tired faces like boys who couldn't win the ball game. They were tired and hungry and demanded food. A couple of soldiers forced some women into their houses to bring out food and they took turns sitting down to eat while others held their guns on the scared and weary people still standing.

The peasants were ready to drop. The officer demanded all the stronger men to line up: about 20 of us including me, the youngest. The soldiers shoved back the frantic women who were grabbing at the clothes of the selected men.

The soldiers bullied us up the road from the village, poking and hitting with guns to keep us in line. I looked back at the women, children and old men watching in horror pleading with the soldiers. The village men trudging beside me worked for us. I'd known them all my life. Some of the soldiers threatened shooting their guns while we climbed up the hill out of sight of the village. The young officer yelled, "Stop!"

Shivers ran all over me. At least, I had on my clothes. Many of the men were in nightclothes, barefoot, and shivering from panic and cold. I could see they were trying to bravely face the unknown. The whole scene seemed like a terrible nightmare.

They lined us up between two small hills. On one side was a row of machine guns. Loud Bulgarian voices rang through the chilly air. I interpreted for the men, trying to manage my voice. "They are ordering us to dig trenches for our graves."

Shocked Serbian voices muttered, "My God, they are really going to kill us!"

"Shoot us and bury us here?"

Facing the soldiers' guns, we slowly started digging with our hands, shovels, and sticks, our bodies shaking from exhaustion and fear. Any man who made a wrong move saw guns and death centered on him.

My throat kept closing up and I strained to get air. One of the young men next to me started to cry loudly and I became aware of cries and whimpers all around me. I don't know what made me do it but I yelled sternly and loudly, "We are all soldiers, we can't cry. Think. Talk. Don't cry!"

Then I said quietly, "The minute the shooting starts, jump in the trench and we'll dig out later. Pass it on." The Bulgarians couldn't understand us.

When the shallow trenches were dug, the village men were lined up in two lines in front of our graves. No one made a sound. Suddenly, shouts and the rapid burst of machine guns startled us. We raised our heads up and were amazed to see the Bulgarian soldiers whirling around, their guns pointed in the other direction. Machine guns spit red fire into the air. Serbian guards burst out of the forest. They screamed at the Bulgarians, "Stop, stop! Lay down your guns. Surrender!"

The startled young officer threw down his gun and yelled "Cease fire!" to his men. His frightened soldiers immediately dropped their guns and raised their arms in surrender.

I stared through the dark. It couldn't be. Like a vision, I recognized my Uncle Budimir running towards us with a man in a high Nazi uniform right behind him.

"Release those men!" the officer ordered.

I found my feet and ran to them, completely bewildered. Who was this Nazi officer with him and where did the Serbians come from? Why did they stop the killing?

The Bulgarian officer tried to protect himself, "Don't shoot, we are all guerrillas!"

"No, Uncle," I cried, "We were taken from home!"

Before I could get any more words out, Uncle Budimir threw up his hand to silence me and motioned me back. "Go back, Mila. Go back to the village and take the villagers with you. Let their families see them alive. I'll talk to you later."

I turned, motioned them to follow me and started running back down the hill towards the village with the others stumbling after me. As we got closer to Kamenica, awful sounds of keening pierced the air. In the pale dawn light, I saw our little Church building draped with blue and black flags of mourning. The woman and children must think all their men are dead, I thought.

"Take the flags down," I yelled. "We're alive. We're all alive!" The villagers turned towards my voice, astonished until they recognized me.

"Miodrag, Miodrag! You're alive." They stood stunned, then held up their hands to God in thanks.

The rest of the men running right behind me, passed me up to find and embrace their families. Tears turned to shouts of joy and relief. I'd never experienced such an emotional scene. Out of the crowd and noise, my Majka, her arms in the air ran to me crying, "My son, he brought them back alive. He'll be Czar, he's a leader!"

Tata came back early the next day and had already heard all about the near massacre before he arrived at the house. His reaction of shock nearly made him sick. Over breakfast, he kept brushing back his thick auburn hair with his hand trying to make sense of the whole alarming attack.

"This war has finally arrived on our doorstep. We'll have to take precautions. Your Majka did the right thing to take the girls to the cellar but that may not work next time. We must make a plan."

A few days later, Uncle Budimir showed up at our house. Around the family dinner table, he told how we actually came to be rescued.

"No one outside this table must know about this or I'm dead. I've been secretly working as a guide for the Germans so I can get information for our guerrillas. When Milan heard the commotion at the house he rode hours to find me. According to the Germans, those soldiers were Bulgarian Communists and the massacre was their own idea. Trying to make a name for themselves, I guess. I got help through my new associate, Commander Schmitz, a high Nazi officer. He must fight for the Nazis or be killed the same as me. He has friends in the Wehrmacht who will help protect us when they can."

I stared at him. He was going against everything I believed in, that I thought my family believed in. My voice was quivering with emotion, but I ask him anyway. "Uncle, how could you work with the Nazis?"

"Schmitz is not a real Nazi, just conscripted into the German army like so many other young men. I saved his life recently. He feels he must protect me and mine in return. Now he has saved your life and all the village men with you. We do what we must for survival. Until we can get some aid from the Allies, the massacres show us it's just suicide to fight. That's how it works." The muscles in his fleshy jaw were set hard and his usually warm eyes blazed ice cold. No more questions were asked.

During dinner, Uncle told us General Mihailovic felt frustrated, also. "He's determined to try to help the Germans and Italians prevent a Communist victory. In November, after fruitless negotiations with Tito, the General ordered Cetnik units to attack the unwelcome communist Partisans, and Tito's central command withdrew into Bosnia. The Cetnici expanded southwest trying to gain local and Italian support."

⌐⌐

Winter blew in hard. Snow banked against the buildings and fences. Our supply sources were generally cut off although our family remained comfortable with our carefully stored supply of food and fuel. Tata and Milan made sure Kulina and Kamenica had plenty and we could only hope other villages did, too.

If it weren't for Tata's high-powered radio with BBC, Radio Moscow, the Voice of America, and the Uncles traveling and gathering information, we would be as much in the dark as the peasants. Germany bragged of their invincibility as the Wehrmacht continued a ferocious frontal attack into southern Russia. I felt frustrated as I wanted to know more and the news often came between crackles and snaps even on our powerful radio.

Britain recognized Mihailovic as the leader of the resistance movement including our ragged leftover Army. They began supplying the Cetnici even though they were not sure who the Cetnici were fighting. At times, we weren't sure either. Churchill believed the balance of influence between Russia and the West did not include Yugoslavia.

In December, 1941, the big news came to us that Japan had attacked America on one of their islands. Now they would be in the war and we knew America was the only country who had airplanes capable of crossing the ocean. We still felt sure they would come by way of the Adriatic Sea.

We heard of many people taken off to prison or taken hostage even near our villages. About the same time, Germany upped their threat to the Balkan people: 100 people would be killed for every German wounded, and 300 for one German soldier killed. That edict immediately hit home.

Chapter 8

1942

One frosty but pleasant spring Sunday morning my family and I rode in our best carriage down to Kulina to attend our Orthodox Church. I noticed a huge dust cloud rising up on the road coming from the opposite direction, too big and moving to fast for country wagons. Tata nervously pulled the horses over and we climbed out and stood by the road nearby the Church.

Suddenly two large army trucks loomed into sight, their engines roaring. Curious people came out of the church. The noisy trucks' brakes screeched, raising the dust as we all stood there mesmerized. Young Nazis in splendid uniforms compared to the Bulgarians, jumped out pointing big rifles right at us.

Their officer demanded that anyone speaking German must step out. My feet froze. My voice cracked when I tried to say, "I speak German."

Majka, alarmed, started pulling on my coattail. The officer pointed at me and ordered me to inform the people that all males from 15 to 35 years old were to line up. I was struck silent until he pressed his rifle right on my heart and demanded, "Say it!"

I shifted my feet apart to keep my balance. "All men from 15 years of age to 35 years of age step forth." The soldiers laughed at my formal, but broken German. "Say it to them!" he ordered. I tried to get it out. No one moved. The priest came running, waving his arms trying to intervene. A soldier rudely pushed him back with a butt of a rifle.

"Shout it again!" ordered the officer. I shouted it embarrassed that my voice cracked.

The men looked at each other, at their families and at the rifles. They began to timidly step forward. The soldiers grabbed them by their collars and shoved the stumbling men toward the trucks and heisted them in. I looked at each familiar man. Thank God, neither my teacher Sir Teacher Slatoje from school nor my cousins were there.

The women wailed in such anguish that I stood still mesmerized at the scene. Majka whispered in gulps in my ear to stand still, hoping maybe they'd think I was too young. My sisters clutched onto her and me, their faces white with eyes wide with fear. Tata stood perfectly still, his lips pinched tight with anger holding his Bible to his chest.

The soldiers scattered to search through our church and the houses looking for other young males. They tried the stores but they were closed for the Sabbath so they broke a few windows and helped themselves to whatever caught their eye. My big, fat Deda stood near his precious store deadly still in shock and fear.

When all the men they could find were loaded in the truck, the officer turned to me and ordered me in, too. Deda jumped to me and Majka started to shriek both trying to hold me back. Tata spoke forcefully, "Let him go."

The officer took hold of my arm and led me to the back of the truck. He shoved me up and I landed on my knees. My eyes adjusted to a whole load of men, many unknown to me from other villages. A terrible dread glowed in every eye. My own nerves were tingling and a tiny, wet drizzle trickled down my bare leg.

The engine revved up and off we went, rattling and bouncing in the dark. Silence filled the crowded truck. Nazi soldiers were crowded in with us holding onto their rifles. The smell of strong body odor mixed with gasoline fumes made me feel dizzy. I had to think. The truck had been headed south and didn't turn around so as near as I could tell, we must be headed south towards Nis.

We rattled along and I tried to calculate our speed and how long it would take to get there. No one talked and soon they were sitting back and dozing off. I smoothed my warm wool suit and gave my coat to a shivering employee of ours. He nodded his head but said nothing. I concentrated on trying to relax and forget the cold.

The truck came to a screeching stop again, and we all woke up. Was this a dream? Hardly. They herded us with pointed rifles through a big roll-up doorway into a huge factory building. In fact, as I looked around in the dark, I recognized it must be a tile factory. Hundreds of strange men were standing there, tired and scared. They stared at this new group as if they were waiting for us. Surely, the Nazis wouldn't kill us here.

A high-grade officer called for attention in German; a Serbian voice interpreted. "You are taken as hostages. You have been warned. You will be kept for 15 days and released only if not one Nazi is killed in this area. If even one of Hitler's finest is killed, all 300 hostages here will be shot! You will be assigned a job and you will obey orders." The officer clicked his heels and raised his hand for all his soldiers to follow, "Heil Hitler!"

Considering these Nazi soldiers represented all I'd ever heard about but never seen, I was impressed. They were well groomed, regimented and serious. I couldn't begin to believe they would kill all these innocent people. The factory looked as if it recently had been a normal working operation.

Upon command, we were herded outside to toilets in the most horrible conditions, then back to a large empty room with straw scattered on the floor, the sleeping area. Soldiers passed around black bread and water to the new group. My stomach growled with hunger and I grabbed the biggest piece of bread I could.

The next morning very early, we were rousted up and given our assignments. I was assigned to the temporary bakery next to the soldier's mess. Much to my joy, I found myself next to a fellow my own age from my school. "Ivan, I can't believe it. Can you believe this?"

We grabbed each other, far from home, anxious about our dilemma, and so relieved to see a familiar face. "Oh Mila, am I glad to see you. Oh, I'm sorry, I didn't mean here!"

"That's all right. I'm glad to see someone I know, too."

"Can you believe the rats running over the straw they call a bed?"

"I may tame one for a pet. How did you like the toilets?"

"They stink!" and we found that together, we could laugh. Inside the bakery, they showed us our simple task of pulling bread and pastry out of the hot ovens with huge paddles and gloves. Talking with Ivan made the time go by and caused little interference. Our Nazi overseers, bored and young, ignored us for the most part. They talked among themselves yearning for battle, not enjoying being stuck in this boring place.

Later, just after our meager supper of black bread, a potato and tea, I was called by name in German. Nervously, I stood up and was escorted to a private office. The soldier opened the door, and there stood my Tata wearing a hat pulled down shading his face, and his long overcoat. He was talking to a Nazi officer! My eyes about fell out, but I quickly steeled myself and acted like I didn't recognize him. He smiled and spoke to me in Serbian.

"It's all right, Miodrag. This officer buys wine from your Deda Jovanovic indirectly. We have arranged for you to leave at night to go to your Uncle Svetislav's house close by. You will hide in the toilets after dark until it's quiet, and the night guard will let you out the gate. You must be back before dawn. Do you understand? I must go. Take care, my son."

Before I could speak, he was gone.

That night, I stayed in the toilet when the others left. I hid there a while, holding my nose, then shaking with fear, I bent over and ran to the guard on duty expecting a bullet at any moment. Some relief came when the little old veteran motioned me out the gate. Running too fast, I fell down and crawled a ways just to clear myself from the factory. Then picked myself up and ran down the road, hiding in bushes when sounds of trucks came passing by.

I searched to find the house of my Uncle Svetislav about a mile away. He and his mousy wife welcomed me quietly, taking me to the kitchen to feed me. They warned me to keep hidden from the servant coming in during the day. That night, I slept in a good, warm bed. Before sunrise, Uncle woke me and suggested I wear some of his old comfortable working clothes under my good suit coat to sneak back to the factory before first light. I could ditch the suit coat later where they wouldn't notice.

Each morning before dawn, I filled pockets with toast and jam, apples and walnuts for the old guard who sneaked me back into the factory. I tried to convince myself that working in the bakery was a real job, and it wasn't so bad. I did feel sorry for the others scratching from bedbugs and rat bites from their straw beds. Ivan and I worked hard and learned to make good pastries for the soldiers. We laughed when I interpreted the German soldiers' jokes that they didn't know I could understand.

On the 15th night, I crept out as usual past the guard. Before I went to sleep in Uncle's soft bed, I thought about leaving the bakery the next day, the end of the term. I would start making plans to keep in touch with Ivan.

Before first light, I grabbed toast and jam to eat and sneaked back to the factory before the shift change. In the freezing morning predawn, as I'd done for two weeks, I carefully approached the factory.

Something was wrong. The air was too quiet and the building appeared empty. Alarm bells went off in my head as I sneaked past the empty guard gate, sneaked up to the big door only hearing weeping and gnashing. I peaked in to see the familiar face of the old German security guard, and some local cleaners.

"What happened?"

"Oh, youngster. All the prisoners, every last one of them were taken out last night and executed. They were all shot because one German soldier was killed by someone!" The old guard seemed to fold up.

"I'm the only one left? I can't believe it. Everyone?" I asked. "Even Ivan, my friend?"

"Every prisoner, every one, even Ivan. All executed."

The guard struggled to say, "You were born under a lucky star, youngster. Now leave quickly before they bring in a whole new bunch to murder for our crazy Furher."

"I'm going. Thank you. You saved my life. And when the war is over, I will buy this factory and you will manage it." That was my plan.

"Go. Go!"

I carefully made my way back to Uncle Svetislav's in the daylight. Why me? I lay in the grass to let a vehicle go by, tears rolling down my face. Why me? All those men and boys dead. What would happen to their families? All the young men from several villages around my own were dead, their families left alone. The enormity stung my heart and soul. I made it to the house and sneaked in the back door. The legs went out from under me and I slid down to the floor where Uncle found me.

"Oh, Miodrag, thank God, thank God. We heard. Your father was right to bribe that officer or you would be dead. Do you think anyone saw you?"

"The guard saw me when I went back and he told me about the execution. Uncle, they killed all those men! The Nazis just shot them dead."

"We're at war. Nothing is fair. I've been here before and I prayed this would never happen again. I thank God your Baba is not here to see this."

"I want to go home," I told him. "Does my father know I'm alive?"

"He'll find out, but you can't go back home, Miodrag. If the hostages had all been allowed to go back home, we'd be safe for now. But you just avoided a massacre and are supposed to be dead. No one will be searching for you here."

My mouth fell open. I couldn't go home and see my family? I tried to come to grips with this shocking situation.

"What about the German guard?" I asked Uncle. "He knows I'm alive."

"I'll check on him. But for now you must lay low for awhile. You can stay here. I'll get a message to Sretein to bring your clothes, and your books, and whatever else you need."

My throat went dry. Images of the men I worked with in the bakery rolled by my eyes like a movie. It suddenly dawned on me the danger Tata had put himself and the family in to save me. By saving my life when all the others were killed, he could be blamed for collaboration with the enemy. No one in our villages could know I was alive, or my family and our businesses would be ostracized. What was the point of saving my sorry life?

I'd never known this Aunt very well at all. The couple was childless and Auntie seemed exceptionally quiet and complained of poor health. Poor old thing, so thin with bags under her squinted eyes. Her hair was a dull gray, and her dry lips were pursed in a funny way. Uncle told me she had awful pain in her teeth. During the occupation, dentists, even in Nis were nearly impossible to find. She spent most of her time in her room where I was not invited.

Uncle Svetislav on the other hand, always so quiet and refined when he visited his brothers gathered at my home, welcomed me so cheerfully and seemed to take a big interest in me now. In our visits, I asked incessant questions about Baba and Ceda in the olden days when Uncle was growing up.

I told him the most sadness I'd ever had as a child was loosing a toy truck I really loved, or when a favorite dog died. I could not even comprehend death until Baba's. Uncle listened to me, and his soothing voice and stories helped me sleep.

On the third day, my Tata showed up, kissed my forehead, and gave me of big box of my belongings. I tried to thank him but had trouble getting the right words to come out. He understood. He took my hands and looked at me with those big, kind eyes.

"Mila, I know you are devastated now at this horror but hopefully, you will have a long life, and I couldn't just risk your death. You will see the reasons for your life later on. The officer will tell no one as he took a bribe, and the old guard was shot to death, not your fault."

"That nice little man is dead?" my voice choked.

"Yes, son, we are at war and I can assure you will experience much death and horror before this terrible war is over. All of us are at risk all the time. We must be brave and carry on best we know how. Oh, my Mila, my son, don't look at me that way." He hugged me to him. "Each of us does what we have to do. I thank God you're alive." He swallowed and paused to compose himself.

"Remember the Nazi officer who helped Budimir in the rescue at Kamenica? Well, I followed that same path and got you out at least at night when the executions were taking place. I had no choice, my son. I had to take the risk. I wish we could have rescued every man there, but we couldn't. Now, I'm taking care of many families who lost their men at the execution, and I'm trying to find new farm workers."

"I know, Tata that you'll do your best to watch over Majka and Drgica and Jelica. Will you take care of Dana for me? You know how she likes her oats and she loves carrots and her treats. She hates staying in the stable too long."

I stopped because I didn't want my voice to crack.

"I'll do my best, son. And I'm working on finding a position for you, too. Just trust God and trust me. I'll see you soon."

Strength came through in his expression and manner. At about my age, he lost his beloved father and experienced a terrible war, his three brothers in horrible prisons, two with wounds. Still, he had the strength to face another brutal and horrendous combat. How could I do less?

I couldn't get out another word around the lump in my throat and walked silently with him to the front door to see him out. I peaked out the window at Milan holding the horses. He probably didn't know I was alive. My eyes followed them pulling away and my heart sunk. But I swallowed and tried to act like a man in front of my old Uncle and Aunt and tried graciously to fit in.

This close up encounter with the Nazis in the factory made me conscious of my poor use of the German language I needed to communicate.

Uncle Svetislav assured me, "Miodrag, I will teach you more, as much as I can. You're going to need it. I'm working on a plan for your future but we'll discuss that later."

Their servant thought I just came for a visit as she came in the early morning and made breakfast for us. No one ever could make my breakfast like Baba, and just thinking about her still hurt. Lecturing myself brought forth the determination and fortitude Baba had taught me. My life must now be that of an adult. If only I'd get some whiskers, I'd feel better.

Uncle Svetislav, his shoulders sagging in his old cardigan sweater, asked me to join him in his study after dinner one night. His expression turned so serious, I knew something big was coming.

"Son, I've enjoyed your company very much, having an energetic, young man in the house and your enthusiasm in our German language lessons. I don't want you to leave but we've found a position for you."

"A job? Tell me, Uncle." Excitement crept up my neck. I was ready.

Uncle continued, "We have made arrangements for you to work for General Mihailovic as a courier."

The hair stood up on the back of my neck. This was big! "What's a courier?"

"The courier runs messages to other guerrilla units all over the country even across the mountains. The courier takes information that is so important, it cannot be transmitted by any other manner for fear of interception. You'll be a critical messenger."

"Important? Hmmm. When do I start?

By the light of the kerosene lamp that night, I lay in bed, thinking about war. Great battles played in my head fought by men with swords and armor. Stop, silly boy, I said to myself. Think guns with real bullets, tanks, planes and killing. I could just hear Baba, 'Put away your boyish illusions, Mila. The Germans must not take our land, our democratic principles, and our men away from us.'"

I wonder if I'll see a real battle where I'm not just taken without a fight.

Once again, Tata, accompanied by Milan arrived at Uncle Svetislav's to pick me up. I'd never seen my father carry any weapon unless he was going hunting but now both men were seriously armed. Auntie quietly waited on the porch. She pulled my head down to kiss me good-by and tell all of us including Uncle Svetislav accompanying us, to be careful until we climbed in the old wagon. She stood bravely alone as we rode off.

I asked Tata why he was dressed in peasant clothes like Milan. "We just want to melt into the background like the farm workers. We don't want to attract attention on the road as you'll soon learn to do."

We caught up on the news from home during the long, slow wagon ride. Majka and the girls knew I was alive but wouldn't be coming home. They had to act as if I was dead along with most of the village women whose husbands and sons had been executed at the factory.

We followed a map in code and spurred the tired horses on to General Mihailovic's hidden, guarded headquarters in Ravna Gora, just northwest of Uztice in Serbia.

Chapter 9

I never expected to meet my hero, Draza Mihailovic in person. A young soldier led us into a small building with messy papers all over the desk in the reception area. We waited when suddenly a tall, strong, older man in uniform appeared in the doorway of the next little room. General Mihailovic himself grabbed Uncle Svetislav's hand and face, greeting him as a friend. The scene reminded me of the old Bishop greeting Baba at the St. Stevon's Monastery several years ago. The two men demonstrated a connection I couldn't really understand.

The General's young aide brought chairs into the tiny office for us to sit and talk.

General Mihailovic sat back and looked me over, then addressed us. The deep tone of his voice held authority, confidence, and appeal.

"We've been restricted from a regular army for now. I am pulling together a new group of guerrillas called the Rava Gorski Pokret Movement. We are at one, compatriots in spirit, ready to defend our beliefs, King and Church. We are people who wish to defend family and farms, not to take from others. I know Miodrag has already experienced first hand the evil of the Bulgarians, and the Nazis. He knows now how it feels to be violated. I ask for this young man's services to deliver secret orders to our guerrillas."

"Miodrag," he directly addressed me causing the blood to rush from my head, "You come from fine stock, and you look much younger than your years. Don't be offended son; that makes you an asset, as you won't be so easily suspected. This job is important, physically and mentally very difficult, and dangerous. You could easily be killed. But as much as you can accomplish will help move us to victory. Are you up for it?"

All eyes were on me, and my tongue dried up but I stood up straight, and saluted the General. He smiled at me, his sun baked face softened to compassion. "I'll take that as a 'yes,' " and he smiled.

The four of us, Uncle Svetislav, Tata, Milan, and myself enjoyed a meal in the officer's humble quarters before we left. Uncle Svetislav told us about the General's training under Ceda who helped him advance as an army officer in the last World War. From Ceda in past and current conversations, Uncle felt Draza Mihailovic really just wanted to stay a farmer, not be involved in another big war at this time of his life, but he had no choice. None of us did.

My voice shook as I said good-by to my Tata, Uncle, and Milan, the three men I loved and admired the most.

The General sent me to Corporal Dihan for instructions. This man who had introduced us to the General, was taller and about five years older than me. He shook my hand and smiled at me. His mouth seemed to droop slightly on one side, but his whole face especially his eyes showed liveliness. Then he became serious to give me instructions.

"You will memorize the messages. Never carry anything in writing. Never reveal your real identification. You will stay away from any soldiers or camps unless instructed otherwise. You can carry your pocketknife, water canteen and your little bag. That's all. If you are caught and interrogated, pretend you are deaf and dumb. You will have to beg your own food and transportation just like the displaced person that you are. We are counting on you."

Then he gave me a message and made me repeat it until I got it straight. My fingers nervously ran through my hair. Dihan and I had a soft drink together, ate big helpings of food and swapped stories. He told me he was twenty years old, an orphan for several years now attached to the military. His father was killed at the end of the last War leaving a young pregnant, wife. She died a few years ago.

We studied the map to find my first destination only a few miles distance. We shook hands and I started walking. I calmed down and my step quickened. I now had an important assignment and I felt like a man.

As I was walking down the narrow, dirt road, alone in a strange place to me, I took out my beautiful pocketknife and rolled it around in my hand. I felt exhilarated. I took in a deep breath and looked around at the dry foliage, the mountains in the distance, and sensed a new freedom. Water from my canteen filled from the frequent clear streams, tasted wonderful. My sturdy calf leather boots fit, and I carried the good coat over my arm when the hot sun took charge. Life is good.

I first experienced the litter of war when I came upon a wrecked truck smoldering in the road. Two dead men in Nazi uniforms sprawled out of their seats, half hanging out the open doors. I stared at them. Some clothing, shoes, and spent bullet casings scattered on the road indicated a guerrilla skirmish. The Partisans had probably dragged their wounded or dead away. A shudder went through me wondering how many peasants would die for those two dead Germans.

The only identification I had on me was a tiny piece of paper with my code name, and address tucked into the sole of my boot. When I managed to take the right roads and arrived at the designation, I realized my sense of direction had really paid off. After proper identification was shown, and the right person faced me, I delivered the message and headed back to headquarters. Well, this seemed simple enough, but I wasn't so naïve to believe this job was going to be easy.

Within a few days I was being sent on longer and longer trips. My feet hurt and needed to be soaked when I returned, but they soon became tougher and so did I. Food was wrapped in paper and stuffed in all my pockets, some sewn on the inside of my jacket.

Often as I walked alone, I talked to Baba, and her spirit seemed to encourage me and urge me to keep going. There is only one truth. See the sun, only one sun. That's the truth. See with your own eyes and hear with your own ears.

Eventually, as trust was earned, the assignments became more important in the vital information transmitted. I learned to hitch rides, sometimes in carts and wagons. Rarely, only near the bigger towns, a car would stop for a poor boy.

I cringed at towns caught in battles devastated by bombs and fire. Over a narrow high section of a cobbled street were huge pieces of crumbling stone arches blocking me off. On hands and knees, I worked my way over the huge clutter, twisting my leg under a moving stone at one point. God, that hurt! I had no choice but to climb over the rubble wall and keep going.

No one else paid any attention to me with more than a glance. When needed, I begged food and found my boyish appearance literally did open doors for me. In contrast to the war torn areas, I walked and climbed over some of the most beautiful mountains I'd ever seen.

When I finally arrived in Bosnia, I came upon a young, light haired girl just sitting beside the road alone. I stopped to talk to her as she looked so lost.

"Are you in trouble." Her pitiful brown eyes stared up at me with a glimpse of trust. She started calmly to tell me the Ustasha men came at night and ordered everyone into the road.

"They took away and killed everyone including our priests and officials in my small town. I hid in our garden and heard all the screaming and shots being fired.

She cried and gulped, "Then after a few hours, when every-thing went quiet, I peaked out and my parents and every single person in our village was dead except me." She tried to gain control.

"We didn't see it coming. We don't have any weapons and who could believe people would treat other people that way. They aren't supposed to be our enemy. They chopped off ears and noses and tortured them." Her voice rose and the tears came again.

"They killed everyone in my family. I'm the only one alive! All I saw when they left were dead people, everywhere, everyone I ever knew."

By now she was throwing her head back crying loudly and moaning to my dismay.

"Get up. You can't stay here." I pulled her up and helped brush her off. I felt so sorry for this girl not much younger than me and walked beside her to the next village where she had some relatives. The shock of her news rattled them but the family composed themselves and kindly took her in and fed both of us. Later, they laid down a blanket for me to sleep on the floor. I sneaked out before the sun rose, found a well to draw water and fill my water bottle, and off I went. I felt such sorrow for those people, but I took my mission very seriously above everything else.

My muscles became stronger by the day but I still didn't seem to grow an inch. And I'd lost weight and still didn't have any whiskers. My only problem was my boots gradually grew big holes in the soles.

Finally, a dead German soldier appeared ahead of me on the road, still wearing a nearly new pair of boots. Cautiously, I sneaked up on the body, ignored the stench, and tugged the boots off his feet. I tipped them upside down and shook them in case of cooties, and tried them on over my socks. They fit fine. Thank you, Lord.

The General was right, I delivered my messages to men who barely gave me a second glance. I kept silent unless sure I was facing the right person and he asked me a direct question.

A man who gave me a long car ride on my first trip to Axis-occupied Montenegro told me he was heading for Greece, and from there to British occupied Africa where he thought his family would be safer. His family carried as much as they could in the cramped car and still picked me up. He talked about how the Italians in this area were courteous and friendly even when facing the Balkan guerrillas who acted so proud, so set in their minds, and warlike that they'd fight any outsiders to the death.

I asked questions as usual. He relayed the message that the German munitions and supplies were trying to get through the Balkans to Rommel's harassed armies on the North African front but our remarkable resistance from our trained guerrillas was seriously upsetting the Nazi plans. I thanked him and his family for the ride and wondered at their bravery.

This little town near Niksic was my destination. Tito was supposed to be someplace around here trying to gain some control in the power struggle with the Chetnik guerrillas as they called themselves. I had memorized a detailed description of him. Early one morning, I caught my first clear look at him coming out of a building getting into a car, but I kept out of his sight. He appeared to be a big, handsome man, with iron gray hair and a somewhat haggard face. A group of uniformed men surrounded him for protection but he still stood out.

My instructions were to lay low for a few days to watch and confirm Tito himself was here and not an imposter. I fell in with some Muslims kids playing on the street. Kids were the safest people to be as they were rarely ever questioned by the soldiers. My face was purposely dirty with a cap over my curly hair. Soon my beautiful coat looked as worn as any boy's on the street. I'd hide my boots and coat when I needed to hide in a crowd.

Barefoot, wearing ragged clothes, people hopefully only saw another poor, poor, poor kid just like all the others. The language seemed difficult to understand very well, but they seem to treat me like one of them. I learned to listen to each dialect very carefully and watch signs and movements.

Even with his soldiers surrounding him, and me staring every moment I could, with other boys in the street were unaware of my mission. There I got a second close look at the man moving out of a building getting into a car. He positively fit the description of Tito, again. I could leave, now. My boots were retrieved where I'd hid them and sneaked out of the town hitching a ride back.

Sometimes, the temporary quarters of General Mihailovic moved before I returned but somehow he always relayed directions for me to find him again. His first officer, the trusted Corporal Dihan gave me that crooked smile of his and greeted me warmly. I think they were always amazed when I showed up again.

Dihan may have been the only man privy to the secret movements of General Mihailovic's resistance guerrillas. Dihan never gave even a hint of the messages given to me or the responses from anyone but the General. The two of us were probably the only people the General truly trusted. I would never let him down even it meant my life.

The new location in Bosnia resulted from the most horrendous situation.

"Ante Pavelic, a man without a soul, now rules Croatia, or the NDH as the Nazis call them which now includes Bosnia," Dihan told me over supper.

"This Ustasha power maniac plays up to both the Italian Fascists and the German Nazis. Now they're recruiting the Muslims for support against the Orthodox Serbs."

My hair stood on end when I heard that. Dihan pulled me close to him and his voice softened to a whisper.

"If they don't convert to the Roman Catholic Church, or leave the country, they are being murdered by the thousands. Supposedly, Archbishop Stepinac doesn't want that to happen in the name of the Church. He just wants to build up hundred of thousands of new converts to look good to Rome. But we're positive he's in with the Ustasha regime and Ante Pavelic.

"God, Mila, you won't want to hear this but we just got word that these mass murderers have already burned down or dynamited a third of the Orthodox churches, often with men, women and children inside. They are butchering thousands. In Drvar, the Ustasha took the Orthodox priest and seventy people into the hills, cut their throats and hurled the bodies into a ravine. Oh, God, Mila, don't get sick on me!"

I had to leave the table to run outside the tent, bile burning my throat, bending over the weeds, heaving my heels feeling so sick. When my body rid itself and I could sit up in the tall weeds, I rationalized that the common German soldiers were also horrified at the barbaric Ustashe! I'd been trained not to show emotion, not to know anything, or talk to anyone else about war or the politics. But I just couldn't ignore the atrocities not from the enemy, but from related savages. Tata was right. Our neighbors can also be our enemy. Get a grip, I told myself. I'm the messenger. I have a job to do.

Dihan sat waiting for me to haul myself back inside. "Don't feel too bad. We all had to adjust and if you get too tough and loose your humanity, you'll end up like the Ustashe, walking ghosts. Sit down. Now, let me ask you. Do you have a girl friend back home?"

He took me by surprise. "No, I didn't have much time for girls and my two little sisters were just a nuisance." Dihan chuckled at that.

"You will, my friend. You will. You're a good-looking guy. You like girls, don't you?"

"Sure, I like to look at the pretty ones. But my family has strict rules about marriage. They all help choose and decide who marries into our family, and they insist the girl must be Serbian." I hadn't even thought that much about women in these rough times.

Dihan, still amused at my expense, "You don't have to marry them, my boy. Just have some fun sometimes. Don't you know anything about sex?"

"Of course, I do. What do you think I am?" Actually, I probably didn't know that much, only from hearing the other boys talk.

"I do know I don't want to make babies with anyone but a Serbian girl. When girls flirt with me, I just kiss them and threaten to take them to the bedroom to scare them. Then I get out of there."

Why was he laughing at me? And slapping his knee? It wasn't that funny.

Later, when Dihan finished teasing me, he got serious and told me more shock about thousands more Jews being murdered.

"Not just in Germany and Poland but here. I saw it myself. They were promised a trip to a better place. Instead, the Germans and the fascist Croat troops were loading them in trucks then gassing them by hoses. Those poor, innocent families screamed and pounded on the door begging to be let out before they dropped dead."

My gut tightened promising me to become tougher.

I brought the General information that Tito's Partisans were now based in Uzice, in western Serbia. Tito was raised in Croatia but was believed not to condone ethnic killing. He'd recruit many antifascist Croatians into Communist ranks supposedly joining Serbs to fight the Germans. Uzice was the only town in the area that Germans didn't control. Tito proclaimed it his "Red Republic" taking over the hotel, bank, factories, newspaper and the prison. We watched in frustration as Tito engaged the Germans in skirmishes causing more reprisal massacres. As a result in November, General Mihailovic had no choice but to order his Chetnics to attack Tito's Partisans, and neighbors started shooting each other. The Chetniks now carried flags with skull and crossbones and "Freedom or Death" printed on them.

⤳

The early frosty morning that I traveled into Uzice on orders, I was walking off the road on the side of the hill for cover. Suddenly, a huge explosion shocked me and I ran closer to see. It was the Red Republic's powder store and armaments factory that blew up. German tanks waiting just outside of town moved right in giving Tito only twenty minutes to get out.

No one knew exactly who set the explosives. But from my vantage position, I actually saw his men and Tito himself prepare to leave in his decorated long coat with his big German Shepherd dog by his side. His men loaded a printing press and several boxes in the back of the truck. Tito's Partisans immediately came under rifle fire but he kept going with the walking wounded ahead of him.

The Germans were smart enough to establish a puppet regime under General Milan Nedic who considered himself a custodian of the government-in-exile. Nedic tried to maintain control over the violence to the Serbs and yet not to appear as a collaborator with the Germans.

Back in Mihailovic's primitive quarters with Dihan, we listened to Moscow radio in Serbo-Croat. "No, it can't be!" yelled Dihan jumping up. "Listen! The fighting in Serbia against the Germans, can you believe Moscow is giving credit for it to General Mihailovic?" He slapped his knee and we both started hollering.

"Tito must be having a fit!" we laughed at the misplaced honor to the Chetniks. Our Resistance group had purposely stayed clear of killing Germans and concentrated on fighting the murderous Ustasha.

To our surprise, we learned Stalin communicated with our government-in-exile and refused to supply arms to Tito. Stalin feared he could not control the aggressive Partisan action that might weaken Allied trust of the Soviet Union ruining their long-range plans.

He even offered a military mission and supplies to the Cetnici. Dihan blue eyes sparkled at the unexpected turn of events. Our working relationship grew to friendship.

Hiking through the mountains, I heard noises ahead of me. The trees provided a shield to move up to the ruckus. Strung out as far as I could see around the path through the trees were hundreds of peasant women and girls kerchiefs on their heads and little boys in their round hats carrying and pulling along their belongings. They were lined up as prisoners with a line of German soldiers on horseback herding them on possibly to concentration camps. I rushed on higher up to pass this pitiful parade to try to go for help. I never knew what happened to them.

By now, we had reason to suspect Tito had abandoned Serbia and was hiding on Mount Zlatibor in Bosnia. Some even said he'd gone to the Vatican to hide out. Mihailovic desperately wanted to know where Tito was hiding.

The winter fury came with no consideration for the Partisans holed up in the rugged mountains. My assignment was to find Tito's hidden main camp where he had withdrawn. I was instructed to insert my presence among them to see what I could find out. My worn but heavy coat, a scarf, and my worn boots even with the heavy stockings barely kept me from freezing as I trudged through the deep snow with an icy crust. All I had was my trusty pocketknife and bits of food stuffed in my pockets.

Wolves were a main concern, but now it started to snow, so hopefully I wasn't leaving a clear track. With little direction, I just followed my nose amazed to find Tito's hidden camp in a high mountain, abandoned village.

I just walked into camp and found only chaos. The lookout guard soldier showed surprise to see a boy suddenly appear out of the heavy snow. It's a wonder I didn't get shot! My cover story was becoming lost from my father on a hunting trip and lost my rifle. No one questioned my story. The guard motioned to another soldier to show me around.

Most of the men slept in wet, sagging tents. A few old cottages scattered among the trees housed the officers. Some bedraggled soldiers were trying to fuel a fire with wet wood, and men were eating bark and shooting rabbits and small game to keep from starving. Suddenly, screaming coming from a tent made me jump. The soldier drew me into his tent.

"The devil is torturing us. Another one of us has suffered frostbite and another soldier who is not a doctor had to amputate all his toes without any anesthetic. Others have lost fingers and their feet. God, I hate this place."

"Can't you get out of here?" I asked him.

"No, we don't have any place to go. Serbia has thrown us out, and Stalin has abandoned us. I'm not so sure about Communism now. Screw them guys. Oh, and wait 'til I tell you the best part. The Germans took advantage of the deep snow and attacked us on skis! Some of us saw them coming and tried to scramble up the mountain to escape. They killed several of us and Tito himself was very nearly killed. But he grabbed his sub-machine gun, got off a few rounds and then high-tailed it into the trees."

"What a close call. Is he here now? I'd sure like to get a glimpse of him."

"Sure, there he is, a couple of tents away." He took me over to meet the infamous man. I knew it was him. Tito greeted me cordially and kissed me on the forehead when I called him "Sir General Tito." He was dressed in a big, worn, wet, double-crested coat, fur hat, a pistol bandolier and high boots. His cheeks sagged and his eyes showed frustration and sorrow. Overall, he was still an attractive man with a wide, smooth face and a scar on his cheek.

I immediately felt awe of his personal power; his confident presence. His beautiful German Shepherd dog stood close to this side. Tito saw my interest and introduced the dog as "Tigger" who growled and glared right through me with hatred.

I wished Tito wasn't a Communist as we could certainly use his leadership in our government as a democrat when the War was over. He asked me questions about troop movements and any news but I played the dumb kid. I was impressed though, when this famous soldier had his man bring me some cold rabbit and cooked turnips to eat.

I turned down the invitation to stay overnight. I needed to move on certainly aware of enemy territory and the danger of pushing my luck. Bringing back the exact location of his camp motivated me, too. I climbed back up the mountain I'd come over. Within a couple of hours, regret set in. The snow came horizontally on a freezing wind. Darkness hovered early. I could lose my fingers and toes like those poor soldiers or even die up here! Damn! I prayed to find shelter. I had learned to climb a tree and tie myself to the branches to avoid the hungry wolves, but now the wind was too furious to try that.

I wished again I'd stayed at the camp, enemy or not. I used my whole body to scramble up the rocks, unable to see down or up for the thick, icy flurries.

I spotted a dark area in the rocks and hoping for some kind of shelter, I struggled up to it. An opening appeared and on my belly, crawled into a good size cave hoping it wasn't full of sleeping snakes. The temperature immediately felt livable. No wind, with air to breathe even if it contained a strange odor but I probably didn't smell so good myself. Still, it beat freezing.

I took off my wet coat and scarf, shaking them out to dry and started to remove my ice-coated boots when I heard cooing noises, like a baby or several babies. I stopped still. My eyes were barely adjusted to the dark when I discovered a bear cub nudging my coat pocket, then another cold nose, and another one. Why aren't they sleeping? Oh, God, where is Mama? Then I heard her soft growling deeper and louder. And the smell! I could see her claws, pale and curved, her hackles bristling and felt fear run through my bones.

I couldn't out run her. I couldn't even move. I could only talk. In my most convincing voice like talking to Dana my horse, I started telling Mama Bear that I was friendly, no weapons on me, and no harm would come to her cubs. I even softly whistled a tune. Mama came nearer, I could see her big eyes and she was cooing, not growling. Then it dawned on me I had some dry corn and walnuts in my pocket and reached carefully for them to feed the cubs. Oh, that made them very happy and the fuzzies were all over me lapping kernels up with their rough tongues out of my palm.

Suddenly a great growl and in comes Papa Bear from his patrol. Mama turned to him and mumbled her odd noise to let him know I was a friend. He *awllwed* back and walked around us giving me the look and went to lie down. When the nuts were gone, the bears all curled up and went to sleep. Exhausted as I was, I did too. At first pale light, I woke up to find the cubs cuddled up to me with Mama and Papa keeping a sleepy eye on us. I thanked them for their hospitality and gently crawled out of the cave to a calm, soft dawn streaked with low, pink clouds.

Papa Bear followed me out watching me stretch, appreciating the air, the scenery, and the good Lord like I never had before. Papa Bear commenced *awllwing* good-by, and watched me work my way back over the mountain. I looked back raising my arms to the sky amazed. Why, Jesus Christ? Is that possible? Bears must be the sweetest animals on the earth. Why can't people just be as kind to each other, trusting even what they don't understand?

⤺

The wind on the trip back blew up my legs with frontal bite. The pain became almost more than I could stand but I continued to rub them hard trying to avoid frozen limbs. When I returned to our camp, the important Partisan information was relayed to the General. I didn't tell him Tito himself kissed me on the forehead. The location of that camp made a big difference in the General's plans.

Late in the evening after a rub down on my swollen, aching legs and feet, we enjoyed a real supper and a glass of wine. I told Dihan the bear story.

He cocked his head at me, screwed up his nose and said, "I don't think you better tell that story to anyone else, Mila. You'd get locked up in an insane asylum!" and he laughed at me. He teased me mercilessly every chance he got. "Talked to any bears lately, Babyface?" and he'd laugh, but he kept our secret.

Dihan also teased me about knowing nothing about the Military. The fact was I didn't want or need to know. Too many rules. I thrived on my own wits to survive. I had no ration card, no ID, no papers. My name and home address were still folded into a tiny piece hidden in the heel of my boot in case I got killed.

Majka would have a fit to see my clothes so disheveled and dirty. No one paid much attention to a poor, dumb, peasant boy. In the towns and villages, I learned to hide between buildings and sneak down alleys. I usually left in the opposite direction, then turned around to avoid anyone following me. In crowded taverns, a great place to hide and swipe food, I could also listen to groups talking to learn the latest war gossip with very little threat. We had no real communication system other than couriers.

At one of the camps, an officer asked me if I could drive a truck. "No," I told him.

"Can you repair a truck?"

"No, I know nothing about engines. I prefer a horse where I have the most control. Don't need to haul gasoline, no mechanical parts to break down. All you need is a good saddle. And I can always find grass and feed."

My thoughts included Dana and hoped she was being cared for back home. I worried over my horse being stolen by the Nazis. Then it dawned on me even a horse would be way too much trouble out here. On foot, I was nearly invisible, could hide in small places, and didn't appear to be a threat to anyone. The freedom was exhilarating.

Sometimes, shell-swept land had to crossed to deliver accurate dispatches between the front lines and our regimental headquarters. I kept silent around unknown high officials and stayed in the background trying to become as invisible as a real mute. When a stranger demanded to know where I came from, I'd lift my head and eyes up to heaven and point my finger up there.

Bosnia was now enemy territory. I saw German soldiers all over in fancy uniforms, metal helmets and warm coats riding in good vehicles. Far more worrisome were still the local Ustasha men. These men usually appeared dirty with heavy facial hair, their eyes glazed over like maniacs, firmly believing any Orthodox Serbian represented the devil.

Even the Germans seemed afraid of Ustasha in Bosnia and were horrified at the indiscriminate killing. General Mihailovic himself knew Berlin feared the slaughter would promote greater resistance from the Serbs, and Germany had no more troops to spare to hold the Balkans.

He also went on about the Germans encouraging the persecution of Jews in Croatia but disapproved of the horrible atrocities on the Jews from the Ustasha. He talked of rape and torture, gouging eyes out, and starving pigs eating dead human beings.

I'd seen some of that, man's cruelty to man. Right while I was thinking of it, I noticed a huge compound from the road. I walked up to the long barbed wire fence where a frantic young woman inside begged me to buy food for her family. I learned thousands of Jews had been rounded up and penned up like cattle.

"We were told we would receive new housing and we're waiting in this heavy snow with little protection. My children are freezing and hungry. I have dinars. Please help us." She pleaded with me.

I did take this desperate, trusting woman's dinars, and brought her back a mixture of groceries from a undamaged store I'd seen on the road. That's all I could do. My heart felt such sadness and failure in humanity.

❧

General Mihailovic sent me around a wide area of the country to deliver documents to his senior officers. Again, I traveled on the eastern side of the Dinaric Alps rising dramatically along the entire Adriatic coast. I found the small camp, sat down on a big rock and emptied gravel out of my boots. I looked up to see a Chetnik officer looking down on me menacingly and pointing his gun right at me until he became convinced of my authority. Then he led me into the staff room. A First Officer read the documents in my presence. I stood there, not moving a muscle trying to fade into the wall, but listening closely.

Mihailovic's ultimate goal was to free Slav territories under the Italians and Germans. Good. Next, he wanted an ethnically pure Yugoslavia, to cleanse all national minorities and non-national elements. That meant forcing Croats, Muslims, Jews, out of the country and most anyone he didn't approve of.

My face remained stoic but inside my heart nearly stopped. Surely, the Uncles didn't know these beliefs. We wanted a democracy for everyone. If this conviction was Mihailovic's true belief, he was as guilty of the religious and extreme social bigotry as Ante Pavelic, the Nazi-loving Croatian.

All the way back, my head thumped. Dihan could see something big was bothering me. I couldn't even talk about it at first. Dihan got me into a meeting to listen to General Mihailovic personal stand. At least, he didn't condone killing people for the "cleansing" like the Ustasha who believed "cleansing" meant murdering everyone who didn't believe the way they did. He explained he was trying to discover a method of understanding and accepting other people that would work for everyone. God help us.

At this time, the Chetnik guerrillas started to affect beards and long hair. They controlled most of Serbia, the barren Sandjak, area, Montenegro and eastern Bosnia-Hercegovina almost to where the Allies could probably disembark.

What we didn't know until it happened, was the Italians wanted to gradually withdraw to protect their own homeland. Italian General Roatta apparently failed to convince Hitler that arming our anti-Communist Chetniks with Italian weapons to use against the far more dangerous Partisans would be practical.

When I carried that news back to my General, he had to rethink his plan of action. He said, "The Germans would never believe we took weapons from the Axis. All we want, though, is help in case of an Anglo-American landing to wipe out the Germans from our land and put our King Petar back on the throne. Of course, Tito will be in a dither when he learns of it since he only wants to run the government himself."

Chapter 10

1943

During the winter of 1942-43, Yugoslavia became a major theatre of war in Europe. Things happened so fast, I could hardly keep track of the players. According to information from the Italian General Roatta, the German defeat at Stalingrad and the loss of North Africa worried them that an Allied invasion must be in the works. General Roatta knew of the planned an "Operation Weiss" into the Balkans to begin on January 20th. Against the wishes of the Germans, General Roatta required some 30,000 Chetnik allies to cover key points along the routes.

General Mihailovic, unable to determine the consequences of fighting against the communist Partisans, ordered all his commanders to prepare for decisive action along the route to the coast. Conflict of interest led to mysterious wheeling and dealing. It appeared for a short time that the Partisans and Germans might fight against the Chetniks and the Italians. Recognizing the terrible chance he was taking by joining the Italians, General Mihailovic sat it out at Lopovo.

Then, between the Lim and Tara valleys, two of the gorges and canyons forming the headwater zone of the River Drina, came hordes of German, Italian, Bulgarian and Croatian Ustashe troops aiming to destroy about 20,000 Partisans.

On the banks of the River Drina, I watched with great anxiety as Tito prepared and then led the Partisans. He seemed unaware of the enormous enemy army hiding in the mountains. Sounds of the huge German bombardment from way behind the lines brought them to alert. The Partisans ran right into a barrage of machine gun fire, dark tanks spraying bullets, and air attacks by the German Stukas diving nearly down on top of them. The sky and earth disappeared in smoke and powder as I ran stumbling to get as far away as I could although part of me still wished hard to be a soldier in the middle of the action.

It seemed like continual motion for me delivering dispatches between our commanders. I quit trying to figure out what could be happening. Just tried to conquer the cold and concentrate on cunning to deliver crucial messages. The Chetniks scattered over the surrounding hills facing the sky filled with German attack planes. Stuka air attacks and heavy artillery fire swept the Partisans into the face battle with the Italians and Chetniks. The Partisans fought to the death but managed to hold their own.

Finally, driven near the River Neretva, a centuries-old trading link between the Adriatic and Bosnia, the army of Partisan soldiers struggled to cross a slippery bridge high over the Sutjeska Gorge. Refusing to give up, Tito and his troops, and many followers just barely slipped across the bridge over the dangerous river to safety in Montenegro.

Seeing fields of blood and wounded men crying out changed me forever just like the regular soldiers.

The slaughter included thousands of wounded guerrillas, civilian women and children, hungry and barefoot in the snow following the Partisans as their only protection against the Croatian Ustashe who drew no boundaries on killing. The hordes of people following Tito found their situation even more horrendous by a typhus epidemic. No one could have ever explained to me the horror, death, and gore, man could inflict against man had I not seen it for myself. No wonder Baba did not wish to live through it again.

Tito's troops escaped over the treacherous bridge, but the Italians were forced to surrender the battle. The rumor came that the entire Italian Third Battalion of the 259th Regiment of the Murge Division was purposely shot to death by the Partisans. The massacre choked the Neretva River with corpses of Italian soldiers.

Much later we learned Tito lost about 7,000 soldiers in that fierce battle, about a third of his army.

That major battle shocked my senses. Man against man, the killing, the horrendous sounds, the blood, and the horror. My imagined thrill of war fell to the ground along with the dead.

General Mihailovic also began to realize his leadership in the alliance with General Roatta in the Operation Weiss could cause great danger from Germany. As Minister of Defense in the government in exile in London, he could not justify his contact with the enemy Italians.

We heard Tito even accused the British of furnishing arms to the Italians or was he trying to convince Russia he was still on their side to turn them against Mihailovic?

The Germans also threw a fit over the Italian's association with us. Quite by accident, we learned the German Foreign Minister went to Rome and even suggested Mihailovic should be murdered. Recognizing my message of the personal danger to himself, General Mihailovic chose to back off in February again leaving for Lopovo to command from afar.

I decided his age and grave disappointment with his involvement in the Operation Weiss must have played a part in his decision to lay low. No one trusted anyone in this confusing time.

In the aftermath, I thought and thought about it. The most amazing part of this long battle to me was that the four main groups, the Germans, Italians, Chetniks and Partisans were all at odds with each other. Even so, the first three joining together nearly succeeded in wiping out Tito's communist army.

After their success in February, Tito got cocky and failed to see the Germans set another trap for him in May. The German "Operation Schwarz, the Fifth Offensive" nearly destroyed the Partisans. Their units began to appear again in the Lim and Tara valleys, at the headwater zone of the River Drina. Soon, about 120,000 German, Italian, Bulgarian and Croation troops tried

own officers to fight the Germans. We heard a hilarious rumor that Tito reported to Moscow that Mihailovic's staff had "about twenty-five Englishmen dressed in Serbian national costume."

That would have meant they would have been wearing the embroidered waistcoats, round caps, knee breeches, and the sandals with curled-back toes. Only festivals showed those old fashioned costumes. Dihan and I had a good laugh over that one.

We also learned Tito was so furious that the Chetniks got aid as well as him, he was ready to join the Germans in fighting the British. Then in the summer, more British officers parachuted into our territory and dropped in much needed supplies of clothing and food for all the guerrillas.

Tito settled down and joined a group of patriots from both Partisans and Chetniks who captured bombers and made a daring attack on the Sarajevo airfield destroying 28 German aircraft. Revved up, our patriots ambushed a German armored train and captured three towns including an important coal-mining center in Bosnia. The blows came down from the Germans who hanged or shot any likely patriot by firing squads. Still, the wrecking of railway lines and key bridges designed to stop the Nazis continued. There was just no stopping our fragmented army or peasants.

At first dawn, I awoke to anti-aircraft guns booming into the overcast sky. The sound excited me. From my mountain top perch, I recognized American planes, possibly come to rescue our country. I ran to a spot where I could look over a valley. American planes were flying high risking the active Nazi reconnaissance ground fire. Looking way up, I was astonished to see one plane burst into fire high in the sky. Moments later, a filled parachute drifted towards earth.

I watched a few seconds more and then as fast as I could headed down the mountain into a deep ravine where I figured the parachute and pilot would land. The forest grew thick, but I spotted his white parachute draped over tree branches and bushes. I climbed over to him fast as I could. His uniform identified him as an American pilot.

"Hey there!" he yelled to me recognizing I wasn't a German soldier. He was slightly burned and dazed but very much alive. He tried to speak to me in his limited German. I assured him in German I was just a Serbian civilian and would not harm him.

He said, "My mission is to fly into Rumania to bomb the oil fields, but very few planes are making it across the Balkans without getting shot down by the Nazis. I made it last time, a round trip of 2,400 miles."

I tried to wash up his small scratches with a little water from a creek. Then we tried to talk for a while. I understood little except his gestures and excitement.

"We go in at low level, about 500 feet to drop the bombs just where we want them on the oil refineries, pumping stations and storage tanks. Boy, you should see those things blow up! Many times we are dropping delayed-action bombs so we can get out before the explosions and the dense smoke clouds! It's really something."

I knew about a remote ravine hiding about 600 American airmen, protected from the Germans by the Chetnik resistance force. He gave me a pencil and a piece of paper and I tried to draw an explicit map through the mountains beyond and walked with him as far as we could safely go together. He gratefully gave me his name on another slip of paper I memorized but had to destroy it. I prayed he would make it to safety.

As I trudged away alone, I thought, I got to meet my first American! My skin was as light as his skin, and my hair was even lighter. He looked so handsome, his features so perfect. My first impression stayed with me and I was sure all Americans were good-looking, more than the British.

A personal problem bothered me. I fell in with some Serbian soldiers bragging about how many girls they'd forced into sex. One loudmouth smiled as he told the others, he had raped 32 girl friends in different places, and had got at least 10 or 12 pregnant. I spit on the ground at his feet.

"You think that's funny? In 10 or 12 years, your children will be asking, 'Who's my father?' Would you like that to happen? Shame on you! I swear men are the worst whores!"

I went off in a huff, kicking pebbles. Maybe I was spoiling their fun but I strongly determined I would respect all women and wait until I fell in love, and then it would have to be a Serbian girl.

During the heavy winter months, our communication lines were often closed. In the best times, we only had radio waves and our couriers. Only through eavesdropping on solemn young German soldiers in a tavern trying to keep warm, did I hear more about Germany's defeat at Stalingrad. And worse for them, they'd had lost all of North Africa to the Allies that they needed for precious oil. They talked about the Tunis area in North Africa and a huge battle with the British and American forces last year.

Now, the Germans' big worry was that an Allied invasion would happen on the Adriatic coast. We had of course, always expected that. But when I relayed this information to General Mihailovic, his lips nearly disappeared, and his eyes took on a cold, frantic appearance.

"If that's the case," he announced, "Hitler will make sure they destroy all the guerrillas, us and the Partisans first if they can." I had never thought of that.

Throughout it all, I continued my mission as courier for General Mihailovic back and forth behind the lines. He sent me off with messages and to see if I could discover any further scuttlebutt.

Then, a shock came when I couldn't believe my hero, General Mihailovic gave a speech in Montenegro declaring he would continue to fight the Croats, Muslims and Communists before he would turn on the foreign invaders. Was he drunk? A British colonel heard the speech and reported it to his superior in London with contacts with our government in exile.

In response, King Petar urged Mihailovic "to reconcile his differences with the Partisans and fight the Germans, the real enemy." I was in the room when the General stated he feared the British would cut off supplying arms if he did.

The torn General ranted and raved. "King Petar and his advisors are sitting out the war in England, while I'm putting my life on the line for this country. Why don't they recognize the threat of the Partisans to the country? Do they want us to live under Russia's devastating style of Communism? I've been in two wars and now I don't believe we'll ever see peace." His voice broke and his head dropped into his huge, wrinkled hands.

Dihan and I quietly left the room, walking out of hearing distance and continued to talk. We agreed General Mihailovic was depressed and failing, and we vented our feelings and frustrations to each other. Dihan kept smoking cigarettes he'd taken off a dead German making me cough. We agreed the General's disappointment with the King's orders must have been the last straw. We both felt terrible for him, our hero, but just a man after all. Dihan eyes showed dark circles just like the General's dark, hollow look. We talked about the war long into the night not coming to any conclusions.

Dihan was the only person I could trust and who knew just what our duties really were and how important we could be to the General and the cause. We stayed loyal to the General despite his obsessions.

Again, under orders, I traveled to Bosnia to deliver a secret message to an important Chetnic commander. In many places,

Partisan soldiers fed me and just treated me like another displaced kid.

Thanks to aid from the British, I could always recognize the Partisan soldiers now in their blue-gray uniforms. Both men and their scruffy women all dressed alike carrying automatic rifles slung over their shoulders. Now they added a small star on the front of the caps, and the officers also wore a star on the lapel of their uniforms.

A secluded trail I knew across the mountains with beautiful cold, fresh water running through the canyons carried me far from the war. Spring flowers blossomed and I spotted many tiny cubs, fawns, and kits testing the territory with their parents. Resting one sunny afternoon, I found a perfect big branch and carved the solid twisted wood into an extremely useful walking stick, just the perfect size for me. I soon discovered it could also serve as a fishing pole.

When I came down to a road, I hitched rides mostly with soldiers, but always was appalled at the scent of smoke, huts torn apart, the smell of burning thatch, and sometimes total destruction in the villages and hamlets. Houses, barns and livestock, all burned, empty, ruined rubble. Sometimes people, still alive in the ruins, peaked out to see how close death could be. Food became extremely scarce but I always seemed to find and raid an orchard and could live on fruit and nuts.

One afternoon, a stray gaggle of geese ran across in front of me. I pounced on a slow one, tied his legs and traded him for bread and sausages from some soldiers.

I finally located the Chetnic Commander in a village surrounded by the Germans. Moving in and out of the small buildings left standing, leaning against the walls at the slightest sign of enemy, the message was delivered at great peril to myself. While still in the room, this commander ordered a circular letter he'd just written to be read out loud. It was addressed, "To Chetnik Intellectuals." It stated in essence, "We seek a pure national state. A couple of million minority people would have

144 • Jean C. Colp

to leave our country. The pure people will share all the land left."

The document he planned to spread in towns and villages, reeked of propaganda. Much to his anger, I made it clear I could not deliver those flyers to anyone.

Immediately, when I walked out the building, my hair stood on end warning me of an armed man following me through the village with hollow footsteps. I quickly took off my boots, holding them under my jacket and dodged quietly down an alley with a lump in my throat.

I ran out of the alley onto the rubble littered street and spotted a group of Muslim boys, kicking an old ball. As a diversion, I ran into the middle of the noisy group and tried to casually join their fun. The ball came straight at me, and I ducked. The raggedly dressed boys starting laughing at me. I waved back friendly, chasing the ball keeping my head down. They continued kicking the ball including me without question.

I stuck right in the middle of the game invisible to the soldier standing aside staring at us bewildered. Guess it worked, as he disappeared. Up to now, I'd assumed I was invisible and the thought of actually being captured and interrogated gave me a cold chill.

One of the tall, ragged fellows came up to me speaking the "Allah" language I barely understood. Their dialect differed completely from those in Macedonia. "You're in trouble, aren't you? I saw that guard looking at you," he gestured.

"I don't know him, but he was following me. I don't want you to get in trouble." I showed him my big walking stick and my pocketknife, smiling trying to let him know I could take care of myself. The Muslim boy switched to a rough Serbian language when he started to trust me.

"Don't worry. Come with me," he motioned. I picked up my coat with my boots wrapped inside and he led me down another narrow street to his house. Their house was a tightly built shack housing the grandparents, three younger brothers of my new friend, and their mother all sleeping in one room on mats.

An odor of spice, deep pungent spice like balsam, almost made me feel sick. The tiny grandmother seemed to read my mind. She decided immediately I was Serbian, an orphan, and friendly. In her generous way, she put out her best dishes, smiling and chatting with me. The boy's mother hid from me. Her son told me she followed the old Muslim religion by laying eyes only on her own family and vice versa. After sharing their meager but delicious dinner, I sat with the grandmother and my new friend, a year younger than me and shared stories.

"How did you find your way here?" they asked.

"I just follow my nose. No one can follow my path. But today I had a close call and I appreciate your family taking me in." I hoped grandmother wouldn't ask me too many questions and she seemed to sense my need for privacy.

My new friend said, "Are you one of us? Say yes or no."

A little scared, I said, "No."

"Do you know what is SS?"

I lied, "No."

"Do you know Ustashe?"

"No."

The boy proudly told me, "They're worse than the Germans and mostly Muslim divisions and believe me, they don't just kill, they try to roast alive and eat their prisoners and strangers. Just make sure when you leave here, you know whose house you are going to! You have light skin and blue eyes. Many degrees of Muslims live here and you must carefully decide who you are dealing with for survival."

That night, Grandmother showed me to a storage area where they kept firewood. I slept there in the chips and dirt. I didn't care. I felt safe and confident they wouldn't betray me. In fact, she took me into their circle like her own.

The next morning I brushed off the lice and my rescuers told me the menacing man still hung about and told me not leave.

Grandmother's old fingers touched my hair and she said, "Boy, you must learn the lessons my boys know. First you will stay with us until we can get you out safely. Most of our men are dead, killed by our enemies, but we have our ways to survive. First, we put a brew of roasted goat fat mixed with crushed garlic and rub it on our faces. Believe me, that keeps our enemy stay away from us." She giggled in her high voice at her clever deceit.

I started to laugh, but held it back so I wouldn't hurt her feelings as my Baba taught me.

"And if you are going to travel around for whatever reasons, you must learn to play deaf and dumb."

"Huh, deaf and dumb? Why?"

If your enemies think you are crazy, they won't bother you. Learning this doesn't come easy. Do you want to learn?"

"Oh, yes!" I had already learned to dress like a peasant, not to talk too much, and to keep a stoic face to melt into the background. But this idea sounded great.

She practiced with me, watching my eyes, my body movements, teaching me not to flinch at strange sounds, and to look and act dumb. These were life saving devices learned by them centuries ago.

A couple of days later, a boom or hard object could drop without me jumping or responding, not even a blink of my eye. All results born out of practice. With my new skills, I gained new confidence.

The next day, I woke up next to the woodpile to discover lice covered me worse than ever. The grandmother put my clothes in a tub of hot water moving them around with a big stick. Her efforts prompted me to wash my body down carefully. Wrapped in a blanket, I fidgeted in their little living room waiting for my clothes to dry.

I started looking around the room when my eyes fell on an icon of the Mother Mary of Jesus high above the door. I couldn't believe it, in a Muslim house? Dressed again, I bowed and asked permission of Grandmother to ask a question. She nodded and I ask what the icon was about.

She told me, "That is our Mary, mother of Jesus. He, too, is our savior."

She smiled at me, "That icon is from our great-grand parents who were Christians. Our ancestors were forced to become Muslims a very long time ago but we refuse to speak the "Allah" language all the time. We don't touch and we don't talk. To have peace in your mind, let your soul guide you."

"Oh, my friend, you are the same as me," I cried, and she hugged me.

The absent father finally visited and gave me some advice. "The Muslims in Bosnia and Macedonia are very different from us. Their worship is different. Don't assume they will be friendly to you as we have been. It could be a fatal mistake. Many will not hesitate to kill children. Look, the street is free for you to go now."

I thanked him for his hospitality, then set my boots aside and asked him and the grateful grandmother to give them to my young friend who had none. This family may have saved my life, and I'd miss the grandmother who taught me so much.

I sneaked out of town hiding behind the burned houses, barns and body remains of a bloody massacre all along the countryside. My bare feet turned tough and callused. I kept a watch for another pair of boots and eventually stole a pair off a dead German soldier again. Maybe I was getting more callous than I thought. In one village I was passing through, I counted 169 houses smoldering plus two Muslim mosques burned to the ground.

The mountain trip back using my wonderful walking stick gave me plenty of time to think. Going from the disastrous war destruction to this wondrous peacefulness shook my senses. But my ability to bring back impressions and the people's view could possibly influence the future for General Mihailovic. Even the illiterate knew how to see and think!

Sometime or other, I crossed the border into Yugoslavia and again saw devastating ruins from the Ustasha killing. Just as I was thanking a soldier for giving me a ride in his jeep, he sped off nearly knocking me down.

From behind, Ustashe bullies grabbed me. One pushed the other one and laughed, "Who wants that scrawny kid to be in our "Honor Guard?" They forced me over to a field turned into a crude burial ground. Several soldiers stood over a hole with a pile of dirt beside it.

A middleaged, well dressed woman, struggling against two soldiers holding her, screamed at them. "I had one son as a Chetnik and another as a Partisan. That broke my heart, but both were better than you devils!"

Their laughter made my skin crawl as they shoved me to the edge of a crude hole and forced me to look in at a young, dead, mutilated soldier

"He's my son, he's my son. Let me go!" the woman screamed.

"Why don't you let her go?" I cried.

"You'll see!" Just then she broke from the soldier and headed for the grave attempting to dive in. The other fellow grasped her arm.

"Oh, go ahead and let her jump. We'll bury both of them," the soldiers continued to taunt the suffering woman with several others standing back enjoying the disgusting scene.

"Stop it, quit hurting the poor lady, she could be your mother!" I yelled. They all turned to me with disdain.

One young guy piped up, "Fine, kid, then you can jump in the grave in her place," getting a big laugh from the rest.

Just then, the woman jerked away and actually jumped into the grave of her son. Two soldiers jumped in to dig her out of the fresh soil and pulled her out. The dazed woman's arm flew up to her chest. She bent over, her screams turning to agonizing gasps. They lowered her crumbling body to the ground and silently watched her twitch in agony. Her body finally lay completely still, and her mouth open.

The soldiers looked at each other, then one kicked her rolling her over. She lay in the dirt, her arms flung out from her pinched, white, lifeless face while my stomach churned. They surely killed her, too. I'd never accept this terror.

"Fun's over, kid, get out of here!" The soldier started to lower his rifle and I took the opportunity to run and disappear as fast as I could.

My miss and hit transportation took me over the southern route through Kosovo. Intending to go north, I took a detour across a field that revealed a strange sight, and the closer I got, the sicker I became. Heads, decapitated from the bodies were displayed on sticks and nearby, bodies were being roasted like pigs on spits just like the Muslim father had warned me. I hid in the tall grass and proceeded nearly on my belly to get past the gristly scene.

ᔕᐤ

When I realized how close my home was, I decided to take a detour to end up in Kamenica. I still didn't want to show my face in the village so I hid until dark. The village looked almost deserted. With so many of the men killed, I supposed some of the families went to stay with relatives. Carefully, trying not to alert the dogs, I crept through the back meadows to my home, sneaked into the wine shed, and spent the night alone.

At first sun, I knocked on the kitchen door, surprised to see Drgica peak through the screen. Her voice quavered a little, "What do you want?"

"Drgica, it's me, Mila. Let me in."

Her hand went to her chest in shock. "Mila, it can't be, is it really you?"

She let me in, hugging me tightly, shoving me into the pantry. "Stay here!" she ordered while quietly going to get the family.

Majka came first dressed in black, her face white. Great, dark circles surrounded sunken eyes. Her body appeared terribly thin.

"Can that be you, my son?" She stood back staring at me, then took my left hand with the crooked finger to check me. Tata came up behind her followed by Jelica. I knew I looked terrible, dirty, matted hair, ragged clothes, rags around my boots, and probably smelled bad, too. Tata and my sisters talked all at once and couldn't hide me from our long time servants gathering around. Tears came up.

Immediately, the servants started up the fire, brought in food, and sat me down to breakfast. Oh, did fresh eggs and milk taste good. Visions of my Baba's special breakfast came to mind. I think I missed good food as much as I missed the family! But the family gathered around me was oddly quiet. I knew I needed a bath.

Tata looked older and strained. The girls' beauty had blossomed but their clothes were old, dark, and dowdy, and their hair hanging loose differed from the luxurious appearance we'd all been used to. I knew the difficult times had taken toll on everyone, including my own family. At least this part of the country had not yet been touched by bombs or serious battles.

After breakfast, the room became silent. All eyes including the faithful household servants went to Tata, "I have bad news, my son. Your Uncle Budimer is dead. He was murdered in his own house, shot up close six or seven times by marauding Partisans. They spared his wife. I'm sorry son, we've all been in mourning and had no way of informing you."

Majka's strained, sharp voice said to Tata, "You will be next!"

Tata patiently answered, "No, I'm not a politician. They won't come after me." Tata turned to me. "There is nowhere else for us to go. We'll stay on our land until we're dead."

Majka turned to me, her eyes blazing. "We can't go anywhere. It's too dangerous to travel with the Nazi's everywhere. We have to stay right here on our land and take care of the people and the farms."

I tried to agree, but Majka slipped out of her chair and quietly left the room. Drgica and Jelica looked at Tata as fear washed over their faces from deep in their hearts. They always supported Uncle Budimer but knew he had his own mind. Would he be next?

I couldn't believe it. My Uncle Budimer, in spite of his position as a Senator, his education in France, and all his dinars and influence, now dead, murdered, not in battle, but in his own home.

In War, none of that mattered. People dying all around us, but not my Uncle Budimer! Tears streaked down my dirty face from all such horror I'd seen. But this was my Uncle Budimer! All his power couldn't save him, or maybe it was his political contacts that killed him. He was trying to please both sides. I looked at my Tata, tears in his eyes for his brother-in-law and his widow. Poor Majka, her only brother! No wonder she looked awful. I felt sick.

"Was he avenged?" I finally asked Tata.

"Yes. Some Chetniks including Milan killed eight Partisans, hopefully the guilty ones. It's still neighbors killing neighbors! Sit down, son, there is nothing you can do, and you must not show your face. You are supposed to be dead. Your Uncles cannot meet together anymore, and we are somewhat out of touch except for the radio and don't get much off that. All we can do is try to survive. Don't worry about me. I'm just a struggling peasant farmer."

"What about Deda?" I felt nervous to even ask.

"He's dead, too, Mila. He died of a heart attack, we think. He was found dead in his store just a week after his son Budimir was killed. He lived a long life. We have two new graves in our family cemetery, now. Your mother hasn't been well since. But, she'll get stronger and we're together. Son, we miss you so much. Now tell us all about your travels and what's happening in the War."

I told them some stories without revealing much gore. I asked questions. Since most of the able bodied men from the villages had been mass murdered back in Nis, I learned how the family suffered from lack of workers on the farms. Many more had been killed by the Bulgarians, and the fighting between the Partisans and the Chetnics made manpower terribly scarce. Fields lay unattended and food was hoarded.

Dana recognized me throwing her head back with a welcome whinney. I walked her, fed her and brushed her down in the paddock. She and Vidion, the stallion had been well hidden so they wouldn't be stolen by marauding soldiers. I kissed her nose and wondered when I'd ever see my horse or any of the family, again.

Majka did quietly visit with me, fixed food, and dug up old clothes to replace my dirty, ragged ones. The luxury of soaking in a bubbly hot tub relaxed me somewhat and after I changed into the clean, fresh clothes, I studied my image in the mirror. I hardly recognized my body so very thin, my hair still thick, curly and long. And I couldn't believe I still didn't have any whiskers. Baba's clear voice told me that was a blessing to keep my disguise as a young boy, even though at almost nineteen, I felt like a man.

My old pair of boots barely fit but it beat going barefoot. Drgica stuffed my pockets with food and one pair of clean socks and underwear.

I went in Majka's room just before I left. Her dark eyes stood out of her thin, dark skin face. She stared at me when I took her hands in mine. "You are dead to me. Your name is on the graves in Nis." I kissed her but she hardly could respond.

I knew I had to leave. Danger lurked everywhere and I could not put the family into any more jeopardy.

When I left, I headed North following the Marova River towards Lopovo to get orders from General Mihailovic. When I found the headquarters, my friend Dihan greeted me, grabbing my head giving me a lively kiss on the forehead.

"Well, Babyface, you made it through. We were beginning to wonder if you were dead. Stay with any bears?" He loved to tease me.

He brought me black tea and bread with a huge sausage, a big treat. We visited all evening catching up on stories. One thing that kept coming up was Tito's looks. We'd both seen him several times, and realized that sometimes he was shorter, fatter, or lacked his scar. Finally, it dawned on both of us that there must be more than one Tito. He must have impersonators doing some of the dirty work and meetings he'd prepared them for. Between us, we figured there must be two or three impersonators.

When we finished fooling around, Dilan said seriously, "The General has changed. You'll see for yourself. He wants to see you."

General Mihailovic, his face thinner with misery in sunken eyes, visited with me just as if I was important. I told him all the secret, essential details. He appeared interested as I talked about my tour, how the Partisans seemed to be taking over although Tito remained in western Bosnia away from the Ustasha. The General frowned. He was most concerned with the possibility of the Brits turning against him and not sending as much equipment and weapons.

I told him I'd heard of the price on his head was 100,000 gold Deutsche marks. His face squinted into a deep frown until I announced the Germans had also put the same price on Tito's head. He nodded his head and smiled at that. His eyes became pensive and he rubbed his head.

"I only want a pure country without the animosity between people over religion. Is that too much to ask?"

I didn't know what to say.

He gave me another assignment back across the mountains. As I went out of the door, I figured I might as well stop at Aunt Milojka's right on the way.

Suhotnothe was a tiny village where Aunt Milojka lived with her husband when he was there. Her small house looked quite rundown on the outside, until she appeared in the doorway.

She greeted me with kisses, smelled wonderful and appeared happy with her marriage to "a wonderful man" The place inside was furnished very well from her trousseau, warm and lovely as I would have expected of her. She pulled the curtains shut in her kitchen while she fed me hot stew and black bread while we talked a while. We talked about Uncle Budimir, Deda, and the war's effect on everyone.

I just stared at her and said, "I hope when the war is over, I can find a beautiful, precious woman like you for myself."

She laughed and kissed me on the forehead again. She drew me back from her and I looked into her beautiful, kind eyes.

"You're growing to be a handsome young man, just like your Tata, Mila. You'll find the right woman, don't you worry."

"Milojka, We know about Uncle Budimir and Deda's deaths, but what happened to Milan? Tata said Milan helped kill the killers but hadn't heard from him since. I hated to ask the family about him as they were all in mourning."

"Oh, Mila. I know how much you admired Milan. So did I. But he was shot and killed in Kamenica and we buried him in the family plot."

"Oh, no. Not Milan; he was so strong and seemed invincible. That's horrible news. He taught me so much growing up."

I thought of the strong handsome man and figured it was probably political, also. Suddenly I wondered, "Buried in the family plot? Aunt Milojka, how could that be? Only family members can be buried there."

Milojka took my hands and leaned toward me. "Dear boy, Milan was the illegitimate son of Ceda, a mistake he made as a young soldier away from home but he kept track of the mother with instructions that if he was killed, she was to take Milan to Milika, my mother. Apparently, the girl did take the baby to your Baba who made arrangements for the girl and Milan to board with a respectable farm family. The girl died soon after.

"Baba always taught him history herself, hired a tutor for him to learn to read and made sure he was raised properly. Your father knew and always treated him as a brother but of course, your Majka could not have him live in the house."

That tragic but shocking news made my head spin. My revered Grandfather Ceda sired an illegitimate child? I would have never guessed Milan's lineage but Tata and I always admired him as an exceptional person and I would miss him as much as my revered Uncle Budimir.

Before I left with a packet of food, she instructed me not to take the patrolled road, but to travel in the nearby stream leaving no footprints. "God bless us all, my darling Mila."

The stream led around the village of Zitkovac about two miles away and would lead back into the Morava River. I thought so much of all my family, especially Milan. Imagine that! What a brave woman my Baba was. I couldn't believe that Milan was dead, giving his life for our family's revenge.

I headed back up into the mountains navigating through the stream. Just between twilight and darkness nibbling some food, my eyes squinted ahead to see strewn piles of something. Slowly, I sloshed my way upstream recognizing the waning stench first.

About forty bodies were piled on top of each other in the water, clothes in tatters. Oh, God, they had been beheaded! Who did this? Staring down at those poor souls in the stream, I felt dizzy. The cold water rushed through my legs as I tried to keep my balance to hold me up.

I recognized at least two people by their hands. I had kissed those hands many times greeting them in my father's home. I'd always felt a little self-conscious about my own crooked finger making me highly aware of other people's hands.

I felt powerless. This atrocity could not even be reported without being sent to a mental institution or a concentration camp. How much do I have to bear, God? I had no choice but to stumble past them through the cold mountain water in the dark.

Every time I saw even big rocks ahead of me, I froze with fear. Then I realized and worried that while I was working my way upstream even before I saw the dead bodies, their blood and guts had been coming down. I washed up in the clean water, dried off, and prayed I wouldn't get sick. Finally, I calmed down enough to find a mossy place to sleep. I rubbed my nearly frozen feet from the cold water.

I crossed the Sandjak, between Bosnia and Montenegro. It was the most remote, ugly province I'd ever seen. No trees, just ground full of stones and rocks, plus primitive, terrible, scary people known to kill one another and drink a person's blood while they were still alive.

A couple of dirty men actually chased me for no reason, forcing me to hide in a damp cave. I had to sneak my way through northeast Bosnia to try to deliver my message.

〜

In July, large German forces had created and occupied big camps, plus small groups in the mountains. They were forced to stay to protect lines of supply to Greece.

In northeast Bosnia one night, I was particularly hungry and heard voices up the road. I sneaked up to see Partisan soldiers laughing and carrying two very drunk soldiers trying to load them in a wagon. I went in close and just stood quietly with the young soldiers.

"Hide our Star Englishman," one called. "Don't let anyone know who he is." Then he turned around and saw me standing there in the shadows.

"Who are you?" The others turned surprised to see a silent, ragged stranger standing there. "Get out of here, boy. This is private business!"

I pretended to be mute and motioned at the drunk and innocently with my hands asked who he was. One of the drunken soldiers yelled, "It's a famous English officer and him and this other officer got so drunk they was having sex with a goat! And then they could hardly stand up!"

"Do you know who Winston Churchill is?" one asked me showing off. They all laughed uproariously. I shook my head, "no" innocently.

"Well, you dumb kid. He's the Prime Minister of Great Britain and this is his drunkard son, Randolph, just like his pompous old man."

And they laughed uproariously slapping each other. The wagon started off with four feet sticking out the back. I pointed at the food and they handed me a bowl of left-over soup and a potato.

But then they threatened me, "Get out of here, Boy! We'll make you completely disappear if you ever tell anyone about this! No one will believe you, anyway. Now get out of here!" He kicked his leg towards me.

I trotted away from there feeling humiliated. After all, of course I knew who Winston Churchill was. I hated having to play so dumb all the time. I kicked a rock in frustration. I'll be glad when this war is over.

Winston Churchill was playing both sides by furnishing the Partisans and the Chetniks supplies. Didn't he care the Partisans were Communists? Guess he thought we all worked together to fight the Germans.

Those English didn't really know or care much about our country. Only that we were against the Germans who occupied our land. Except for the Croats, of course, who allied and aided the Germans killing Serbian Orthodox peasants. What an upper crust bore that English snob Churchill was anyway, or at least that's what I'd heard. He probably wants to rule the world just like Stalin and Hitler. He's no better than they are! And that gross story about his son. A goat? Is he demented? God, what am I doing here?

I guess I was also feeling disconnected and upset about my hero, General Mihailovic. Why couldn't anything be the way it seemed? The darkness just amplified my foul mood and my strength seemed to seep out of me. Better concentrate on avoiding the wolves. I searched and found an old tree with strong branches and climbed up to just the right spot to sleep until first sun.

A few miles away, I made sure no one was in sight, stretched and climbed down. After quite a walk, I spotted smoke, wandered into a busy Partisan camp and decided to blend in and get breakfast.

I reported the incident just as soon as I could to at least save Randolph Churchill. I lied that my family had been killed, and I would do chores for food. I could say whatever came to my head now, truth or lie. Or I could stay totally silent. I just flowed with the circumstances at the time, all rather unreal anyway.

Then a really unreal thing happened. There in the midst of the Partisans stood a Chetnic, Commander Boja Mitrovic, a man I recognized, known to me through Tata and the Uncles, and whom I'd seen in the presence of General Mihailovic. He stared right at me, came over without changing the expression on his face, turned me around by the shoulder and kept walking with me beside him. When he was sure we were out of earshot, he said, "What are you doing here, Boy?"

"Commander, with all due respect, what are you doing here?" I answered.

"This is no place for you, Mlodrag. I know you are a courier for the General. I knew your grandfather Ceda and your family and your connections. Get as far away as you can!"

"No, Commander, I'm just a poor orphan boy. You have me confused with someone else."

"I don't think so. You're Miodrag Cedic, I'm sure. What a coincidence!" He paused to stare at me a minute or two.

Finally, he said, "I've changed my mind. I'm taking you to see someone," he said and herded me off to a cottage where he introduced me to a young blonde woman in civilian shirt and pants and left me there.

She smiled, took my hand and said, "Miodrag, I know who you are. I'm the wife of Branko. Won't you sit down?"

I almost fell over. Branko was the youngest son of General Mihailovic. When I could get the words out, I asked, "What are you doing here?"

"The tides of the war are changing, Miodrag. The Partisans under Tito are in favor now, and they our only chance to beat the Germans. Please understand. You should come over, too. Branko and his friends are all coming over.

"We are not Communists but the Western Allies believe the Partisans are the only Yugoslav resistance group actively fighting the Germans. Do you see? Since losing so many men at Sutjeska Gorge, they've built the army back up to about 26 divisions to match the Germans. With all the arms they took after the Italians left, Tito has managed to double the size of his field army from the materials he took from the Italians. We are hoping that by allying with the Partisans, we can help win the war earlier for our country."

She stopped and asked me if I was hungry. Startled as I was to find myself in this position, I nodded my head and said I'd appreciate a hot meal. I just couldn't believe what I was hearing.

"The Partisans gained control of the coastal territory as you know, Miodrag, and now they have begun receiving supplies from both Britain and the United States through Italy."

She talked so sincerely as she fixed me breakfast.

"Those countries increased support to the Partisans because they have been showing aggression like a real army and recently proved much stronger against the Germans than the Cetnici are now.

"Last fall, we were in on secret meetings called Anti-Fascist Council for the National Liberation of Yugoslavia. They are proclaiming support for democracy, rights for ethnic groups and property, and economic initiative. See, Miodrag, we really are all on the same side. Branko's brother doesn't know yet and the General may never understand.

"More British officers have parachuted in to help the Partisans, and the RAF has started to drop in supplies of clothing and food for the guerrillas. Fitzroy Maclean has been sent from Churchill to aid Tito and we are very impressed with him.

"We are just waiting to meet again with Tito. He's a remarkable man, Miodrag. He has great strength and can discuss any subject and make decisions. My father-in-law is a great man and I admire him as much as you do but he is getting old and past accepting the new Yugoslavia we want to build if we can win this war."

"Why are you telling me this? I'm not qualified to know this. What should I do?"

My senses were frantic going every which direction, but I kept eating. She poured more coffee for me then took my hands and smiled at me so sweetly.

"We want you to go back to the General and explain what is happening Miodrag, and we want you to find out what we need to do to get him to join us. We've been trying to figure out how to approach the General and by the grace of God, here you are!"

"He'll never believe me. I'm just a courier." What a fix I'm in, I thought. What's going to happen to us?

"I trust you, Miodrag. Don't worry, no Partisans will know who you are. You use your own judgement which is what I hear you do anyway. Let us know what you decide to do. Go. Here, take some food with you, young man." She kissed my forehead and sent me out.

My heart was beating hard as I casually walked through the camp hoping I was invisible. I worried the highway would be in the hands of Germans, but no vehicles came. No tanks, trucks or troops.

Finally out of the silence, I heard a jeep coming up the hill. I had no place to hide and just trudged along like a weary kid, my back to the noise of the motor. I heard it pull up behind me and a German soldier call out. I turned around with my best innocent look. Two of them climbed down, blocked me and ask for my identification.

"I don't have any," I said in German.

"Then who are you?" they started towards me.

"I'm no one, just a little boy. I belong to him," and I pointed to the sky. They laughed, tossed me a big hunk of black bread and an apple and drove off without any more interference. I swear my heart didn't slow down until I traveled deep into the forest.

When I settled down, I started to review our war again. What should I do? Mihailovic himself, urged by patriots like my Uncles, had started to fight against the Germans invasion in May, 1941. That was long before Tito got into the action supposedly because of his association with Stalin.

But the savage punishment to the peasants after the massacre at Kragujevac that October stopped the Chetniks from further attacks of the Germans for fear of reprisals. How close I came to being killed along with friends then. And I thought, Britain is harboring King Petar. What will happen to our King? How will they influence him?

I half-heartedly completed my mission and went back to headquarters. Finally, Dihan, his antics gone, found a chance to talk to me alone and being the only person I could confide in, I told him what happened with Branko.

"Well, for one thing," Dihan said, "I'm not surprised that Maclean 'bloke' is sucking up to Tito. Tito is impressive but Michael Lees, General Mihailovic's British liaison officer says Maclean is taken by Tito's charm and could influence the British to do damage to our General and the Chetniks."

"What do you think I should do, Dihan?"

"Don't pay any attention to the Maclean thing. We can't do anything about it. About his son, Branko, I don't know. This is one of those times, no matter what we do, it won't be right. The truth is Mila, the General has accomplished so much for this country but he's getting discouraged. And tired. Right now we have three factions, the Ustashe, the Partisans and the Chetnics all having a three-way civil war with each other. The General is very discouraged about our chances of winning without communism. If we are going to chase out the Germans and keep our country together, we have to pull together. That's first."

I felt heartsick. He's right. We just couldn't continue to waste lives and our resources fighting each other. What a fiasco!

"Don't look so discouraged, Mila. I got good news. In November, the AVNOJ is going to hold a big session. They are supposed to have representatives of all the various ethnic and political groups and build a basic government for Yugoslavia after the war. We may get out of this mess yet."

He never called me "Babyface" once. Dihan slapped me on the back, smiling at me trying to cheer me up. I told him the story of Randolph Churchill and the goat. After our silly laughter and settling down, I looked at him closely. Dihan, my friend and confidant looked older, shabby, and told me how morale was low, men were deserting, and how discouraged he was at the futile killing with no end in sight.

"Now, go on and take a bath before you meet with the General. You stink!"

Clean and fed, I met with the General. His weathered face had grown thinner and he appeared worn down. His tall figure slumped down in his big chair behind his desk, his long legs sticking out. But after we discussed our business, he spoke in sensible terms, obviously not giving up easily.

"I know many of our men will go over to fight with the much advanced Partisans. Brave men who will never be communists, though. Tito wants to run our country if he lives long enough. He's strong and determined and I have reason to believe he'll never give in to Stalin's shape of communism anyway. He wants to pull all our nationalities together and that goes against their Marxist theory."

He paused and his eyes narrowed and he continued.

"It's really a matter of religion and power. He wants the power, and the countries want their religion. And that doesn't fit into the Marxist scheme that divides people according to class.

"In the meantime, my boy, the men who are the real guerrillas will follow me. We still have plans. We will protect our large group of downed Americans pilots hiding in the hills for one thing although we may not be able to get them out until the War is over. We will protect the villages as we can. We will still fight. I want to live to see our country built back up and become free and prosperous."

He smiled at me, a strong man and a good man, misery in his eyes, still forceful and dedicated to his own mission. I just couldn't bring myself to tell him about his son. He was the General and he would function for his country in his own way. I admired him as my family did before me.

⌒

At the second session of the AVNOJ in November 1943, representatives voted to reorganize the country on a federal basis, elected a national committee to act as a temporary government.

To my great surprise, they named Tito as marshal and prime minister of Yugoslavia. We did hear later that Tito enraged Stalin by failing to notify him about the plans for AVNOJ. The western Allies who believed the Partisans were the only resistance group fighting the Germans anyway, took it in stride.

At dusk near to our base, I heard shouting and a crowd of village people crowding around. Walking into a thick grove of trees, I sneaked in as close as I dared and peaked around a tree. I came upon a dreadful sight.

A small group of guerrillas were holding a man down in the snow while he struggled for his life. He was being interrogated while stripped naked. One person stood over him with a knife throwing down a sharp glint from the last light on the poor victim. The knife whirled not to his heart but to his penis. My hand flew to my mouth as it was sliced off to horrible screams. The person held the penis up.

The victim's screams drove away the birds before a soldier stuffed it in his mouth. Bile came up my throat. Then the soldier cut off his ears while he bled profusely.

The murderer laughed. It was not a man's, but a woman's high pitched horrible laugh. She held it up for all to see.

"For my husband, the priest Milosevic, and our son, Slobodan, the peacemaker who will one day rule Yugoslavia," she screamed.

Myself was frozen to the spot until they started to move away leaving the dying man writhing on the ground. Grandmothers and children started to cry and keen. The women were crossing themselves with their left hands as they could not believe what they had just witnessed.

"Oh, my God, A priest's wife is doing this? Is that possible?"

I ran to the bleeding, dying man and knelt down. He was one of Mihailovic's men. He gurgled, took his last breath and died as I held him. God help us.

↜

General Mihailovic learned the U.S. President Roosevelt, Churchill and Stalin had met in Teheran in December and had decided to support the Partisans. The most difficult result of that meeting was Britain stopped supplying the Cetnici and heavily threw support at the Partisans.

The General showed encouragement only from the Americans. They seemed to appreciate our heavy influence against the Germans and saw the importance of keeping a military mission with him for all his efforts to save the downed fliers.

Our world appeared like it may explode at any moment. Even though we nearly became used to living with the horror, I felt a surge of hope for our country. Maybe we could still overcome all the factors against us.

Very soon, I began to wonder. The Germans came back strong with the Sixth Offensive. The former Italian zone of southern Slovenia, the Adriatic coast and the islands were hit hard and the Germans smashed all three Partisan divisions in northeast Bosnia. The only island left was Vis that had Royal Navy and

RAF protection. I looked it up on the map; about the middle of the Adriatic far out from the shore.

The General remarked, "I've always felt the Germans anticipated an Allied invasion of the Balkans just as we did. They know we would aid the Allies and would continue burning up men and materials trying to stop us. I'm certain the Chetniks will make a big comeback aiding the Americans at the shoreline. I dream of that even knowing the sacrifice we would have to make. I know Hitler has not given up his 'Dream for World Domination.'

"Winston Churchill supposedly sent a personal letter to Tito. My Partisan source assured me that by sending his son Randolph with the British military mission, he had shown his support."

I laughed, "Are you kidding? Churchill is probably hoping his pitiful son will be a dead martyr."

Chapter 11

1944

The whole experience was such a letdown to us that the General sent me home for a rest. The more I walked the more I shivered from cold, disappointment, and growing rage. Yugoslavia must become a democracy. Now Tito was in power, War or no War. The General had planned carefully, used caution, analyzed, and commanded as best he could. What had gone wrong? Again, the more I thought, the more time passed quickly.

An old peasant farmer stopped and gave me a ride in his wagon from Aleksinac, nine miles from home. I rode on the seat beside him. It seemed still no one owned trucks or cars in this part of the country partially due to lack of gasoline. And danger lurked as even a wagon could be confiscated by the Germans any minute. The wheels squeaked in rhythm to the horses' hooves. My head vibrated, my bones ached with exhaustion. Even so, the old man seemed to appreciate my company.

No lights were visible in my house so, once again, I stayed in the wine cellar that still looked the same. I pulled a dirty blanket over me and went to sleep for the rest of the night.

Dreams entered of clear fields, orchards full of blossoms in spring, the air clear and sunny and Tata and I surveying all that we owned. I watched my Tata sail over the fence on Vidion, the huge black stallion followed by me on Dana, my beautiful mare. I could feel us flying through the air, free with clean blood rushing to our heads.

Reality came back awaking with the first sun. When the first smoke came out of the chimney, I sneaked to the house to surprise the family.

"Oh, Mila, you are so lean and muscled. You look so old!" Drgica's welcome made me laugh as I hugged her.

Majka welcomed me without much feeling. Her pale face showed stress, still with deep, darker circles under her dark eyes. Drgica and Jelica pulled on me, happy and vying for attention. Both were lovely young women ready for marriage but obviously still kept very sheltered by Majka. The stress of war interrupted everyone's lives.

Tata came in the back door from the barn, a huge grin on his face, "Son, my son."

He grabbed my head and kissed my forehead. "You're alive. I knew you were. I pray for you everyday." He held me away from him, looking me over.

"You have grown, son. But still only a tiny fuzz on your chin," he laughed and teased me. I hugged him with all my might. For all the worry and hard work pressing grooves in his forehead, he still looked good. All the family appeared dowdy but adequately fed. We talked late into the night.

"I'm so proud of you, son. You're doing your country a great service and I've heard from General Milailovic's headquarters that you've turned the tide of battles more than once with your confidential information they would never have known otherwise."

The next day farm hands and I helped Tata get ready to leave for Jakovlje to ground his grain into flour at the mill. He would supply the Orthodox Christmas holiday coming up in a few days on January 9th.

"You stay here and visit, Miodrag. People must not see you. I won't be long. I'll be back home tonight."

The family talking and laughing with me cheered me up immensely. I felt so relaxed that I fell asleep in the big upholstered chair in the living room while waiting up for Tata.

I woke with Majka shaking me, "What are you doing sleeping in the chair?" A weak ray of sunlight was coming in the window.

"Where's Tata? Wasn't he coming home last night?"

"I don't know. He must be here."

She started to panic. "He should be here. Oh God, where is he?" We searched outside. He wasn't anywhere, the wagon was still gone and no one had seen him. "I'm going to find him," she insisted.

"No, Majka, I'll go. Where would he be?"

"I'll go. You must stay hidden here. I know everyone in Jakovlje. Don't forget I was born and raised there. They know and trust me, and I can track him down or will be told if anything bad has happened." Her face was white, drained but her thinking seemed fired up, clear and determined.

"I'll take Drgica. Better for me to go. You stay here with Jelica and the servants in case he comes back."

Just before she was ready, she rushed to answer a knock at the front door. I heard the hysterics and ran to the door behind my mother. Jelesic, a trusted neighbor stood there, hat in hand. I grabbed hold of the man crying with Majka.

"What happened?"

"It's your father, It's Stretein Milanovic. He's dead!"

Never for all I'd seen, did the blood leave my head so severely. I still managed to catch sight of Majka going green and grabbed her before she hit the floor and carried her to the couch to lie down. The neighbor was still there staring at me. "Who are you? You can't be Miodrag. You're dead."

"No. What happened to my father?" Tears were slipping down my face but I didn't care.

"Oh, Miodrag, I was in Jakovje yesterday when I heard he had been captured by Partisans. He was taken by surprise right off the street to the City Hall. They tortured him trying to get him to talk about the guerrillas movement in the area. He knew nothing but they hung him up barely alive in the Town Square for all to see. He finally died. That's where I came upon him just before dark. I'm so sorry."

Majka said, "I'm going there. He can't be dead. I'm going to get him."

"I'll go." I tried to stop her but she ordered me to stay. She took off with Drgica and the neighbor Jelesic driving her carriage, whipping the poor old horses down the icy road.

I can't stand this. After so much death, my innocent Tata can't be gone. I waited for several hours with the terrified Jelica, only thirteen years old. Villagers already aware of big trouble, began coming by asking the servants if they could help. How could anyone help? Finally, I heard the noise outside and ran out. Majka and Drgica, pale and wrung out, were helped out of the carriage into my arms and taken into the house. The men lifted the mangled body of Tata wrapped in a blanket out of the back of the wagon.

Majka grabbing onto me cried, screaming and choking, "I didn't believe it. He's dead. I couldn't believe it. We saw him hanging in the Town Square for everyone to see."

Her voice sobbed up to a scream and down to a whisper and fell through my arms to the floor on her knees.

She couldn't stop talking. "Oh, Miodrag, they told me the soldiers twisted his body on a table and tore out four ribs from his body while torturing him to get him to talk. He never told them anything before they hung him up. He died for all to see. My Sretein, so kind, so good. Where is our God?

"Sretein never hurt anyone in his life. I knew this would happen. My poor, poor Sretein."

She sobbed loosing her strength. I held her head in my hands but she couldn't stop talking, her voice strained between gulps and choking.

"I never should have taken Drgica. What was I thinking? She collapsed at the sight of his body hanging there. I just didn't believe he was really dead. I begged them to take him down. And with people's help, we got the body into the wagon and raced home."

I tried to calm her but in her hysterics and keening, she pushed me away. The vomit came up my throat and my legs started to buckle. Friends took over.

I ran to the wine cellar. Not my beloved Tata! I felt so helpless. What if it was my fault? What if someone thought I'd gone over to the Partisans? Did someone see me? I picked up a large knife and in my horror and sorrow, I meant to plunge it into myself. The door flew open. Aunt Milojka and Uncle Svetomir burst in seizing the knife from me.

"No, oh Mila, NO!" cried Milojka. "Oh Mila, No, No, your family needs you. We love you. And we all loved our dear sweet Sretein. He would not want you to die. We all want you to live."

Her voice broke into sobs. She held me and rocked me for a long time it seemed. They lifted me to my feet and we stumbled our way back into the house where Uncle Svetomir held onto Majka.

"Selimka, Selimka." He cried out trying to console her.

Drgica had come back from Jakovje in a serious state of shock. She had fainted when she saw him hanging and stayed in a semi-conscious state all the way home. The servants carried her to her bed, and she had not moved since, just stared at the ceiling with a blank look on her face. Jelica sat in the big rocking chair at bedside holding Drgica's hand and rocking herself back and forth crying.

All my Uncles, Tata's brothers, and their families arrived filling the guest house bedrooms keeping our faithful servants busy cleaning, preparing and serving food.

In the next few days, Tata's body was prepared and laid out in the great room of our home. Late at night, I came by his side to sleep on the floor near him until the frosty early morning. I don't remember much more.

In the next days, so many people, including high officers and diplomats, all came through our home. Peasant villagers from all around brought food and even cows, trying to console the family in traditional ways. Scores of Chetnik and Partisan soldiers and supporters came by. Some stood guard at all times and others just passed by his body. I kept hidden.

The Kamenica and Kulina villagers were building a sturdy casket for him. When it was finished, a big funeral was held at our Orthodox Church in Kulina. The villagers took Tata to be buried in our family plot beside his parents, Ceda's empty plot, and my Baba.

The soldiers restricted Milojka, her husband, Radojako, Uncle Svetomir and myself from the funeral. Maybe they were to watch me so I wouldn't use the knife on myself. Or maybe we, too were targets for disaster. Milojka never left my side. I could barely think straight. Even after all the death and gore I'd seen, losing my innocent Tata was just too painful.

Later, it became clear to me most of the village people believed I was dead. My name was listed on the board in Nis with those 300 men minus one who were executed in the factory at the beginning of the war.

One night later Jelesic, the same man, who'd seen Tata hanging before his death, came to the door to speak to me again. When he came in, he lifted his jacket to show me a large belt around himself. He proceeded to take it off and released the buckle off it. I stared at him first with curiosity then horror creeping around my neck. He handed me the antique buckle. I stared at the huge, heavy, white gold and silver piece burning into my hand.

Just holding it made me feel faint. It belonged to my Tata. I pushed it back at him. "I can't! I can't take it!" The pain was indescribable.

"You must take it, Mila. It's your heritage." Jelesic raised his voice to my protests. "Your father's tailor happened to have it for measurement of a new belt the day your father was killed. He told me the buckle is an antique passed down many generations of your family from the 1300s. Take it!"

I still couldn't take it. It burned my soul. I begged the trusted, long time neighbor to take it back home to bury it for me for now. He was the only surviving person who knew I was alive outside the family and as far as I ever knew, he never told anyone.

The buckle loomed in my thoughts in dreams. At first sun, my thoughts became clear. I'd heard the buckle was a prize from the Battle of Kosovo or so the legend went. Ceda, my Baba, and Tata always were so proud of it and I couldn't fathom why it was out of the house at all. But I still could not look at it and would find out where it was hidden and retrieve it later. Jelesic's son was a good friend of mine and we would keep in touch.

I tried to help Majka who went about working with our faithful household staff who were still there. Everyone pitched in to feed the animals in the winter weather.

I visited Drgica in her room every chance I got. Her weak, pale face and blank eyes tried to smile at me but couldn't quite make it. I'll just give her time, I thought and read to her while she just sat in a chaise lounge with a blanket over her. Jelica tried to wash and comb her hair but she barely responded to us and had to be helped even with feeding and personal care.

I told Majka about the belt buckle when I felt she could discuss it. She said, "Your Tata meant to give that important piece of our heritage to you on your twenty-fifth birthday. The buckle is yours, Miodrag. Where is it, now?"

"I told Jelesic to bury it for now. I'll get it from him soon. I just couldn't touch it right then. I know he will take care of it for us."

I tried to cheer her up. "Did you know his son joined the Border Patrol and learned to speak Albanian fluently?"

My Majka looked blank, her eyes so sad. "I don't care anymore. All is lost. We have nothing left without Sretein. Nothing but you children matter."

We learned Tata's tailor had also been murdered, hanged in Jakovje soon after Tata. It was amazing we got the buckle back before he died. Several villages shared one Town Square with one mayor so everyone knew about the murders.

For about four months I stayed home with the approval of the General. I took charge of the farm's management. I began begging an old village man who'd worked for the family for many years to act as foreman. Now only the very old and the very young could continue to grow and furnish food for everyone. I did my best but knew the farms could not last long without Tata's expertise.

In my free time, I read Karl Marx because my father had been reading him to learn about communism in its pure form. I wanted to carry on Tata's studies. My old Sir Teacher Slatoje and his wife, Desaska wrote their condolences and announced they were now Socialists. I recalled them intellectually promoting it as an advanced system. Then, they personally believed it a much better way to live.

They had taught us in school, "We're going to be fighting again and everyone including God will be in it. God will not be against the Christ who was a communist, according to the communists." *One world, one government.* Propaganda, I knew, but as Baba said, "Even the illiterate knew how to think!"

Jelica told me that before Uncle Budimir was murdered, he had arranged for our teachers, Statoje and Desaska and their family to move to Kosovo for safety. All the Uncles admired them and wished them no harm.

My back rested back in a big chair as I reminisced about Slatojes' young son who helped me to pass the math test, my hardest subject. I smiled at memories of school. I couldn't sing or paint well, but other than math I had excellent grades, and if not for the war I would be attending university now preparing for my business future.

I pushed back in my chair, chuckling over a school picture episode. About the time all the children were lined up ready for the photographer, I ran up on the hill behind them, climbed into a little apple tree alone posing holding apples above my head. One of the teachers heard some giggling and ordered me back in my place, but the photographer intervened and told me to stay up there. Guess he thought it would make a unique picture.

The picture did turn out great with all the children smiling and me in the tree. The teachers had it blown up and hung in the hall of the school. Tata loved that picture. Wonder if the tree is still there? How I loved to show off.

Then I thought about Tito who also loved to show off as a communist, although he was not in very good standing with Stalin. Would he end up our president or premier or dictator? His organization of the Partisans was remarkable. Overall as a group, they were much more educated and effective than the unruly peasant Chetniks.

The Chetniks controlled and defended the countryside in an erratic manner. Of all Slavic people, the peasants were often the most stubborn, closed minded people. Like the Bulgarians, they often acted like rabid animals.

And what about King Petar? Would he ever be welcomed to come back and rule?

Men issuing loud orders and hoofs hitting the bricks around the horse barn brought me straight up out of my reverie. I stood helplessly at the window. Oh, God! Marauding, armed Nazi soldiers were stealing the best of our terrified horses. They threw on bits and reins and led them right out of their stalls and down the road.

I watched helplessly as the hidden Dana and Vidian, our beautiful thoroughbreds were discovered, throwing their heads up and whinnying in resistance but still stolen along with anything else the enemy wanted. Had they no respect for a house draped in mourning?

Uncle Svetislav's sick wife had died many months ago, and he had attended Tata's funeral alone. I hadn't seen him since I joined the General. Finally, he came back with Uncle Svetomir to talk to me about the future.

Both entered the main house looking worn out and old. We hung their coats up and went into the big dining room. "I miss our talks around this table with the men, Mila. I watched you mature and now you are such a fine, young man," said Uncle Svetomir.

Tears came to his eyes. "I couldn't tell you before, Mila, but we also lost our Vladislav in battle several month ago."

"Oh God, Vladislov is dead?" Now my wild and favorite older cousin, Vladislov, the boy who teased me so, who tested my skills, who was my best friend, now dead with the others. Was there no end to the killing? "Oh Uncle, I'm so sorry."

I gulped trying to hold the tears back. I'd been sure I had none left over from all I shed over my Tata. Memories flooded back on me, and Uncle seemed to want to hear them to remember his bright, first son. His other son, Zivadin was also fighting and angry over his brother's death, but so far as we knew, he was alive somewhere in Bosnia.

Uncle talked of the present. "Someone else you know was murdered, Mila. Drazik Kodlj, your Tata's friend and business partner who came here for the funeral was also hung like your father. I'm sorry."

"We must talk about a place for the women. They cannot remain here. The property is too big and too dangerous. Milan is gone and you have your responsibilities. There aren't enough men around to care for them and the fields and the orchards. And we're short on kerosene and fuel and soon not enough dinars will be coming in to maintain it all."

They told me the bank accounts had been confiscated two years ago for the war effort. I thought of the fortune in gold coins buried somewhere on our property. Oh, no, Tata never told anyone where the coins were buried! Then I thought of the ancient belt buckle. I hoped to retrieve the belt buckle very soon so I could sell it but who could afford to buy it?

Later over dinner, we laughed with Jelica about when we were children at the festival and the boys were trying to ride the goats in front of Prince Peter. Drgica still could not bring herself to come downstairs.

After dark, I dressed in the oldest clothes out of the tack room and walked down to Kamenica dodging around houses. At the Jelesic house, I greeted his wife who answered the door and handed her a basket of food. She did not recognize me but gave me another shock. Father and son had gone off with the

Chetniks. The mother breaking into tears, told me both had been killed and she didn't know anything about the belt buckle. She gave me permission to look for a buried place but after searching in the snow covered ground and trying to dig for two hours, no sign of the belt could be found anymore than the gold coins hidden on our property. I stood there leaning on the shovel while despair rolled over me.

At least Uncle would be there to help me find a home for the women. He mentioned Tata had dinars stashed in the tack room that we did retrieve, thank God. All the relatives were offering accommodations.

When Uncle left, I talked to Majka who showed much interest in leaving this big house and the sorrow in every corner. She looked at me seriously and talked to me as her equal. "I have no family left and I don't want to stay with any of Stretein's family. I want to go to Aleksinac. So far it has not been bombed or burned and we can rent a house there from my father's friends. We'll still be close to the rest of the family. Most of all they have a small mental hospital there where I can get help for Drgica if they haven't turned it completely into a German hospital. What do you think?"

I was amazed she asked me. She went on.

"I can't live here with so many memories," her voice shook. "He is in every inch of this house and the whole property, the guest house, the wine building, the barns and tack rooms, even the village is so depressing. My whole life of importance centered around Sretein and you children. And Drgica is not getting better. Will you try to talk to her, my Mila? We must move into a safer place if there is such a thing in this filthy war."

I took her shaking hands in mine and assured her I'd take care of the arrangements.

I looked into the pretty, pale face of Drgica, her light blue, sad eyes and reddish, blond hair so like Tata. Her voice was so soft, barely audible.

"I want to feel better, Mila, really I do. I've been training to be a teacher. But, I don't want to teach communism, Mila. I just want to teach the basics. Little children need to be taught like we were." She was so thin but her eyes revealed she was trying to come out of her depression.

She paused several minutes looking at me straight into my soul. "Of course, you had Baba which most people, no matter where they live will ever have a teacher like her. Someday you'll go back to school, Mila and become a famous man. I pray for you."

Then her voice faded and she could not speak any more. She rolled her head back on the pillow and stared at the ceiling. She never should have seen Tata hanging in the Square. It was just too much for anyone. I feared Majka was right. She may never recover.

We started making arrangements. By March, we had closed down all we could, left our faithful servants to continue to live here and keep up the house as some had all their lives.

Maybe for the last time, I rode an old horse around the vineyards, the gardens, the fields, the orchards knowing the peasants would take care of the property as best they could. We packed goods from the root cellar, flour, salt, potatoes, cabbage, wine, preserves, and ammunition for Majka's pistol. Jelica, Drgica and Majka, wrapped in blankets were loaded in the carriage with another loaded wagon following behind us driven by our armed old servant couple.

Finally, we arrived in Aleksinac and drove towards their new little rented house. The town seemed nearly deserted with only a few poorly stocked stores open. Only old, broken men and very young boys lived here with all the women. A small, pleasant, house on a small garden plot had been rented for them. The house could barely be seen from the road and we prayed it would be safe.

I helped move the furniture into the house and made sure Majka and Jelica were settled in. Actually, without servants, the space was just right. Majka could handle it alone.

She sat across from me drinking her heavy coffee and I noticed she had also lost weight drastically and her warm dress hung on her. Her dark skin revealed heavy, darker circles under sad eyes; her mouth set in a straight line rarely moving into a semblance of a smile.

"My parents are dead. I only have you children. My youngest brother Obren died when a rope caught him and dropped him into a well," her voice wandered in the past.

Tears came down her face. Another death, losing Uncle Obren in the War far away in Bosnia shortly after Budimir died. It was no accident.

I rallied her into the future and talked to her about spending the dinars I'd brought from home. Enough dinars for them to live well were hidden on the back porch of the little house where she could grab the metal box and escape with it in an emergency.

I had not yet found the buried fortune of the wine gold coins anywhere on our old property. Tata hadn't left a clue. But the women would be set for life even if something happened to me. Jelica cried and hugged me threatening never to let me go. Majka gave me a real kiss on my forehead, an unusual gesture for her.

"I promise to be back soon and I'll have someone check on you often and the family will be nearby."

I didn't know what else to say and turned my back and left. I felt guilty and deeply concerned leaving my Majka and sisters behind but I had no choice but to go back to the General.

My stay ended after I made one last trip to check on Drgica settled in the nearby tiny but comfortable hospital for the mentally unbalanced near a larger hospital. Only one doctor and just a few assistants were still there. Drgica seemed comfortable and safe.

Several patients, mostly German soldiers appeared normal enough to me. Germans soldiers heavily guarded these patients. The guards hopefully would protect Drgica and maybe she could recover. I felt responsible and hated to leave her there.

Turning north, guilty feelings continued. I'd left Majka with fuel and water and all the available comforts and prayed they would not see any enemy. Word spread that the Americans were still bombing to the East and I needed to be with the General.

Chapter 12

I walked all the way to General Mihailovic's quarters, dodging and ducking into dark corners and hiding behind bushes after all my possible exposure before and after Tata's death. The horrible three-way civil war made the enemy besides the Germans difficult to recognize.

Dihan's eyes lit up when he saw me trudging dirty and tired into the old headquarters building. He expressed his sincere regrets about my father, got me something to eat, then hit me on the shoulder and teased me a little.

He took my face in his hand, tipped it one side and said, "Aha, a little fuzz on the chin, my friend. And by the look of your pants, you've grown some, too. Better get yourself some uniform pants, my friend. Guess I can't call you 'Babyface' anymore." He motioned for me to sit down.

"Got a lot to tell you. The English are all over the place mostly bragging about Churchill's son here on a mission as a big favor to the Partisans and how they loved Tito. How dumb can you get?

"Seems the Americans are different even though they don't know much about their friends or foes, either. Roosevelt doesn't like Tito much but doesn't begin to understand our Country as a legitimate state. At least he continues to support our King Petar just like English are doing. He's sent four U.S. planes to the 'Royal Yugoslav Air Force.' Imagine that!

"The General thinks he wants to control the route to Suez and India just like the Germans except Roosevelt wants to rid the world of empires so they can be the foreign policy decision-makers. The General believes the Allies are more worried about the Russians than us anyway but they did sent a high-level mission to General Mihailovic. He must still think the United States will rescue us from the Communists."

Dihan finally took a breath. I swear I'd never seen him talk so much and I got a kick out of it.

"I'm telling you all this, Mila, because the General has a tight, intellectual knowledge, but he is discouraged and still feels the Ustasha and the Communists took millions of lives and caused far more damage to Yugoslavia than the Germans did, bad as they are.

"Now the worst part. The General has reason to believe Tito influenced the Anglo-American Air Force to spread blanket bombing of Belgrade and some towns in Montenegro for three days running with the excuse German tanks were passing through. That just happened on our St. George's Day just like they did on Easter Sunday three years ago."

"I didn't even know all this!" I realized that in the last few months my world had turned in on me as if the war had ceased to exist.

Now reality was staring me in the face. The war didn't go away after it killed my Tata. The killing continues. I had to steel myself, not to kill but to do my part as a courier. I was almost nineteen and a man. No more tears from me.

General Mihailovic also expounded his sorrow over my father's death. He then told me not to worry over Tito being named Marshal of Yugoslavia and Prime Minister. He's had word that Britain will not abandon King Petar. He also knew Britain was leery of Tito's hidden agenda but needed to use him against the Germans. I didn't ask any questions.

~

I just took my orders and started off for Bosnia, this time riding most of the way in an open army truck, huddled in a corner, the only one in civilian clothes. No one paid any attention to the young civilian hitching a ride. These soldiers were hard to figure out as so many Chetnics had joined the Partisans to fight the Nazis. I listened carefully to the talk of the soldiers, many not much older than I was. I learned a lot.

We were right in the middle of the German "Operation Kugelblitz (Thunderbolt)" called the Sixth Offensive. The Germans were fighting to retake southern Slovenia, the Adriatic coast and the islands, and wipe out the three Partisan divisions in northeast Bosnia.

The men argued over the fact Tito was against the Brits establishing a base on the coast. The Brits had moved into the island of Vis, the farthermost island in the Adriatic for protection of the coastline. For now, that was our only line of defense. The men also seemed to know about the military mission to join the Partisans after a long period of being ignored.

The gossip I heard was that General Korneyev of the Red Army's Soviet Mission had his men parachuted into Yugoslavia but he landed by plane; some said he had lost a foot at Stalingrad and couldn't jump. His plane was filled with many colonels and cases of caviar and vodka. The officers were all dressed in bright uniforms with gold epaulets and shiny boots, hardy an equal view of communism.

The rumor continued that Russian General Korneyev was an incurable drunk. Then he insisted he wanted a lavatory that no one else had, even the British General Maclean, who used the nearest tree same as the regulars. So they dug a deep hole, left piles of dirt on the ground, put up a wooden hutch, and whitewashed it.

Right off, a German plane must have noticed the white building, flew in low and bombed it off the earth. These Partisans laughed and laughed at the Russians who supposedly came to help them but who couldn't figure out who was in charge.

Our rations were black bread and water from the passed-around canteens. Listening to the men, I understood how everyone was caught up in such a horrible situation, not knowing if one or one's family would be alive by tomorrow. Many patriots in that truck wanted to just fight the Germans, yet would fight each other in a minute.

We finally chugged through the mountains into Bosnia. The open truck drove through ruined villages, shelled houses torn apart, woman and children's bodies lying torn and dead in the roads. Smoke hung over the ruins smelling of flesh of people and animals. Abandoned children were crying on the side of the road with no one to answer.

Just a few miles away were Germans and tanks. Why didn't the peasants leave? Where would they go? Could they survive the big guns and planes diving out of nowhere? At one point we saw bodies smashed into the road by German tanks. Did we do this or did the Germans do this? All these tough men became quiet and deeply saddened by the sight.

At my signal, the driver stopped. I said nothing, just jumped off the truck and watched the truck drive away making a lot of noise and found myself on a road alone in the last stages of dusk.

My instructions were to connect with a commander a short distance away. I heard nothing, no sign of people on the post, only owls. Which way do I go? I started walking slowly when I heard a vehicle coming and crouched down in the weeds. A jeep came up slowly and I recognized a high grade Chetnik commander ordering the jeep to pull up. I rose up and just stood there.

"Are you Miodrag Cedic?" he called.

I asked for ID, although I had none to show him.

"We've been looking for you for days and I figured a civilian boy on the Army truck must be you. I have good news. We have the executioner of your father."

My blood ran cold. I stood motionless. They took me to the post and introduced me to the commander I was to speak to, and another high officer named Janko Stefanovic whose hands were tied in front of him.

"This man has been found guilty of killing your father. He headed up the committee and named your father as a spy and we know that was a false accusation. He is responsible for the assassination and he actually took part in the torture and the hanging and must be punished."

I still stood there frozen. What was coming? I just stared at the bound officer, his face fixed without expression avoiding looking at me.

The officer spoke, "You, Miodrag Cedic will have the honor to shoot him for his crime." I looked away from the guilty officer to his accuser trying to take in this totally shocking situation.

I could barely think. Kill this man for murdering my Tata? Would that bring him back? Would that heal my sister? And make my Majka happy? God help me. I stood silent as they all stared at me, my blood pounding in my temple. Finally, words came out.

"I respect you, Sir, but I don't want revenge. We are at war with the Nazis and ourselves. My mother and sisters are alive, and would also agree with my decision. And I must protect them from further retaliation. My father was a good man and he taught me that revenge only leads to more killing. We are all human beings. He taught me the process to learn how to live in peace and freedom for all time."

"You want no revenge? You mean you want to save the life of the man who murdered your father, an innocent and prominent civilian? That's a crime!" the officers looked astounded and stared at me.

"Yes, I do want to save him. God will punish him. You'll have to kill me first before you kill him. I want no revenge!"

All the men just stared at me. The accused Janko Stefanovic fell to his knees, moved towards me and grabbed me around my knees.

He whimpered, "Thank you, thank you. Forgive me, forgive me. I am sorry and deeply regret my mistake."

My voice rose full of emotion, "Then talk to your comrades to stop the killing!"

All the confusion suddenly brought me down. I stood looking at the commander after they took Stefanovic away. My head felt dizzy, and I felt disoriented. I guess I was still in shock. The commander politely invited me to dinner. His officers joined us around the table, but we didn't have much to say. They gave me a bed for the night, and I left before dawn into a cold darkness.

As I neared a valley, I heard the drone of planes and looked down to see ripples of flame in the valley. German Stukas were attacking a town. I walked down the road closer to see, intending to keep my distance to just watch the action.

As I neared a farm, the roar of an airplane came from behind me, lower and louder. I whirled around and stared at it all in flames swooping down seemly so close, that I put my hands over my head. The burning plane barely swept over me into the field with the family already at work, bouncing and scraping the ground for quite a ways crashing into the barn. I ran towards the crash and heard burning cows screaming inside the barn.

My instincts must have guided me in the smoky air because I ran straight down into the burning barn. Ammunition was exploding all around in loud pops. I took out my knife and started cutting ropes from the stalls to let the frantic cows loose. I pushed them towards the door. The dumb animals were nearly frozen in fear from the fire and explosions.

Flames grew all around me and suddenly I spotted an injured pilot in between the cows. He looked no bigger than me in the smoke, so I grabbed him by the shoulders and dragged him out of the flames, through the cows heading out, and kept dragging him across the road and into the stream I'd just crossed. He was burning from the oil. I dunked myself and him in the water up to his neck and then rubbed sand into his scorching hair and face first to quickly stop the burning as best I could.

All the time he was looking right at me, moaning and talking in American all the while, but I kept talking to him in German just to reassure and soothe him.

I got the flames out just as I heard the roar of motorcycles coming closer on the road. I peaked out between the bushes and saw a German Patrol stop and dismount close to us. I had no choice but to leap up and leave the soldier alive and alone.

I spent the night in the forest away from the plane crash and early the next morning sneaked in to check out the village. The Germans were gone. An acrid stench of explosives and the fire still hung in the air. The villagers close by were going on to their work excitedly gossiping in the street about the incident. The barn and the house had burned to the ground. But mercifully, many of the cows were saved.

I played innocent and asked what happened to the airman. The Germans had rescued him and questioned the villagers as they couldn't figure out how the airman escaped the fire and managed to crawl into the creek. The villagers told the Germans nothing. But they looked at me curiously and asked who the boy was that saved the cows and the pilot. I remained silent.

~

This time, I realized I was stuck in Bosnia. The Germans were everywhere, making a big show of strength. Hitler apparently never figured on so much trouble and local resistance in the Balkans.

With all our internal strife, we had become a big pain. Thousands of people had been taken to prison, killed, ruined, our precious country losing its identity. Comments and insults from other countries' peoples confused me and I continued to try to understand why all this agony was happening.

God knows I had plenty of time to think while traveling on foot. Occasionally, I helped myself to a stray donkey. The only vehicles on the road now were those of the armies mostly Germans. Rarely, they became isolated targets for the tiny Balkans Airforce.

I saw one very long convoy smashed every which way all over the road, papers, tin cans, and a broken frame of a gun carriage beside smashed trucks smoldering on the roads.

At another point I saw a tank burning. Was it ours or theirs? Bodies contorted in every position became a common scene. Passing through one village, poor peasants gathered around a parked abandoned tank poking and feeling and climbing up on it. They probably had never seen a big truck before much less a tank and were crawling all over it.

I stayed off the road as much as possible except when I was hungry which was most of the time. At least the weather broke, less rain and occasional warm days. My boots needed new soles and the lining of my good coat was coming apart. I wondered what day it was as it might be my birthday. That cheered me up a little. I would be nineteen years old.

Maybe I should join the army, but which one? The Chetniks were falling apart and the Partisans remained mainly communists. God, I don't really belong anywhere! That realization took me back. Tata said I have to make my own way. My life is mine to handle as I wished. I couldn't begin to understand what that meant. Will the war ever be over?

I traveled through the Drvar valley and mountains on my way to Tito's hideout. I had a message for the General's son, Branko supposedly in Tito's enclave hidden in the mountains. Tito had retreated to a cave, again from threats on his life.

I hoped if I did find it, they wouldn't shoot me. My civilian clothes helped, but I'd grown and couldn't pass for a child anymore. My directions were to turn east at the town of Drvar, and then to a cave that I should find by the next day. At dusk, I made myself a comfortable bed of leaves and moss to sleep high on the hill above Drvar.

Just as I awoke in the forest, I heard two German Focke-Wulfs fly towards Drvar. I couldn't believe my eyes, the planes swooped in so low. I knew from the deep, steady, roaring thunder sound, they weren't alone. From my perch above, I shaded my eyes and watched about fifty bombers swoop in dropping bombs to flatten the town.

As soon as the heavy smoke cleared, six Junker transport planes dropped paratroopers. Then gliders bringing in more soldiers with heavy equipment followed in one after another. I stood high on the hill, my mouth open in amazement.

The Germans are so organized. They started hiking right for Tito's cave high up on the other side of town. I could hear the constant machine-gun fire and some sound higher pitched from the cave.

My fascination turned to horror. No way could Tito and all his army with him survive. All of them must be dead and I'd better get out of here. If I'd been a day earlier, I'd be dead for sure. My survivor skills kicked in.

Scrambling around the hill keeping low, I knew I was headed south and stayed in the mountains, climbing, then sliding. The calves in my legs were strong, yet they pulled hard in my frantic exit causing cramps. Food did not cross my mind.

I finally stopped. I heard noises ahead, not animal. Was it the Germans, or peasants hiding out? I peered through the trees blinking and staring harder. Uniforms. I edged closer and saw they were Partisan. Could it be?

I approached cautiously. Surely, it was Tito's people so I called ahead with my hands up. I stopped in full sight, holding my breath and was motioned in. Slowly, I walked forward, hands still over my head and let the guard search me. All he found was my pocketknife and nut shells.

I asked to see Branko but no one knew who he was, so I was taken to Marshal Tito. He looked older, his face drawn and wrinkled, and he had gained weight. He could only offer me bread rations, but he got a kick out of telling me the story of their escape.

"The Germans brought in about 1,000 troops," he said. I believed him, not revealing I had watched much of it from my vantage point on the other side of the town.

"They sneaked right up to our cave, spraying the entrance with machine-gun fire, so no one could leave. What they didn't know was we managed to climb up our escape route through the watercourse of the falls at the back of the cave then up through a tunnel at the top of the cliff.

"Rankovic and his squad held off the attackers while we got away. They got away, too, after they piled dead German bodies in the entrance to the cave."

I parted with them as they resumed their escape, thinking Rankovic was a real hero.

Later I learned from a Chetnik commander that Tito had lost his whole wireless communication system so they could not function at all. So they left there and holed up on the Island Vis, in the Adriatic Sea. The small island, only 16 square miles of scrub land became his headquarters in a tent village protected by the British.

The really big news came in bits and pieces over the BBC. The British General Montgomery and the American, General Eisenhower, planned a secret invasion of the coast of Normandy, France. In spite of delays, the huge battle took place on June 6.

We heard about 5,000 ships and 4,000 small landing crafts hit the beach facing a heavily fortified German defense. I kept asking and getting details. I wondered if it could be true and tried to imagine the bravery it must have taken to jump in the water with big guns shooting at you trying to cross a beach full of mines. Imagine planning something that big! Even with thousands of men, what chance did they have?

I started daydreaming I'd taken part in the invasion, joining men who scrambled through heavy waves up the beach into the face of the enemy dodging machine-gun and artillery fire, running bravely knowing I could be killed any second. Inching, sinking in the sand, smoke blinding me, men falling all around me. I'd just keep struggling into the line of fire from the Nazis, driving them back.

My on-going fantasy as a hero popped into realism when we later heard about thousands of men killed on that beach in one of the most fantastic battles of the war.

All this time we had been sure Allies would come through our Balkan beaches where we were prepared to aid them, but they fooled us and went bravely head-on into the heavily armed enemy in Normandy and miraculously made it through the heavy line of defense. They called it Operation Overlord, later known as D-Day.

In July, a great Soviet drive pushed down the Dvina River and cut off the Nazi troops holding the Croatia and Bosnia country. That territory had been under German control since 1941.

The big news came as Hitler himself went on the radio on July 21, and announced he'd been conferring with his advisers when a bomb exploded six feet away causing bruises and burns.

Hitler announced he'd appointed Heinrich Himmler as Gestapo Chief and Commander of the Army within Germany. Word came that a clique of officers wanted to kill him, seize power, and make peace. We couldn't even imagine what really went on.

Not until August did all allied troops including Canadians, break out of the Normandy coast and struggled on through Isigny and Cherbourg to clear out pockets of Nazi resistance, fighting their way on to Paris. British and Canadian troops took Caen, a strong Nazi stronghold, much to the appreciation of the French. When combined armies moved on through Belgium towards Germany, we all gained heart. Russians had taken many cities back, from the Baltic to the Carpathians. At last, it looked like the Allies had a chance to win this God-awful war.

In September, King Petar succumbed to British pressure and summoned all Yugoslavs to back the Partisans in fighting the Germans. General Mihailovic retreated back to Ravna Gora, for safety. I eventually joined him there in the Flat Mountains on the Serbian side of the River Drina. Dihan warned me the General's mental health had been compromised by all the discouragement.

The General invited us to his private quarters. He did look thin and worn down. His eyes had lost their vitality, and stress and wrinkles aged his face. His voice lacked its usual confidence.

"Your family would not have liked the way this war has gone, Miodrag. Britain is supporting the Partisans for their efforts against the Germans. At least Tito understands Churchill would not like it if the Partisans turn their guns on the Chetniks and not the Germans. I swear the other allied countries have no idea of the fact that the guerrilla warfare here is separated in two factions. Our fierce Chetniks guerrillas are still fighting but overall are discouraged. Even in the beginning, these peasants seemed to believe it was their choice whether to go into battle or not. I swear, sometimes, they just choose to stay home.

"The Partisans and the Germans were running us down and it seems certain the Partisans will win the civil war even though the Chetniks are receiving support from the Americans. I fear our Yugoslavia will become communist after all, my dear Miodrag. Tito has no intention of bringing our King Petar back to the throne even though Britain is trying to reconcile the two of them. Tito will take over the country in his obsession for power.

"My days are nearly over, my boy. I've done everything I could for our country." He sagged back in his chair like a broken man.

To distract him from his sorrow, I cleared my throat and asked, "General, each time I've seen Tito in person, he appears differently. I think I know the real Tito but other times including years ago in this office with you, I think he's used impersonators."

The General sat up straight, his face awake. "Have you seen that, too? Sometimes, even his voice is different. You are very observant, my boy. I have secretly believed there may be as many as three imposters this strong man uses for his purposes. And I have reason to believe that none of them knew about the other ones." He leaned forward with a twinkle in his eye.

"Over the years of this war I've heard wild rumors that Tito himself was a Russian officer, a Ukrainian, a Polish count or a Polish Jew. In fact the secret file I have on him says that Tito was really Walter Goerhing, born in Linz, Austria, same town as Hitler and that he is the biological half-brother of General Herman Goerhing with same father, Stovac. His mother Stavania, from Boslovinia bore him out of wedlock. Tito came out of the Tan (secret) Intel Terrorist Organization. I heard the name 'Tito' is actually an acronym for the 'Third International Terrorist Organization.'

"So you see son, people can be anyone they want with the right connections. The funniest one was when I heard the British novelist, Evelyn Waugh say he thought Tito was really a woman!"

At that, the General actually laughed out loud, one of the few times I'd ever seen him really laugh. He seemed so cheered up by the gossip, that in a jovial mood, he ordered a hot roast pork dinner inviting the faithful Dihan to join us. He told us we were the only two people in the entire world that he could trust. How sad. It was the last time the three of us were together.

After a few days of rest and good food, the General sent me back to Tuzla in Bosnia with possibly his last message. By now, the beautiful mountain trails were familiar and I made excellent time. Signs of war were everywhere.

I smelled smoke from one small village in the lower range where I had stopped for the night several times. As I neared it, the scent of smoke of burning thatch penetrated the air. I saw it was demolished. No woman hanging over the fence offering shelter. Just heaps of plaster and slabs of wood, crockery mixed with bedclothes lying in puddles of dark sticky blood.

Hardly a building or house had been spared. I wondered where the people had gone as I didn't see anyone, just a few dogs barking and the eerie sound of hungry, hysterical cows and horses in the pastures. I did stop and fill my pockets with walnuts.

A few minutes later, I came to the edge of a ravine and tried to force myself not to look down. I couldn't seem to help it. I stepped to the edge and peered over. Scattered down the steep slopes all the way to a creek far below were the torn bodies of men, woman and children, even dogs littered among the rocks and bushes. Under my feet, the ground covered with empty bullet casings seemed to shudder or maybe that was my own body reacting to this vicious, sickening scene.

I mouthed a prayer. When I opened my eyes, I saw a baby's rattle near the edge, another child victim. I jumped out of my reverie as sounds of artillery fire resounded in the distance and black puffs of flak rose into the air.

I started down the road hearing the whistling and explosion of shells ahead. The hair on the back of my neck bristled. I felt deep fear. The drone of planes becoming targets of the artillery file appeared in the sky ahead. German Stukas bombing aiming to wipe out the guerrillas preventing their army's progress north.

The sky went nearly black. I looked around and thought, I could go back to the burned village, head straight down a steep gully away from my destination, or sneak around the battle. I decided I could skirt on the edge without losing much time and plotted out a route.

The firing on the mountain built to a roar. Whistling in the air and the sound of explosion of shells promised a rip-roaring battle. Maybe our forces could push the Nazi's back, a breakthrough. But God, how do I get out of here? The battle seemed to be moving my way. I couldn't be safe in the ravine or on the road. It was crushing right into me.

Gravel began flying much too near and soldiers suddenly materialized right in front of me through the smoke, falling dead around me. I ran as low as I could heading back down when wham! my whole body jumped off the ground and came crashing down again. I'd been hit. I fell on my stomach, and crawled as fast as I could to a bank of earth to hide my head. My fear went to protecting my eyes. I couldn't go blind. My side burned. I looked down shocked to see blood spurting out of my calf, then my thigh. God, I am shot up! I can't believe it. I'm not a soldier. I felt my bowels squeeze up and a hot drop of urine on my thigh.

Out of this revelation, I heard a voice calling, "Mila, Mila!" Was I hallucinating? "Mila, help me!" I couldn't believe it. With my eyes squinted, I recognized a guy from school wounded clear out here in Bosnia! I scooted on my belly toward his sound just a few feet away.

"Help me!" He must have spotted me and cried out at the same moment he took a bullet in the chest. I tried to get to him, but the air was popping with bullets separating us. I couldn't reach him. I hesitated a few minutes watching with awe the flying dirt in front of my face. Between the bouncing dirt and smoke, I saw him roll on his back, and his mouth fell open and his eyes closed.

I turned away, crawling, rolling down the hill, finally separating myself from the battle and crawled into the forest alone. I wiped off my finger and stuck it in the bloody wound. It felt like it probably wasn't life threatening, just stung like fire. I tried to tie up the wounds by tearing up a hankie and a piece of my shirt. When the silence came, it became more intense than the battle. At least I knew where that was.

I kept thinking of my dead friend. What a strange coincidence that I knew this man so near but yet unreachable. I lay there feeling stupid and helpless. My breathing slowed down. No, don't go to sleep. I've got to move, to find help. The late afternoon sun setting in the West offered me directions.

How did I get around the town of Tuzla? I tried to walk until the pain got so bad, then I scooted and rolled. Sweat ran down my brow into my eyes. I may be near the little town of

Maglaj. Finally, I spotted a big house set way back off the road surrounded by a high wall and locked covered gate. Through the pain, I climbed over the locked and rotting gate in the rock wall landing on my back with my legs up.

The big house looked like once wealthy people must have lived there. It appeared so quiet, it was probably deserted. I dragged my wounded leg up the snowy driveway wondering how I could get in.

Suddenly, a weary woman younger than my mother opened the door. Her voice sounded so good, but afraid. "Come in, come in, quickly."

She was Serbian and told me several members of her family had been taken away and shot because they refused to convert to the Roman Catholic Church. She admitted to me she finally told them she would convert but only to save her life and her children.

All the while she was telling me that, she was cleaning my ugly, bloody, wounds. That beautiful, kind woman brought me corn bread and bean soup and some heavy slivovitz.

Soon, I just lay down exhausted in front of a huge fireplace on the hearth and fell asleep. The pain woke me burning through my skin at dawn. She brought me mush and milk, and stuck an apple in my jacket.

"You must go. If the Germans find you here, they'll kill you and me and what's left of my family, too."

I no more opened the big front door to leave, than men burst through the front gate. At least they were Partisans, not Germans, bringing in more wounded soldiers and male medics.

A doctor astonished to recognize me called out, "Mila, you are here!" much to the surprise of my hostess and especially me. He knew my family and knew I was connected to General Mihailovic. He helped me back into a bedroom while I begged him not to reveal my identity.

These men were mostly from near my home area. I learned my friend who had called out my name on the mountain, died along with hundreds of others setting artillery against the Stuka planes. They had been surprised by Germans pouring in on them.

The doctor started trying to pick out the shrapnel with an instrument. "What is shrapnel exactly, Doctor?" I tried to distract myself from the excruciating pain.

He worked as he explained it was a hollow projectile containing bullets or the like, and a bursting charge explodes and sprays a shower of missiles or shell fragments.

I stayed another night among 40 or 50 Army people getting patched up, most of them leaving the next morning except the most serious wounded.

The doctor picked out all the shrapnel he could find and cleaned me up with sulfur and bandages. I thanked him and the good Lord for my luck of connecting with him to get help. Many died from these shrapnel wounds.

The woman owner cried real tears, "You must leave with the soldiers so the Germans won't find you here. It's very dangerous to all of us." She walked me to the gate, and kissed me all over my face.

"You could be my son!" Guards stood outside smiling and let me go.

Outside, heavy snow began to fall. I kept walking, not wanting to follow the other soldiers but three or four older Chetnik soldiers surrounded me and one said, "Look at this snow, it's getting colder. He'll freeze. Let's just kill him and take him out of his misery!"

In my drugged up state, I couldn't tell if they were kidding or were going to shoot me like a horse with a broken leg. I couldn't run or defend myself.

One of the men grabbed me by my flimsy belt and held me up. "You heard the Doc. He's somebody. We'd better not kill him. Let's take him with us."

They pulled and pushed me all the way to a tiny Muslim village outside Zavidovic and gathered outside a house with candlelight inside.

"Don't worry," the soldier said. He pounded on a door. "Open up!" waking a sleepy man. The soldiers barged in dragging me along. Flickering candles and incense in a crevice spilled into the smoky room. The men arranged themselves grasping their guns to their chests and fell fast asleep.

The Muslim with no teeth looked at me and said in his jumbled talk, "Youngster, you're wounded. Lay down by me." He was a tall man with a full beard and flowing dress. He didn't smell so good, but apparently his intentions were safe.

He whispered, "I heard one of the soldiers say he would kill you and 'blame it on the Muslim,' so I'm saving you to save my own sorry life. Don't be afraid."

In the morning, the soldiers raided their host's food stuffs and left, ignoring the Muslim, my protector and me. He fixed some gruel for us and gave me directions to Zavidovic's railroad station. I thanked him and left.

The snow came down in big, lovely flakes, piling up. Even abandoned animals were quiet; the whole world seemed still and peaceful, the snow covering the ugly remnants of battle.

I walked slowly, dragging the swollen leg along. The cold seemed to hold down the pain. Before long, the exhaustion took command of my body. Just when I didn't think I could go any further, I spotted a trailer parked away from the road just outside of town. Probably Gypsies. I couldn't tell, so I dragged slowly up to the back of it, lay down and crawled under it where it was dry.

I slept a little, and woke to find a silent world, no sound from the trailer above me, no sun, just more snow. I didn't know what time it was but ate some of the food the kind Muslim gave me. I stopped chewing and heard a noise. Crunch, crunch. Someone was coming through the snow. Sounded like big German boots. German voices confirmed that, and I held my breath.

"Look, the footprints end here. Someone is hiding under the trailer!"

"Come on out from under there," a strong German voice demanded.

I peaked out looking up into their big faces, scooted out. They grabbed me upright and I spoke perfect German. "I was wounded in my leg," I said meekly looking up at these huge, warmly dressed soldiers. Just their boots were as high as the top of my legs, it seemed. It was dark, no wind, with light only from their flashlights.

"Goot Got, your bandages are falling apart!" the officer spoke in a rough German, maybe Austrian. The soldiers broke the lock on the empty trailer to take over for themselves but they showed me the wood box under cover outside, dumped me in, and brought some rugs out of the trailer to cover me.

Late the next morning, the officer woke me up and said, "Young man, do you know what is today?" I shook my head. "It is Christmas Eve!" That is, the date the Germans celebrated, December 24th. Good thing though, or they might have killed me. The officer brought me inside. "My name is Kurt Gunter," and he introduced me to the others, fixed some hot tea, large tins of porridge, sausages, and white bread with honey, a wonderful treat. He looked at my leg wounds in the dull candlelight. My whole leg was red and black, swollen and painful.

"You must go to hospital. We'll take you to railroad station and send you to hospital." I wondered then, did he think I was a German? What was I doing here, then? I went out to relieve myself and realized I was full of lice from the woodbin. What else? The tall, good-looking officer about the age my Tata would have been, hauled me up onto a horse in back of him and off we went.

On the way, he started talking out loud to his soldiers. "The American, President Roosevelt has met with Premier Stalin and Winston Churchill in Teheran. Oh, how I'd love to have been a mouse in the wall! This is not good. We've had the Russians bearing the brunt and now if the others become prepared, we may be in serious trouble."

We finally arrived cold and stiff at the train station in Zavidovic. Only problem, it was a cattle train sent here for the

German wounded soldiers. The German officer Gunter helped me off the horse, up into a boxcar and laid me down on the floor with no stretcher, blankets, or mat. Just many wounded German soldiers, some already dead. This kind man Gunter, told me he just found out we may all be taken to Doboj in Austria. At that point, I had no choice. I began to worry the horrible looking leg would have to be cut off. I couldn't get off the train so I just accepted the situation nervously. I had no choice.

He left me to go to an officer's car to join his comrades. I didn't blame him. As soon as they slid the box car door shut with a bang, the wounded moaning, I started to smell dead men mixed with cattle manure. God, how was I going to stand the stench? No choice, I just laid back and prayed for air, and dozed on and off. Clickity, clack. Clickity, clack.

Screech, the train was braking, causing the screams and moans again inside our dark, dirty car. I could hear angry voices and gun shots. Now what? The big heavy doors slid open. For a minute, my eyes tried to adjust to the light. I could see men lined up outside with their hands held up. I recognized from the ragged uniforms, they were Serbian Chetnik soldiers being murdered by Croatian Ustashe!

God save us from those maniacs. These renegade Ustashe were cutting off dead Serbian heads as they loved to do. I turned my head away and kept as dead still as I could. Not a sound came from the wounded inside the train car.

I heard Ustashe soldiers brag they were placing the heads in buckets to present to their Croatian ruler, Archbishop Stepinic to show how Serbians were punished if they would not convert to Roman Catholicism. I put my hands over my ears and prayed for the Serbians knowing the Partisans and Germans had been killing the deadly Ustashe off by the dozens for months.

Gunshots very close startled us! The German officers starting shooting at the Ustashe murderers but the car door was slammed shut and I couldn't see what happened.

After we were fed cold tea, boiled potatoes and bread, the train took off again. Many hours later we stopped and an officer told us we were in Austria. I couldn't believe it. I'd never even been in Croatia much less clear out of the Balkans. No one knew where I was. I've never felt so isolated and worried. Clickity, clack. Clickity, clack.

Chapter 13

1945

In Ljubljama, near Vienna, they unloaded the wounded onto the platform in the cold. Some of the men still had dried blood on their faces around dirty bandages wrapped loosely around their whole heads. I barely had any feelings left for others.

After a long wait with little care I heard the officers announce no hospital was available and we were all loaded back into the cattle car again and started off north. My leg throbbed all the time and the lice were eating me alive.

The train from hell just kept going north, through mountains and heavy snow, slowing up for the weather I could only feel, not see. I learned we'd crossed all the way through Austria and were going to stop in Brno, Chekoslovakia, the only place who would take the wounded German soldiers who were still alive.

I just couldn't believe I'd been stuck in this death train. I worked on not losing my mind and remembered my Baba's words, "Keep your head clear and your faith in God." I did pray a lot, for myself and for the dead and dying men around me.

In the little town of Brno, soldiers came with stretchers to carry off the few wounded soldiers left alive. The orderlies tied me to a stretcher and set me down on the side of the tracks in the snow. I was the last one off and I could hear them discuss whether or not to do anything at all with this young man, meaning me.

The German officer, Kurt Gunter who took care of me originally, walked up in a few minutes and told them, "Take him with the other soldiers. He's a Partisan soldier working with us."

What? Did that make me a traitor? Well, maybe it'd be a good cover. I hardly had any choice. The date was January 7, our Serbian Christmas day. My already limited range of vision evaporated in the swirling, blurry snow.

Eventually, everyone else was loaded into trucks and ambulances. I realized I was the only one left there when no more sounds of engines and orders were to be heard. Just silence. My stretcher's thin blanket couldn't keep out the cold. I lay there scared, freezing and in pain. "God, what happened? What did I do? Are you punishing me?"

Finally, just as all hope was nearly gone and my whole body had gone numb, I heard a motor. I could see the wheels of an ambulance appear near me. Two men in white picked up the stretcher, slid me in the back and drove me to the hospital. Once there, inside a warm room, I thanked God. but couldn't understand the Chek language.

First, on arrival, they took sponges dipped in a bucket and cleansed me with kerosene to burn off the lice housing all over my body. After that miserable experience, they rolled me in a wheelchair to a soapy, hot water bath, so soothing and so wonderful. I relaxed for the first time in sheer luxury.

Dirt, filthy, crusted, blood, and dead lice colored the water. Just as I became completely unwound, they picked me up and set me into icy cold water shocking my body and pointing and teasing how skinny I was. They assured me the ice was part of the therapy.

A German soldier came in, put a shirt thing over me, threw me over his shoulder, and carried me a real bed dumping me in like a slab of pork. Ah, it seemed like forever since I'd laid in a warm bed.

He asked my name in German. I paused, should I give him my real name? What would the General want me to do? I could barely think, but decided I'd want my family to have a chance to find out if I really died, so I told him, "Mila Cedic" using my nickname hoping it sounded more German. It didn't, but the nurse wrote out a tag with my name to put on the bed for identification.

They put my infected leg in an iron brace pulled up on pulleys. Maybe the fight went out of me in that warm, soft bed. I guess I passed out. I didn't care if I died. I couldn't eat or speak for two days. Most of the nurses spoke Chek so I didn't know or even care what was happening. At one point, I dreamed I'd been captured and would be tortured to death.

The first thing I remember was the doctor standing over me speaking in Greek then German which I understood.

"So you're awake huh? I guarantee you won't be executed. Now, eat!"

What did he mean by that, I wondered. The nurse speaking German told me later that I had mumbled and yelled when I was out of it, "Ask the doctor when I'm going to be tortured and executed."

He told me my leg was swollen three times thicker than it should be from blood poisoning. Were they going to take my leg? I couldn't think about it. At least the lice were gone. Many of the German patients around me complained they were still full of lice.

After a couple of weeks, the crumpled leg was still there, but my temperature went sky high. Oh, no, I thought I was feeling better. Then a huge building fell on my head. Bombs again, at least that's what I thought. My head exploded with pain.

A few days later, I woke up aware of intense itching, intense pain in my back and arms. The doctor told me I'd been unconscious for couple of days and had been diagnosed with typhus. Many of the men had infections picked up from the lice. I still had my leg.

I was stuck right here with many other soldiers in the same predicament isolated into a crowded ward. Typhus killed many soldiers who had escaped wounds and injuries otherwise, and they were being hauled out every day. At least, after about two more weeks, I felt better and had food in front of me three times a day and pretty nurses offering me water and juice.

Even after another week or so of recovery under the best care and eating good food, my weight still was down. The doctors had hardly let me out of bed and I felt all the strength had drained out of me. When I chanced to look in a mirror, I saw an older face and duller eyes. Is that me? I no longer looked young, more like 30. I smiled, though, when I saw actual whiskers starting to peak out.

Many seriously wounded soldiers were pouring daily into the hospital. So I was scheduled to be tranferred to Tuzani about 10 to 15 K away to a converted hospital. I couldn't walk yet but was a lot better off than many soldiers coming in with grenade and bullet wounds. Some were badly burned. Many had lost limbs, open bullet or knife wounds, beyond repair.

Wrapped in pajamas and warm blankets, a real pillow and socks on my feet, they loaded me onto a truck along with the other typhus victims. My lice filled clothes were gone forever and I'd have to worry about new ones when the time came. All I had left was my pocketknife.

Just as we reached the small hospital, a Chekoslovakian soldier stepped into the truck to check my transfer papers. He whispered to me, "I see you are a Partisan soldier from Bosnia. When you see Tito, be sure and tell him he has a secret organization right in this hospital."

Oh, Oh, I wonder if they see Tito as a great marshall, or as a communist? Soon a friendly cleaning woman approached me and we became acquainted. She visited me each evening teaching me to speak her language. She whispered, "I heard you were a Tito Partisan."

I nodded and she began bringing me special food to me on the side. At first I didn't catch on that these people didn't even realize Tito's urge for future power, just saw him as a great general. She asked if I would like to meet other Partisans. What could I say?

In about two weeks, I was ready to go out for a short time so she brought me civilian shirts, pants, and shoes from her dead son about my size.

I told the nurses I was going to evening church service and checked out. Many of the buildings on the street were hulls, bombed out and mere shadows in the dusk. Instead of pretending to find a church, I found the restaurant she'd told me about, still nearly in one piece. When I walked in, all I saw was SS military. I still wasn't very strong and broke into a sweat.

I went to a corner and kept silent with my ears open as I'd been trained. The word came that Chek resistance people were having a meeting in the basement. I crept down stairs with my beer and spoke Serbian as a greeting. These young men and women just stared at me.

Then they all started speaking at once questioning me carefully wanting assurance that I was the person they had been led to expect through the trail from the cleaning lady. I nervously clutched the beer but never tasted a drop that night as I was still quite dizzy from the typhus and needed a steady head.

When the time came and I'd gained a little confidence from them and for them, I asked if they wanted to become Communists? NO. Do you want to learn to become a guerrilla group against the Germans? YES. That's what they wanted but first I told them how difficult and dangerous it would be to try to form such an outfit. They were anxious but willing to try anything against the hated Germans. I hated war but thought how certain German individuals had been good to me and saved my life.

These young patriotic people told me that Russians had penetrated into Romania and Czechoslovakia to fight the Germans. Also, the Red Army had entered Yugoslavia and with the Partisans liberated Belgrade in October, 1944.

Then the Red Army chased the Germans across Yugoslavia into Hungary. Listening made me more aware that people everywhere wanted freedom and would do anything including killing and giving up their lives to get it. Gaining freedom is as compelling as gaining power.

My very limited experience on how to recruit and train others took several evenings at great risk to all of us. People seemed to trust my sincere looks at the hospital and in the basement of that restaurant. Or so I thought.

In a few weeks, I got word I was being released from the hospital. My leg felt much better even though I had a slight limp, and the typhus was tamed. I was ready to go. I was told exact arrangements were made for me to take the train back to Bosnia. This time I'd be riding in a real coach.

Two Germans soldiers armed with rifles escorted two of us to the train and came on board with us into a stuffy, crowded coach. The other fellow had also been a bullet-wounded patient. We weren't allowed to visit with anyone else including the soldier escorts who played cards and watched us at all times. It was obviously still wartime. I felt good. I was going home.

We traveled south into Austria and stopped. I looked out the window as we rolled up to a small platform filled with Nazi soldiers holding rifles. The other people on the train were all filing off the train grasping their bags and sacks with terrified looks on their faces. What was going on?

I soon found out. We were escorted off by our two soldiers holding their rifles down on us pushing us into the long line of the other passengers. Other soldiers appeared roughly managing the people.

Are we prisoners? I spoke to the soldier with us. "Wait, there's some mistake here. I'm going back to Bosnia! I don't want to get off here. Are these prisoners?"

"Silence!" He said harshly and poked me with the butt of the rifle.

"Turn right, keep walking!" they ordered us. I realized I'd been duped. "Turn right!" "Look ahead" "Don't talk!" we were ordered in German. My heart sunk and the blood sunk out of my head as they searched us and took away my precious pocketknife.

My head spun from anger. I yelled "We are not from the Resistance, I think you made a mistake!"

Don't talk!" the soldier hit me with the butt of the gun. I reached in back of my head to feel blood, realizing I had no control of this situation. Rivulets of sweat ran down my brow.

All the men looked horrified as reality hit; we were going into an ugly looking labor camp. The older men were marched inside a low building separately. Each person was then assigned to a barracks. They took away our clothes, and searched us. We were forced to all wear their black and white striped outfits no heavier than pajamas. I felt like a ghost floating around without purpose. They stamped numbers on our hands and shaved all my thick curls off, making fun of me. No one had names, only numbers.

Sleep seemed impossible in the smelly, airless, dark barracks. The rough wooden platforms, one on top of the other were in rows with a number on each bed. The first days I walked around like a zombie. Each morning we were ordered out by numbers to keep track of us. We had to line up to call out the numbers like one-twenty, two-twenty, three-twenty, and so on, to see if anyone was missing.

My German stumbled, and I couldn't keep track fast enough so I said the wrong number. The guard hit me on the head with his stick because I might have been answering for a missing person. I learned quickly to listen closely, concentrate on my German and soon I was only getting the stick on my shoulders until I got it all straight. My German became more perfect with all this motivation.

We couldn't talk in line when standing or going back and forth to the barracks. So many more prisoners came in, the wooden beds became scarce. Soon I got transferred to another section with the "difficult" people; Russians, French, Polish, and Jews. We still were supposed to use no names, only numbers. We could only speak to each other with someone else listening, and then only in German.

One guy, a Serb, lay down on the hard bed and couldn't get up. The guards picked him up and dragged him out. I thought he was dead but heard him moaning. When they dumped him back in two days, he'd been beaten nearly to death.

Then he whispered to me, his words broken, "I was betrayed by my own people in Bosnia, taken from my home."

He struggled on admitting he had helped finance the Partisans but his own cousin, a Chetnic betrayed him. The Nazi SS picked him up and brought him here to die.

How does a man recover from all this and ever trust anyone again?

The Guards treated the Russians the worst. They didn't seem to like the way they acted and walked and didn't consider them humans. I had never talked to a Russian before and found them quite colorful. Their language sounded impossible but they loved to tell stories and laugh. I laughed with them even when though I couldn't really understand what they said.

The only word from home from a new prisoner was that Milan Nedic, a General of Serbian Army who had persecuted the Serbian Jews and demanded Jewish prisoners be separated from Serbians in detention camps, had ended up as a prisoner himself in Germany.

Deep droning sounds of groups of planes flew over us. We prayed they were American and secretly signaled a freedom sign to each other.

Gradually, I picked up pieces of all the languages of the people around me as I did love to talk to everyone when I could. In almost every case, people had not committed real crimes but politically, or like the Jews, held the wrong religion, or were in the wrong place, said the wrong thing, or had killed the enemy and stood up for what they believed.

No school could have taught me the lessons I learned about people in prison. One lesson I could have done without was surviving on being fed once a day. When I delivered messages all over the country, I often ate at odd times and sometimes not at all, but here we had little to do and hunger became an obsession. All we got was thin, meatless soup, and one slice of bread per day.

After about the slowest time I'd ever spent hanging around this ugly, dreary, drizzly, place, I finally got assigned work orders. I guess they considered me safe as my assignment sent us up the Danube about three miles west into the nearby town of Linz.

An old, noisy, rattling truck picked up our large group just after sunrise. We were so packed in, we had to stand up trying to keep our balance against each other. The fumes about knocked us out and we were just thankful we weren't locked in a closed area.

Leaving that dreary, camp gave me the lift I needed. At first, I felt self-conscious wearing these ugly, queer "pajamas" while people on the streets stared at us. My assignment turned into street cleaning rubble from a bombing in the main square, "Hitler Platz." The sun shined on us melting some of the remaining spring snow.

The pretty part of town not too far from Bunker Street looked historic and I ask questions of my fellow Austrian prisoners. Other prisoners cleaned and removed bricks around the old, gothic railroad station very close to our section of Hitler Platz. The old Austrian Bohemian settlement of structures, theaters, and the old Library surrounded us.

I let my mind pretend my lovely lady friend and I were strolling across the Platz to visit the theatre. We would enjoy a wonderful meal in one of the restaurants later. I had to believe I could lead a normal life sometime in the future just to keep my sanity.

Chores were assigned by weight and strength of the men. Our group was reassigned to cleaning up debris from a building project to build a protection high wall. The rumor was that the Nazis were afraid the Russians were coming as if a high wall could save them. We snickered over that. Piles of loose, unbroken bricks had to be carefully loaded into a wagon. My sturdy body was really skinny and continually hungry.

Just outside of the railroad station, a big, fat, Austrian woman managed the vendor food carts. She also took coupons from displaced people who had been bombed out and had no food to eat.

I watched them for days and finally couldn't stand it any longer. Slowly, I shuffled in closer to the long food lines keeping one eye on my guard and the other eye on the friendly looking big, blonde lady selling to the civilians. My chance came when the guard turned his back on me to talk to another guard, and I just stepped in between some mothers and their children in line who pointed at my prisoner costume.

Austrians spoke a more sing-song German. I would listen closely to them to learn. Only four or five people were ahead of me in the line. The big blonde in charge spotted me and frowned menacingly. She obviously didn't want any trouble.

Then suddenly several other prisoners jumped in the line ahead of me. That immediately brought the attention of the young, soldier guards who starting pulling them out of the line and beating them with bully clubs. I bent down, shocked and scared and slinked back.

The Austrian vendor woman grabbed me by the collar and jerked me right out of line. In one motion, she shoved me under her arm and wrapped me into her skirts, protecting me from the guards.

To my horror, I could barely breathe from her tight hold. I could hear the prisoners, and women and children, screaming and crying. Right in the middle of this sickening scene, the big vendor woman stuffed a packet of food under my loose top.

I waited until the coast was clear, and sneaked back among the other distraught prisoners. They whispered to me that the guards had continued to beat the other line-jumping prisoners until they were hurt or dead and then threw them in the trucks to take back to the work camp with the rest of us.

In spite of that, I shared the food when we were safely back in our shack. The line-jumpers were never heard of again and I lived with guilt and fear to have caused the whole incident. I felt even worse when the other prisoners treated me as a hero instead of the stupid rogue I was.

Our work routine repeated itself without any excitement after that day, just long days of work and boredom. We worked like the most ignorant donkeys, starving by night, trying to sleep. When we had a cold spring rain, my leg ached bad but no sense complaining.

When I was alert enough to think, I wondered what was happening to General Mihailovic? We received very little news of the outside world. I missed my family and worried over Majka and my sisters. I prayed for them especially Drgica. I prayed for release for all the weak, heartbroken prisoners.

On a day when no sun shone through dark rain clouds, my feet began to squish in the wet street as my soles of my shoes were nearly completely gone. We were being marched on a narrow street of Linz with seriously armed guards on both sides.

My wet sore feet were dragging along with my spirits. When would we get out of this situation? I knew how lucky I'd been to somehow escape the beatings and killings we heard about of many other prisoners. I still felt rotten.

The rain came down harder; rivulets running madly down the street. A huge, army tank came rumbling up the street and the guards turned around to see what was going on. I spotted a building's lobby door close to where I was standing and impulsively reached over and opened it. I slipped inside and walked backwards looking outside to see if anyone saw me escape. As I turned around, I ran right into a tall German officer just as surprised to see me. My mouth flew open and I nearly collapsed. I thought I'd had it.

The officer spoke in German, "What country are you from?"

"Yugoslavia," I replied shaking.

"Do you speak German?"

I replied, "Yes."

"Follow me."

No one else was in the lobby and he shoved me into the first office. Speaking perfect German, he revealed he was an American intelligence officer in a German uniform.

"Hey, kid. Don't jump out of line like that any more! You could be killed."

He asked me questions and I told him, I'd been a courier for General Mihailovic. He was impressed.

"I've been watching you and saw you get away with your move to get food that day. Don't try to escape just now. We're waiting for bombardment to Berlin to end this war. It will come soon. I need you to give me useful information you may have observed or heard in prison.

"Look, the guards have herded most of the prisoners under the building shelter across the street. They won't miss you just now. Stay to eat!"

From his pack, he handed me delicious sandwiches and poured real coffee with sugar from his thermos. I devoured the precious food almost making me sick. Then he sneaked me back in line with the rest of the prisoners when they were being rounded up into the back to the truck.

Imagine talking to a real American, a rugged, handsome man wearing a German uniform and both of us speaking German! He never appeared suspicious to the other young guards.

As the days rolled by, the undercover "German" officer nudged me while I worked and I'd tell him rumors and anything I'd heard that might be useful.

The weather started to hold that mellow, clean air of spring. At first light, I remembered my 20th birthday would be May 5th and hoped the Americans would get here soon. I was working on the main bridge over the Danube River on the west side of downtown buildings. Slowly I became aware of deep drones coming toward us.

Suddenly, American or British fighter planes and bombers swooped in low. Air raid sirens came on too late over the tremendous noise of planes, then ach ach ach. Anti-aircraft fire and machine gun ammunition filled the air aimed at the Germans. We all scattered off the bridge. I ran following civilians running for the underground bomb shelter.

Just as we went around a curve, a mother and her screaming child both slipped on the damp stairs and fell down. I grabbed them both jerking them back up on their feet again before they were trampled. My head went up just in time to see our guards tearing down the stairs abandoning prisoners and pushing aside civilians. I turned and tried to run back up, my face to the wall. The frantic guards looked at me and the mother yelled, "Leave him alone!" It was everyone for himself.

On the street again, I shaded my eyes and looked out at soldiers and prisoners lying wounded and bleeding all over the broken up plaza. I threw myself down with the dead ones. Then sliding on my belly a few inches at a time, bullets whining over my head, I slid across the plaza about 100 feet, then down the banks of the Danube. I could only think of escape. Even with soldiers and civilians running helter-skelter, some shot and dropping down, I stood up, ran as fast as I dared, crossed the bridge, and headed back towards camp.

I followed the houses facing the river, weaving in between them. If caught, I planned to say I was going back to camp. But I remembered each morning when the prison trucks drove here, I wanted to tip my hat to the Church of Saint Magdelena on a hill overlooking the town. At this moment in the midst of the roar of airplanes and some shooting, something told me to head for the church. I crossed empty pastures near big houses running up the hill to the church. When I got to the top and looked down into chaos, people still scattering all over, some fires, and our clean streets once again littered.

When the incredible show of planes disappeared, trucks and jeeps with American Flags started crossing the Danube moving toward the main square. I reveled at the sweet sight of German soldiers holding up white flags to surrender.

Alone in front of the magnificent St. Magdelena Church, I yelled with all my lungs, "Freedom is ours. Victory is ours."

I felt free and thrilled. Then the euphoria settled down and I stood there in my shabby prison garb not knowing quite what to do next.

I stared down thinking of escape and laid out a route from my vantage point on the hill. I tried to stay out of the turmoil, sometimes crawling on the ground between houses headed for a village beyond. I spotted a farmer's house on a big square land of farm. The barn held cows in an uproar from the air attack, or so I thought, until I peaked into the center of the barn and saw hundreds of German Wehrmacht soldiers huddled together also trying to hide.

I sneaked out of there through orchard trees to another nearby house. A woman saw me and yelled, "Don't come any closer. Go lie down in the woods over there." Pointing to a close stand of trees.

Later, I heard her call, "Young man, where are you? I brought you food." Then she laid it down by a tree and left.

The boiled potatoes, corn bread and water the woman had so graciously left me smelled so good. I tried to sneak deeper into the forest for peace and safety but suddenly bullets started flying again. Still in prison garb, I stood out like a dart board and ran away as fast as I could with my head bent, clinging onto the sack of food.

Chapter 14

It was the end of the War, I could just feel it. I sat in a secluded spot in bushes eating the wonderful food slowly. I thought back. My General thought the Chetniks should wait to fight the Germans until the Americans invaded at the beaches. But instead, the Americans flew in, probably already bombed Berlin to pieces. I visualized the smoke, the rubble, a final finish for the Third Reich.

The road was closer than I realized and I heard a Jeep motor stopping and then heavy footsteps coming towards me. I just knew it was more SS soldiers finding a place to relieve themselves, and would kill me the minute they saw me. My mouth was full of food but I couldn't swallow and couldn't spit it out and started choking. As they got closer trying to see what the odd noise was, I heard a different accent. One pushed branches of a bush back and there I was sitting in a prisoner uniform making a silly little smile.

The soldier started laughing and yelled to me in broken German. "What are you doing here?"

I swallowed my food and answered in German my name and the name of the prison camp, and he motioned for me to walk out with him. To my amazement, they turned out to be American soldiers from the 11th Division, Third army under General Patton.

An American Lieutenant came up. From my position on the ground, he looked about eight feet tall. "Well, what have we here? Camp 2, huh? Are you Jewish?" he spoke in a thin broken German.

I stood up, brushed the crumbs off my embarrassing suit and looked up at this tall, blond, ruggedly handsome man. I lied, "No, I'm Chek."

"Really, well I'm Chek too. My parents came from there. I learned a little of the language and learned enough German to get along here. How about a Coke?"

I could not believe my good luck. A real Coca-Cola? I'd never even seen one. Another soldier traded chocolate bars for my corn bread and we all devoured the food.

"Come on, get in the jeep" They boosted me into the Jeep and sat me on the top of the back seat. Elation rolled through my veins. The worst is over; friends have arrived.

The Lieutenant asked me, "Do you know of the Gehring Tank Industry?" I nodded yes, having seen it every day on the way to Linz. I can show you the way there."

Driving down the narrow road through the forest onto the highway, the French were on one side, screaming "Viva Americans" and Russians soldiers on the other side, wide eyed at probably the first Americans they'd ever seen. I knew how they felt.

One of the Americans translated as they shouted, "What is that prisoner doing sitting up there eating chocolate and drinking coke?"

I couldn't keep a huge smile off my face. I felt like a king. I motioned to the Lieutenant and ask in German, "What are the Russians doing here?"

"Don't you know? The Russians took Poland months ago. Chased the Germans right out. You probably do know they liberated Belgrade last fall with the help from the Partisans, now in charge in Yugoslavia.

My face fell. My worst nightmare: the Allies won but we lost.

"What's the matter, Mila?" The American Lieutenant seemed compassionate, a trait the Germans never showed.

"I'm really from Yugoslavia. I've been in prison for months and don't get much news from the outside. I'm just a little shocked, that's all."

My worst nightmare was Tito at the helm as we'd never be a democracy now. I'd prayed we might still have a chance. But the war was over. Baba would have been happy over that but I'd have to find a new life. I tried to keep smiling.

We passed over a bridge on the Danube and went to the deserted factory where Germans manufactured big Panza tanks. Just the Lieutenant and I went in. It was nearly dark. After looking around the deserted director's main office, I sat down in a big office chair, put my feet up on the desk, drank coke and thanked God. The American Lieutenant starting looking in the files logging the big Tiger Panza tanks. All at once, he grabbed his hat, threw it to the floor, yelling what must be obscenities.

I nearly choked again. My feet flew off the desk, "What's the matter?"

He shoved it in my face "Look at this paper. Look at this! This is not possible!"

When he quit waving it, even I could read the heading in English. I started to laugh

"What are you laughing about? The letterhead says 'Chrysler Corporation, Detroit, Michigan.' "

"I could read that much, that's why I laughed. In the early days, business was going on as usual. The Germans' technical system didn't know everything. They were busy making rockets to use on England before America joined the Allies and they bought material and parts from America and Canada."

I felt free and cocky and couldn't resist saying, "If it wasn't for your country manufacturing parts, this war would have been over a long time ago."

I knew he didn't want to hear this.

The Lieutenant jumped around furiously. "How do you know?" he asked.

"I listen, I read."

He angrily stuffed the files in a leather case and off we went again. I rode this time in the front seat with the driver and my new friend, the disillusioned Lieutenant.

The sky and the ground still smelled of smoke from the attack and fires. The battle came back to me, the vision of the terrified mother and little girl running with civilians to escape the bullets.

"Why did they shoot on civilians and the prisoners? Why did they have to kill all those civilians in the Plaza?"

He answered nonchalantly, "We bombed the hell out of Berlin and finally put the Krauts on the run. We were under orders and had to end the War. That's the way it goes. You ought to know. You've probably seen it all."

We drove to the labor camp just a ways away already taken over by the Americans. The Germans were gone. He laid out his orders to me. He wanted me to stay in the military personnel barracks with the other prisoners until I was formerly released to avoid problems as an escapee in my future. That made sense to me. I knew I had his word on it.

The prisoners who had survived the killing in Linz or had not tried to run away, stood in the yard guarded by American soldiers. The men looked bewildered at this amazing turn of events. When I jumped out of the jeep, they were wide-eyed and started hollering, pointing, and making remarks.

The Lieutenant and his crew took over the administration buildings where prison guards had worked and lived, and the crude barracks we'd lived in for months. As I looked at the place through the American's eyes, I felt ashamed. Ashamed at being placed here and ashamed for the Wehrmach officer who betrayed me and put me here. How could people do this to people? We are all God's children. Would we ever learn? Baba didn't think so and now I didn't have much faith in people or their need for power, either.

The Lieutenant started reading files on the prisoners. I stood by him helping with the German language and answering questions. In camp 2, of all the prisoners, I was one of the youngest. I also learned only 10 or 12 Serb prisoners here were with General Mihailovic, and the rest were listed as Partisans under Tito, or collaborators.

By the prison rules, we never were permitted to tell our past, and wouldn't anyway. In such close quarters, enemies could be dangerous. As prisoners, we all were one.

With the Americans living in the former German military quarters, medicine, blankets, good food, and the precious freedom to talk to each other came with them. The prisoners were slowly processed and shipped out.

But we Yugoslavians were far from home and weren't quite sure what to do now. I told them I'd been with General Mihailovic and would help organize the Yugoslavians to get them back home in one piece. Two older Serbian guys were now interested and we made our own plan to get home. We never believed it would be easy or had any idea how we would be welcomed back.

I got permission to take five guys into the forest on top of the hill to try to teach some guerrilla tactics to help them survive not knowing what else to do.

That night we listened to the radio with the Lieutenant. About 9:30 an importance announcement was about to be made. We sat through about an hour of music, German operas and Bruckner's Seventh Symphony nearly fallng asleep. Then at 10:20 they announced Hitler had fallen, fighting at the head of his troops. We sat frozen. Could it be true? Then all the guys danced around, so happy. Could this be the final end of the war?

The next day, it was announced that Hitler had not died a glorious death but had committed suicide in Switzerland but they could not present his body. Where was it? Was he really dead?

My Serbian and American friends celebrated my 20th birthday in the military camp on May 5th with a real cake and a keg of beer. These Yanks treated us like friends.

On May 7th, the Americans learned that Germany formally surrendered to the American, General Dwight Eisenhower. We began to hear German troops were coming from Poland and Chekoslovakia to Austria to surrender to Arms.

They purposely traveled long distances to surrender to Americans rather than the Russians who had arrived in Berlin before the Americans. The word was out. Russians would probably kill them or send them to terrible prisons back in Russia.

A few days later, my Serbian group of five practiced up on the hill in our borrowed clothes. One yelled, "Look. Look, down on the road, A German convey!"

The Germans with their metal hats were holding up white flags of surrender causing us to yell with joy at the glorious sight. Germans with white flags!

As we ran down to the first truck, pointing an automatic machine gun we'd found and never fired, they raised their arms, and we stopped them right on the road.

I took charge, speaking German, ordering them to give us their weapons in my roughest voice. The tired, scared, young soldiers handed them over so easily that we ordered the weary soldiers out of tanks, cars and motorcycles, confiscating a few of the machines.

That was so easy. I told the leader to go to the military camp to surrender to the Americans. Then I yelled in my most fierce German voice, "Go, Go!" The Germans scattered, jumping in the vehicles we'd left them and headed for camp, dust flying.

I've never felt so elated. For a moment, I thought I'd won the war myself! I knew how my grandfather Ceda felt at times in the first World War. My men couldn't believe how those Germans, those feared Nazis were just weary young humans like the rest of us. God, what a thrill!

We jumped into two big trucks. Only two of us had any inkling of how to drive, and we swerved down the road killing a dog and hitting a fence. We hid the trucks close to camp in the forest as best we could.

Now we had two good running trucks but we needed fuel to make the long voyage home. After dinner, when I figured the Lieutenant had a couple of beers, I approached him with my best manners.

"I wonder if it's possible to give us gas and oil?" The Lieutenant knew nothing about what we'd done with the Germans.

"For what?"

"We're going to Yugoslavia! And to hell with Tito! We took a truck from the Germans who were going to surrender anyway."

"What? You did what? Where are the Germans you thought you captured?"

"They were the ones to came here to surrender a couple of days ago."

"Well, you can't have fuel. That vehicle belongs to the United States Army now. Mila, what were you thinking? You have to give the truck back to us. You can't just turn into highway men."

"You can't take it back," I felt crestfallen. "We took it by force, it's ours. We need transportation home!"

"No, my good friend, I don't know what you thought you were doing. You must return it, and how did you pull that off, anyway? I want to hear this story right now!" He had the twinkle in his eye and took another slug of beer.

He bought me a beer, and I sat down across from him and told him the sequence without too much exaggeration. He laughed and we laughed.

"I can't wait to tell this to my men, of how you and four prison guys held up a convey of Germans with one dirty machine gun that probably wouldn't have hurt a fly! I need to get you guys out of here! You might start another war!"

He laughed and laughed. But he won the vehicles back, not knowing about the other truck I'd kept hidden in the forest.

A few days later, the Lieutenant sat next to me at dinner and said, "Mila, I have good news to tell you, you can leave this miserable place. General Patton, our big boss of the whole Third Army tells us the big three, American, England and Russia are meeting to divide up the land between Russia and Britain, and we're out of here. We've made arrangements for you

Yugoslavians to go on a cargo ship down the Danube to Belgrade and I want you to be in charge for the Captain.

I stared at him for a long silence. "I've been thinking about it and I've changed my mind. I'm not going there."

His expression turned serious.

I raised my arm for silence, and my voice raised and nearly cracked, "What's the difference between Tito and Stalin? They're both the same power mongers! My country is dead to me. Besides, most people think I'm already dead. And if I show up alive, I'm connected with General Mihailovic who's in great trouble now. I'll be killed. I can't go back."

The Lieutenant grabbed me by the shoulders. He knew exactly how I felt. "All I ask is that you must all stay in the barracks area until the ship leaves. My orders are to get you all on it."

I begged my Serbian friends from the prison to stay. "I know you want to go home to your families but think about it. Tito has taken over. Already he's canceled an election he promised the people and has killed many people that don't believe in his idea of communism.

"Go to the American zone or the British zone. If you go to Yugoslavia, you'll be back in six months if you're alive. The war is not over there. Not the civil war. Unless you are a communist, you'll never make it there because of Tito's intentions."

They listened. One guy said, "I curse the land where I was born."

They all signed up to go home.

I had not received one answer from my letters to my mother or the sisters and thought they couldn't answer or were dead. I didn't want the Lieutenant to get into trouble but I knew I never could go back.

"You must go back with the others," the Lieutenant explained to me.

"Yes, I understand but I have my own plan. Listen to me. I'll board the ship so you won't be responsible. I kept one of the

German trucks in the forest. Now, hear me out. You will send that truck with one of your men to my assigned place on the banks of the Danube and wait for me. I'm jumping ship."

His mouth fell open, dropping his lit cigar on the desk, and he stared at me, then the spark came into his eyes.

"If you live through that, we'll hide you out! This friggin' war is over. Maybe I can still get you back to America. By God, you are the craziest son-of-a-bitch I've ever known."

My prisoner friends and I decided we needed better civilian clothes than the odd ones the Americans offered for the trip. So we waited until night and slipped into the abandoned locked SS officer's former quarters and took what was left from the chests. I spotted an expensive suitcase with a label from under a bare bed and suspected good beautiful clothes were in it. I grabbed it and ran. When I showed them off to other guys, they tried to steal my booty so I took the suitcase into the forest up by the church and buried it in a big cardboard box under some brush with a rock over it.

Before the ship was to leave the next day, the Lieutenant and his buddies invited me to drink with them. Those guys sure knew how to have a good time, singing and telling stories.

"Have another one, Mila. We appoint you now an 'Honorable American Citizen!' "

They all lifted their glasses to me. I was deeply touched. But through the fun, felt guilty about the plan brewing in my head to abandon the other guys.

Just after dawn, we were officially released and taken to the river wharf where the cargo ship was ready to go.

"You have to get on the ship with the rest, my dear friend. Good luck," the Lieutenant told me in front of the others.

I walked up the long, high ramp with the rest of my prison buddies, my heart pounding. I'd never been on a ship before or even seen one up that close. The ship started down the river.

From the rail, we waved parting to Linz, to Austria, and to the stinking War. Our stubborn group was jubilant to be free and on their way home to families. Down river to the designated spot when no one was looking, I walked slowly to the rail.

"See you later, sometime in the future, my dear comrades," and jumped overboard into the Danube. My body hit the water with a painful shock and continued to go straight down. After what seemed like a long time, I came back up, took a lung full of air and paddled like a puppy to shore as best I could. I dragged my wet, filthy body up from the water onto the shore and starting looking for the truck. Please God, let me find it before someone finds me.

Suddenly, I spotted my truck parked a downstream. I ran stumbling and dripping to it where a young soldier G.I. a Private Foster for waiting. He was supposed to take me to the barracks but I pleaded with him, "Take me to the St. Magdalene Church and I'll give up the truck. Just stop to let me off when I tell you."

The G.I. looked anxious and asked, "Where are you going to go?"

"Just up the road, don't try to find me," I jumped out, thanked him, and off I went. I climbed downhill into the forest following my barely marked path to retrieve my suitcase. Then I took care not to call attention to myself. Just a guy walking along with regular pants and shirt swinging a suitcase. Keep calm, I tried to convince myself. I'm still in enemy territory, full of conquered Nazis and angry Austrians.

From the church area, I walked down a narrow road where we'd captured the SS movement and smiled at how much fun it had been to see the scared looks on those big Nazis and take their huge vehicles from them. Where to, now?

⮎

I noticed a large garden where a couple of people were working, and an old bench along the road. I sat down on the bench like I was waiting for a bus. A while later in the afternoon,

I watched a man older than my father, come walking by. He nodded at me in a friendly manner and headed for the big house on the property behind me.

I didn't want to approach anyone until just before sunset and waited. Then I went up on the porch, rang the bell, and the man came to the door. I introduced myself in German.

"Any chance I can get a piece of bread to eat?"

"Come in, young man," he invited. "I'm Karl Pickler, owner of this property. What is your name?"

"Miodrag Cedic. They call me Mila."

When they were inside the living room, he asked, "Where are you from?"

I told him the truth; that I'd recently been a Nazi prisoner of war from Yugoslavia and showed him my wrinkled, official release papers, a bit worse from the dunking in the Danube.

Herr Pickler introduced me to his wife and invited me to share dinner as they were just sitting down. What a wonderful meal it was, served on real plates with real silverware. He related how he'd been in a prisoner in Russia in WWI.

"My elder son was killed fighting on the Russian front in the winter offensive last year in this miserable war. We have missed him so. My younger son, a flier, is still missing in Russia. I also have two daughters. My daughter, Cecilia works at the revenue department in Linz, and you met our baby, twelve years old, Greiti who helps us here on our property."

He smiled at Greiti who looked a little miffed to be called a baby.

His wife seemed pleased to share their dinner with me and joined us for coffee and a visit in their parlor later. There was no picture of Hitler in this home. Herr Pickler commented on how no one still could verify how Hitler died.

After a while, I got up my nerve, "Herr Pickler, any chance I can stay overnight here?"

"Of course we'd be pleased to have you for our guest." He motioned for me to follow him up the stairs and showed me to the bedroom of his dead son. "You will feel at home here," he said kindly.

"Herr Pickler, thank you very much. When should I get up in the morning?"

"Sleep as long as you want, my son. I get up at 7 A.M. to go to work at the Post Office. My wife cares for the milking cows very early and we have a servant girl to cook and clean. We managed not to receive much damage like some of our neighbors during the war or the allied invasion. Oh, it's nice to have a young man to converse with again. You must stay here."

This sincere and kind man had appeared like a present from heaven.

That soft feather bed put me right to sleep until 11 A.M. the next morning. I rubbed my eyes looking around the nicely furnished room, solid furniture and wondering for a minute if I'd actually gone to heaven. I stared out the window as I'd always done as a child and absorbed a similar scene, orchards and fields clear up to the hills. My heart filled with happiness.

Greiti started pancakes on the wood stove although the clock ticked close to noon. She seemed quite comfortable with me and chattered on.

"We don't have any electricity and we still don't have any telephone nearby. Our food is still scarce but we trade vegetables and potatoes for fish. My parents say we are fortunate because many people are starving. We had to give most of our food to the German soldiers but we had a lot stored in our root cellars, too."

She was a small, pretty little thing with shiny, light brown hair reminding me of Jelica.

I felt a little self-conscious, visiting with such a young girl with no adults about. "When will Herr Pickler be coming home?"

"He usually is here by four or four-thirty. Mama is in and out. Frau Weiss, our housekeeper also comes in and out. And my big sister works all day and I never know where she goes."

She looked at me sweetly. "I must go now and do my chores."

"Of course, I'll see you later, and thanks for breakfast," I politely answered as she skipped out the back door.

Fraulein Cecilia bounced in after work, not too thrilled to see me there but introduced herself formally and hurried upstairs. I stared after her, her blonde hair bouncing. Her oval face and blue eyes just fit in with her cheerful personality.

When Herr Pickler came home that evening, I asked, "Herr Pickler, would it be possible to stay one or two more nights? I'd be happy to sleep in the barn."

He put his arm around me and said, "You will sleep in my son's bedroom now and you can stay as long as you want. May I call you my son? You remind me so much of my dead son."

I said, "Yes, and may I think of you as father? My father was killed during the War."

A tear came in his eye and his voice shook a little as he said, "Of course."

I sometimes did playfully call him Papa, as did his daughters. "Tata" was reserved for my own father's memory.

I called "Frau Pickler" just that, out of respect. When I first met her the day after I arrived, she looked dowdy. Little strands of hair fell loose from her bun. The skin under her eyes sagged, and her eyes carried a bundle of grief from the loss of her sons. Oddly, she reminded me of my own mother, serious and full of business, not an affectionate person.

Herr Pickler appeared sad and slightly bent over, but through it all, remained a warm and caring man who could light up easily.

On Sunday, they invited me to go to church with them. That's the first time I thought of all the deaths in the Balkans promoted by differences between the Catholic Church and the Serbian Orthodox Church. My Baba would want me to be in God's house in spite of the difference.

After the Catholic services at the Church of St. Magdalene with the family, I asked permission to go and look up the

American Lieutenant who rescued me. Walking the several miles to the American's military site near the prison made me straighten up and breathe in as I marched right into the office without knocking to find him at his desk.

"Lieutenant! I'm back!" He upset his chair getting up and his face actually went white. I really enjoyed shocking him.

"Mila, what are you doing here? God, I thought you were dead."

He came over to pound me on the back then held my shoulders staring at me like he'd never seen me before.

"I don't believe you're standing in front of me. The word came back that you had disappeared off the ship, that you must have committed suicide. I knew you'd never do that and figured what happened when Private Foster brought your stolen truck back. But I sure as hell wondered where you went when he told me you insisted on being dropped off in the forest. Where the hell are you staying?"

The words were just pouring out of his mouth and he kept shaking my shoulders. I finally put up my hand to give me a chance to talk. By now my English had improved as I had lots of time to practice in my head.

We sat down, opened a couple of beers, and I told him the whole story while he just shook his head, and laughed. We agreed the Austrians were not all Nazis politically and had been forced to knuckle under to them. They were in recovery mode themselves trying to cope with shattered lives and ruined cities after such a devastating war.

"So that's where you ended up. It's a good thing the war is over, you rogue. I suppose you killed Hitler, too!" We laughed like old times.

We drove back in the Army jeep to meet the Pickler family. They were quite pleased and honored to entertain an American in their home. The Lieutenant made a good impression convincing the Picklers that we both knew not all the Austrians were to be blamed for their conscription into the Nazi's war.

When I had a chance to be alone with the Lieutenant, I pulled his arm. "Let me show you my bedroom that was their dead son's, better than any barracks or hotel you ever saw here, I bet."

We went upstairs and I proudly showed off the clean and tidy room with sturdy furniture and a rug on the floor. I pointed out the wash basin and mirror on a stand just like mine at home and bragged I could use my new Army razor and shave my whiskers right here.

The Lieutenant laughed, "Oh, Mila, I still have to look close to see many whiskers. Hmmm, I guess there are a few here," he teased me looking around.

"No wonder you stay here! Wow!" he exclaimed. "What happened to the suitcase you stole?"

"You aren't supposed to know about that, but I have it here. I hid it and then retrieved it from the forest after I jumped ship."

I showed him my new wardrobe including some pieces Herr Pickler gave me that belonged to his dead son that would fit me. As soon as I visited the tailor in Linz to shorten the pants and make some adjustments, I'll actually own a nice wardrobe for the first time in years."

The Lieutenant looked around, brushed back his hair back and said, "I can't get over how you found such a great place to stay, and in former enemy territory. Now you, a ragged prisoner owns stolen groovy clothes," he teased.

"No wonder you didn't want to live in the barracks even if I could have let you stay. I wanted to, you know. How can one guy be so lucky?"

A few days after his visit, I was listening to the radio with Herr Pickler after dinner. Suddenly, I heard the name of the cargo ship I'd jumped from. Shock sent shivers down my back. The ship evidently hit a hidden mine in the Danube River near Belgrade, exploded into a giant fireball and burned. Everyone on board was killed. "God, save us," I cried out.

"God did save you from death, son." Herr Pickler said, a tear rolling down his cheek thinking of his own sons. He never knew about my ship-jumping incident.

When I next saw my Lieutenant friend, we were both feeling guilty and horrible about the dead men, but I felt terribly glad to be alive. Both of us thanked God again.

Nearly everyone was working to maintain a normal life. I tried to fit right into the Pickler household and helped with the chores tending the vegetable garden and even washing dishes right along with Frau Weiss. I also cleaned the paddocks and brushed down several brown horses every morning.

I asked for permission to ride a beautiful white horse with the comic name of Gogol.

The Lieutenant drove his jeep out to visit as often as possible. He too, was warmly welcomed by the Picklers. He even joined the family attending St. Magdalene Catholic Church on Sundays to worship with the Pickler family who could finally admit their Catholic preference.

Chapter 15

Waking up a few days later brought terrific pain to my head. I hadn't been drinking. What was wrong with me? After taking my temperature, Mrs. Pickler looked worried and contacted Herr Pickler who called Cecilia to find out where to take me in Linz. She contacted the Emergency Control of Jews in General Hospital where they wouldn't ask questions. The trip in the back of a wagon into town blurred into a coma for me.

I heard they did blood work and located a Dr. Kitchner, an expert in terminal diseases. He entered me into another hospital for two weeks of examination to confirm typhus. Vaguely, voices came that a reoccurrence such as this would almost certainly result in death.

Dr. Kitchner tried pumping blood into alternating hands for about ten days. By now, I felt a little less fuzzy and learned the name of every nurse who gave me much attention.

I didn't always swallow the medicine Dr. Kitchner tried to give me to sleep. The hospital swam around me. The voices didn't believe I could live.

"No relatives. No family plot. He'll have to be cremated," Then Dr. Kitchner's familiar voice sounded like he was in a tunnel.

"I'll make arrangements for a family from my church to give him a permanent grave plot in place of their son whose body will never be recovered from Russia."

My head was so fuzzy, but sick as I was, I couldn't stand staying in bed and insisted on leaving, then threatened to jump out the window. I don't know how I got the strength but I walked out right through the front door intending to get on a streetcar. The street scene started to blur out of focus. Just as I reached for the pole to board the car, I fell back and collapsed.

The voices came through discussing my death again. They had placed me in with the terminal typhus victims, but Dr. Kitchner never gave up on me. He brought in his young son just out of medical school in America during the war. I could hear them talking and understood that together they tried all the new methods. Afraid I might miss something and be totally out of control, I still refused to take shots to sleep. I didn't want to die.

Everyday they took one or two dead from the room filled with smells of medicine and body odors. Eventually, I couldn't stand it and started to pray to die. From a deep sleep, a clear vision of Baba came to me.

She said, "My dear Mila, it's too soon. You have so much life to live. Remember, only one truth, look out the window and see only one sun, God's truth. You will live, my son."

She kissed me. I felt it. Her spirit was so real, so soft; she'd spoken to me, I knew it. I knew I would live.

I forced my eyes open. Dr. Kitchner eyes looked straight into mine. "Your fever is broken. It's a miracle. You're alive, Mila." He shook his head and tears actually came down his cheek. His son came up behind him smiling, and put his hands on his father's shoulders. Baba and the Doctors Kitchner had brought me back to life. No way could I thank them enough for sticking it out.

When I became well enough to leave the unit, nurses and doctors murmured that in their experience no one had ever recovered from typhus a second time. Several of the staff, especially the attentive nurses came to see me off.

The Picklers insisted on taking me back in their horse drawn wagon into their home for recovery for a few weeks. We all agreed their good food had helped save my life. I had no doubt fresh vegetable helped to fight off any stray germs and build me up from that horrible disease I'd caught from those lice during the war.

I lounged in my bed, until I could sit in the rocker trying to read. With lots of time to think, I came to understand good people are found everywhere. Why had these people taken such a chance on me? Why had so many died? People must stop the killing. No war must ever be fought again.

After a few days of complete rest, being waited on and all that thinking, I took a few steps. Then I felt ready to go downstairs, then outside into the yard with leaves turning colors. The food and care I received at Karl Pickler's home kept me alive and improving by the day. I thanked God many times over for this blessed family. But at times, I felt a deep guilt about being alive when so many thousands and thousands of others were dead.

As I felt better, the Lieutenant came and drove me to Linz in the jeep. The trip into the heart of Linz was almost spooky. Flashes of explosions and rippling flame from the air raid came zooming into my head. How did I live through that? We reminisced about the first time his men picked me up when I was in prison garb. Now I had a box full of a Nazi's clothes and a dead Austrian's clothes to take to the tailor. Life just moves right along.

The streets were now nearly cleared of debris again. It was obvious these industrious people took pride in their surroundings even with no prisoners to work at the hard parts.

The Lieutenant drove me to his choice, the best tailor in town named Herr Atzmuller. This short, plump man with white streaks in his hair operated his small, exclusive shop not far from the Hitler Platz where the people had already changed its name back to Linz Platz. The Lieutenant plunked himself into a big, soft chair, lighting up his big cigar, his huge feet spread out, and watched me being measured for alterations.

Herr Atzmuller was quite the talker. Most of these people after the surrender wouldn't mention the name, "Hitler." But this man bragged he was Hitler's personal tailor, that nearly all the clothes and uniforms Hitler owned were "fashioned by Atzmuller."

"Of course you know Linz is Hitler's home town," he said. The Lieutenant and I looked at each other quizzically. "Now, hold still, please, young man.

"Oh, yes, my friends, I knew him when he was very young. This is his home town, you know." His eyes twinkled at the expression on our faces. Was he kidding? "He was born in Branau, you know. Very close to here."

"You knew the bastard?" the Lieutenant asked seriously.

"Oh, you must not be so hard on him. The poor boy was born illegitimately. A wealthy Jewish merchant impregnated several young women in the villages around here and never lifted a finger to help those poor ruined women. Poor Adolph grew up so poor, he had no chance to be accepted. Just a lonely misfit until he went into the army in World War I.

"Then he mixed with the class of educated boys, the 'pure German race.' He'd always wanted to be accepted in the professional, the artistic class. Although that class had been exempted from fighting earlier, they were now incorporated into new regiments for emergency training and Hitler found himself suddenly thrown in with society he'd always craved. He determined to show himself as a brave soldier and a courier runner, a very dangerous job and one for a sturdy individual, you know. He won merit from the officers."

At that, I about fell over. "Hitler was a courier?"

"Yes, he was, and he was wounded three times, then gassed in 1918. I know he's highly out of favor now but people don't know the whole story. Well, son, I'm finished pinning and will have all your alterations finished in a few days."

The Lieutenant and I got back into the jeep and he started snarling ironically on the way back. "Could we believe that old windbag? Trying to make the worst, twisted maniac in history into a real person? I don't think so."

Back at the Pickler's small farm, The Lieutenant and I went out to the stables and to show him the horses especially Gogal, and told how I was becoming known as quite the horseman racing across the fields.

One day bored British soldiers roaming the countryside on horseback challenged me to race them across fields. I couldn't resist the challenge and we ended up racing right through some neighbor's gardens. To complicate matters to my embarrassment, I was supposed to be working. People complained to Herr Pickler about us ruining their gardens.

He asked me, "Did you do this?"

"Yes, father," I answered as contrite as I could, "I'm terribly sorry."

I did feel worse knowing how this new crop was the first one the local farmers wouldn't have to give to the Nazis and after selling, it was barely enough left to feed the household.

Herr Pickler started to laugh. "My son, my missing, youngest son also got in trouble for doing that same thing more than once before the War! But that was better than racing jeeps like some young Nazi soldiers did running right through our fields and gardens with no excuse."

He scowled at the memory, then cheered up again, "Don't you worry. We'll take over some fresh produce to the neighbors to make up for it."

His wrinkled face became serious. "Son, I can't tell you how refreshing it is to have you here. My wife feels the same way and Greiti thinks you are 'just wonderful.' She misses her big brothers terribly, and now she has a big smile for you. You just stay as long as you like."

On our visits, I watched the Lieutenant intently. The tall, good looking pal of mine flirted with the attractive, levelheaded Cecelia, far more forward than anyone I'd ever seen.

They both were about three years older than me and looked great together. He taught her quite a few American words and she seemed interested in him personally. I hoped maybe they'd get together and the Lieutenant would stay in Austria. So I managed to make an excuse to leave them alone a couple of times.

Later, from hints, I became convinced nothing very romantic was taking place in that situation. I asked the Lieutenant why he wasn't interested in this pretty girl.

"Hey, she's great! Pretty, funny but for one thing, I left a girl behind in the States that I love. And did you know, Mila that Cecelia was in Hitler Youth Corps? That shocked me."

"No, I didn't know that, either. How could that be?"

We decided to ask her. We choose a time while we three were sitting out on the porch out of earshot from her parents.

"Was I in the Hitler Youth? Of course I was, everyone was during the early days. All the children got to wear a uniform with a lovely scarf and a little hat that they furnished. We marched together, ate together, and even got permission from the officers to tell on our parents if they didn't follow Hitler's rules. We were made to feel important and quite grown up.

"Don't look at me like that. You must understand we believed Hitler was almost God, and we'd all rule the world. We started young, guess I was about 10 years old when my friends and I joined the troops and they had much younger children than us in there. Actually, it was fun and did you know they held all their meetings in St. Magdalene's Church? It was full of Nazis who had taken it over. I shudder now when I look back on how easily we were influenced. I know now my parents had no choice just trying to survive."

Oh, the look at the Lieutenant's face! He turned pale. A staunch American through and through. That was the end of the flirtation right there.

Good thing because her parents would have had a fit if their precious daughter left for America with an American soldier as many Austrian girls were doing.

Near the end of the summer, the American Lieutenant announced he'd received his papers at last and was being released and sent home. He wanted me to go to America with him. He worked the system hard to make arrangements but the Army's cumbersome paperwork and strict rules prevented it. Under ordinary circumstances, it might take years. I could speak some English, with a lot of slang by now, but I had no proper identity papers, birth certificate or any other form of identification. I could be classified as dangerous.

Just as they were ready to leave, we heard General Patton had been killed in a jeep accident. The irony! All that brutal fighting on the most dangerous front and then get killed in a jeep accident! We just couldn't believe it.

The Lieutenant gave me his full name and address in America and wanted him to come visit in the future. I stared at the name and realized I'd never called him by his real name, just "Lieutenant." For a farewell present, I'd brought him honey in heavily wrapped jars from the Pickler's beehives. He gave me all the Austrian money he had except for a few coins to take back to America as souvenirs.

"Thanks, Lieutenant. That's the first spendable money I've had in years. Thanks for being my friend." I promised with good intentions that I'd come to America and visit him.

His whole unit moved out leaving a terrific void in my life. Feeling much sorrow over the Lieutenant's parting, I realized I had no plans for my future. I was still living on the edge.

The radio news announced Ante Pavelic from Croatia had fled to Argentina. That criminal had ordered the murders of about 350,000 ethnic Serbs, Jews, and Gypsies. No, I can never go back. My presence would put Majka and the girls in jeopardy. I couldn't risk writing any more letters as they would be confiscated and reveal my location. There, the war is not over.

Please, God, take care of my mother and all the rest of my families. I really felt depressed for several days like I had a fever. I took my typhus medicine and felt a little better.

The Picklers finally received news their son had volunteered into a special Nazi SS unit during the war and was now in prison in Russia, maybe for decades. At least he was alive. They continued to hope. It was so hard to watch their continuing grief.

Despite their shock and hurt, the family diligently started paperwork trying to find a way to get him a release. I came to understand what a difficult position all the Austrians had been placed in by that maniac, Adolf Hitler.

The nights had become chilly and the beautiful leaves began to fall spreading on the ground from the huge trees in the yard. I remembered how I loved to roll and play in the leaves as a child.

What now? I checked the calendar. I'd been here since May and now it was October.

As soon as I was able, I made the decision to try to get a job in Linz and discussed it with Herr Pickler. "I could still use you here on the farm, Mila, but now that harvest is nearly finished, you won't have so much to do.

"Why don't you enroll in school in Linz? You can still live here. Housing in town is almost impossible. I'll lend you my son's bicycle for transportation. No one has any gasoline, yet. Or maybe the tailor can give you a little work. Besides the government, he's one of the few making any money. The country is in dire straits until we can recover from the war."

〜

Herr Atzmuller welcomed me, "My dear boy, where have you been? I heard you were very sick and in the hospital. I have your clothes all ready for you. I hope you soon will allow me to make you a suit."

"I have money to pay you for today but I have to get a job first before I can order a suit, Herr Atzmuller. Could you use a helper here?"

"We'll talk about that. How would you like to meet my wife? She is downstairs and then we can discuss it. First, you must try on your clothes."

His work seemed perfect to me. I changed into one of the hemmed pants and checked myself out in the mirror. The Pickler son's pants were no longer dragging on the ground and the Nazi officer's aged, stolen English suits now fit perfectly.

A funny thought bounced into my head. I heard Tito loved good clothes and wondered if he'd stop wearing his fancy uniform now and wear fancy civilian clothes. Another thought crossed my mind: what happened to his impersonators who probably knew too much just like myself?

I admired myself in the full-length mirror; slim, my curly hair grown back, clean and cut, no scars showing, and looking pretty good for a dead man. Now I looked like a normal person with a reasonably good wardrobe.

Herr Atzmuller boxed up my new clothes for me to tie on the back of my bike.

Satisfied, I followed him downstairs to find a clean, nicely furnished apartment that probably had also served as a shelter during the bombing. The real surprise came when he introduced his wife. I guess I expected a frumpy little woman.

Her height equaled his and her buxom figure "groovy." What a lovely smile! Her pretty face was surrounded by coifed blond hair. She must be as old as my Majka but better looking. I nearly lost my tongue as she shook my hand. I looked down and suddenly realized my shoes looked like beggars. I'd forgotten about shoes and probably wouldn't have been reminded if I hadn't looked at my feet through this lovely woman's eyes.

"Welcome, Mila. I've heard a lot about you, how you were a prisoner and how the Americans rescued you from prison. You were so fortunate that you were not in a death camp and killed. We hear thousands of people, mostly Jews were gassed at the end so they wouldn't be discovered. Now sit down. I'm almost ready to serve some fresh coffee and pastries just out of the oven.

"Did Herr Atzmuller tell you I am also from Yugoslavia? My family and I are from the Shilzie providence from generations ago. I also speak Chek from where I lived before I met Herr Atzmuller.

This wonderful woman reminded me of my Aunt Milojka, lovely and friendly. I suddenly realized I hadn't even thought of Milojka for a long time. How was she? Did she ever see my Majka? They lived close to one another but they were so different from each other and never close friends.

"What are you thinking of, Mila? Home? I know you must be lonely. You are welcome here anytime."

"In fact, my dear," said Herr Atzmuller, "the boy will be helping me in the shop. Some of the work is hauling materials and running errands, you know. What do you think, my boy?"

"Thank you Herr Atzmuller. Just tell me what time to be here."

I rode the bike five miles back causing my shrapnel leg to ache but it beat walking. Herr Pickler seemed pleased. He agreed I could use the bicycle for transportation like so many others. The tailor work was light and I enjoyed the company of the Atzmuller's. To my great surprise, I found out the famous Atzmuller had just begun making suits for well-dressed Tito now that Hitler was gone.

Frau Atzmuller invited me to come downstairs late one afternoon and introduced me to her niece, a woman in her late twenties. In her younger days, she may have pretty but now she looked haggard and older than Frau Atzmuller. I couldn't help staring at this sad woman; her eyes l blank and dead.

She looked up at me and said, "I didn't always look this bad. I'm a widow, now from the war. No, that would have been honorable. The truth is, my husband committed suicide!" She picked up her mug and downed a large swig of beer, drops dripping off her chin.

"Oh dear, please try to be calm today and appreciate the fact we escaped the bombing and are alive,"

Frau Atzmuller tried to console her. The niece waved her off and looked at me.

"I want you to know my husband was a personal guard to our Furher, Adolph Hitler for many years, all of his army career. He saved Hitler's life when those bullies he had for officers tried to murder him. He was devoted to Hitler and wanted to protect his Furher the rest of his life. He was with Hitler in the Alps outside Salzburg.

"His whole purpose for living was protecting Hitler but suddenly Hitler decided he would go back to Berlin without his faithful personal guard. My husband felt completely rejected as he'd never been separated from his Furher and he was afraid the Furher would kill himself," she finally paused, tears bubbling down her cheeks.

She bent her head holding out her hand and Frau Atzmuller handed her a hankie. "Here, my dear, don't cry," she cooed. Her lovely face looked so stressed.

"My poor, dear dedicated husband came back here where he was born and shot himself," the woman continued.

"Can you imagine? This strong, brave man killed himself and left me alone." Her voice became louder building to a shriek.

"I begged to get a pass from the Russian zone because I had to come here and see where they buried him."

She burst into tears and started crying out loud. Frau Atzmuller jumped up and put her arms around her niece who pushed her away.

"Everyone is dead. Everyone I know, everywhere. Hitler owes me. I know that son-of-a-bitch is alive. He owes me big!" She fell into angry sobs again.

I sat glued to my seat at her outburst wanting to console her. I felt most of the Germans and Austrians were sincere and had been totally abused by the Nazis regime.

Frau Atzmuller turned to me and apologized for her niece's outburst. She told me, "Many people here in Linz grew up with Hitler, not that they accepted him then. But during the War, they liked to brag they knew him as a friend."

That woman wore me out and I thought of her all the way pedaling home. Poor thing; so many victims of the War.

I worked at the shop pedaling the five miles each way from the farm to the tailor shop. I bought shoes in a second hand store. They probably were taken off a dead man. New shoes along with everything else, were extremely hard to come by in this post-war time.

When the shop wasn't busy, I took off early and dropped in to a beerkarten close by. I locked the bike up outside. Inside, I sat down at the bar and ordered a beer. It didn't take long to get into conversation with some students from the university. I asked if they knew about Hitler.

A young man who introduced himself as Werner glared at me. "Keep your voice down. Our fathers knew him when he was poor and stupid. My father sat next to him in the lower grades. He dropped out of school and went to Vienna but he was just a drifter before the first World War."

Then a big argument started on whether Hitler was dead or alive. Rumors ran everywhere. Was he dead by suicide? Was he in Switzerland or the Austrian Alps? Was he preparing another battle? I remembered when the first reports stated he died a hero heading his army, but later suicide stories were rumored all over Europe.

The young man named Werner took me to the school and showed me exactly where Hitler sat. I sat down a few rows away and tried to envision a homely, unwanted boy sitting there. Just the thought gave me chills, I decided not to try to continue school there.

At dinner one evening with the Atzmuller's, Herr Atzmuller confided to me that his grandmother was related to Hitler's grandmother by marriage.

"His poverty and hatred for the Jews left him quite crazy, I believe. I can say that now. But it wasn't his fault. I don't believe he knew anything about the slaughter in the camps. I believe he just thought they were labor camps and it was that mad villain Himmler who ordered all the murders. Himmler was the beast responsible for all the death camps, not Hitler."

Frau Atzmuller lowered her pretty head over her plate. Obviously, she'd heard all this before and didn't interfere.

"Yes, and did you know his beloved mother was killed by gas iodoform given to her by a Jew doctor while she having an operation at an young age. No wonder he hated the Jews. He hated the Army, too and tried to avoid it by going to Vienna and living in shelters and soup kitchens.

"I helped him find lodging with a tailor family in Munich, a city he loved as he loved the Germans and wanted to be a "pure" German. He then went into the Army in World War I. I've heard he was a warrior.

"Later he found a place in Nazi activities. He discovered a great talent, as a political orator of genius to recruit people into his Nazi way of thinking. He later said, 'To be a leader means to be able to move masses.' And he did. He was not a monster. He gave presents to children, and he hated blood sports and he was always neat and clean, almost fanatical. He never knew about the concentration camps."

"Please, could we talk about something else? Frau Atzmuller glanced up and asked plaintively.

"Forgive me, I do get carried away about the poor man. Just think how far he did come!"

Frau Atzmuller looked straight at her husband and glowered at him and he didn't say another word about Hitler.

⤸

Late one afternoon, I decided to ride the bike over to Linz Platz where I'd worked as a prisoner the day the Americans arrived. I wanted to see how the rebuilding was coming. Memories flooded back. How could man take man prisoner? Would we never progress passed the tyranny, the terrible blood sacrifice, the destruction?

Just as I raised my head from a little silent prayer, who should I see, but the American officer who, posing as a German officer saved me in this very spot. It took me a moment to recognize him in his American uniform as he stared at me, too.

"I can't believe it. It's you, Mila, the cocky, young prisoner. I'd have known you any place with that curly hair," and he shook my hand hard. "The information you were able to give may have helped end this war!"

These Americans love to exaggerate, I thought to myself. I was so happy to see him, I even kissed him on the forehead. I had to ask his name as he'd never told me his real identity when I was a prisoner.

"I'm Colonel James Cortner from Connecticut, U.S.A."

"And I'm Miodrag Cedic from Serbia but you can still call me Mila!" He smiled. We went to get a beer in a quaint, old Bohemian building still standing.

"Well, look at you now! You just disappeared off the face of the earth. I thought you'd probably been blown up on that cargo ship of released Yugoslavian prisoners."

"I boarded with the rest, but jumped into the Danube before we left sight of Linz. And I'm looking out for my future right now."

The amazed officer just stared at me and shook his head and then asked me to dinner. I excused myself to call Herr Pickler to let him know I would be late coming home even though I knew if I spent the whole evening with the Colonel, I'd have to ride home in the dark. Colonel Cortner insisted on buying dinner and drinks.

"How do you happen to still be here? Are you assigned permanently?" I asked.

"I'm in a special American Army unit now, Mila, called the CIC. Just trying to keep order."

"It is a good thing you aren't assigned to Yugoslavia, Colonel Cortner. I don't think the fighting will ever be over there. Many German soldiers are still hiding in the mountains and our country is devastated. I read in the paper that King Petar's group returned from London and had taken up residence in

Salzburg, still in exile. He wanted to return to Yugoslavia but the people loudly voiced their grievances against the king and the former monarchy."

The Colonel told me, "Forget it Mila, your King will never return to Yugoslavia. Tito has taken charge and all his dedicated Partisans are backing him. He's won control of the national assembly and now is planning to abolish the monarchy and is declaring your country a federal republic, in other words, his take on Communism.

"And he may be too much for Stalin. We cannot trust those Russians. We shall see. We're watching closely." He continued to question me, staring me right in the eyes.

I told him, "I wanted to go back to my homeland and family but knew I couldn't because of Tito. He and his men knew I'd worked for his archenemy General Mihailovic, and would surely have me killed. Better to have him and everyone else continue to believe I am dead."

"I'm sorry that's the situation."

After a few quiet minutes eating and thinking, he ask, "How would you like to do some work for me? I'll make it worth your time."

My blood started to run faster in spite of the sluggish feeling from the beer and big slab of roast beef and potatoes I'd just eaten. I wanted back in the action more than anything.

"What I need from you is to help round up and interview displaced people in this area who want to go back to your country or immigrate to other countries, and to help us get them papers. You speak the languages and could really help me."

That didn't sound very exciting but I felt it would lead to better things if the Colonel could trust me. The fact I had no real papers myself seemed a joke. When we parted, I rode my bike down the dark, lonely road to the farm. The atmosphere threatened snow and my leg was killing me but I still felt exhilarated about the prospects of doing some tasks for the Colonel.

The process of meeting my fellow countrymen stuck in Austria, or displaced persons as the Colonel called them, meant trying to sort out their personal and mental health problems. I met the challenge head on.

In the meantime, Herr Atzmuller kept me busy doing odd jobs around the shop, learning interesting details about good clothes, and enjoying good meals in the downstairs apartment with the beautiful Mrs. Atzmuller who made my breath come faster.

Later, I started on my first assignment. I walked back across the Danube bridge in Linz. The purpose was to meet Serbians who had ended up here but wanted to go back home. I tried to talk them into staying in Austria and find any job in the American zone or British Zone. I was afraid if they went back home, they wouldn't be welcomed because of Tito's intentions.

I reported to Colonel Cortner on our follow-up. I heard an election was planned in Yugoslavia and many hoped and prayed things would get back to normal. But thinks got worse. Rumors ran around that Tito forbade and canceled the promised election again.

At the end of October, the Colonel called me to our tavern meeting place. "I have a proposition for you if you wish to accept," he bent towards me and my heart leaped.

Chapter 16

1946

"My contact in Salzburg at the Central Committee of Austria needs a man there to do this business and travel all over Europe. Would you be interested?" the Coronal asked.

I nodded. Traveling and responsibility appealed to me.

"They can't put you on the payroll as you are still considered 'underground,' but all expenses are paid. Your King Peter is there."

At the house, I sat down and explained the situation to Herr Pickler. He sat smoking his pipe for several minutes, looking very serious.

"Oh, son, I knew you couldn't stay forever. This family will miss you very much." He sighed. "We'll help you any way we can as you have helped us out. But you must promise me one thing. You are a member of this family and you must keep in touch with us."

I looked in his wrinkled, kind face. This family saved me from living like a wandering Gypsy and housed me, fed me, clothed me. I loved them, too. Nothing could make that up.

"I will be back," I promised.

After I settled with Herr Atzmuller and boarded the train, I realized most my traveling out of Yugoslavia had been in a freight train with no windows. Now I was traveling first class, dressed in my made-over suit and preparing to eat in a dining car. I sat up straight, smiled to myself, and began to feel quite important.

My destination was Salzburg near the border of Austria. The beautiful country in the Alps with wooded mountain peaks from 7000 to 9000 feet reminded me of all my time in the evergreens and beech trees of the Balkans. The late autumn leaves fluttered down into the streams. The scenery softened my pounding heart.

The Nazi party had started here 25 years ago. Supposedly, Hitler's hideaway, the "Eagle's Nest" was near here on a mountaintop. We'd heard rumors of Hitler trying to gear up for a major last stand battle from a mountain fortress near the end of the war. Ally airmen had risked their lives to save Salzburg, Mozart's birthplace.

I arrived with my valise in hand, immediately looked up the address, and found the huge, grand building where our government-in-exile rented offices. I walked up the wide marble steps to present myself to the guard outside. He asked for my Identification Card and I showed the brand new one the Colonel had made up for me. He asked if I spoke English and I answered in German.

"I have a letter of introduction to see the President of the Central Committee, if I may."

Another guard came up and said in Serbian, "Where are you from?"

"I've traveled from Linz but I was born in Yugoslavia." His eyes lit up.

"Ah, what village are you from?"

"I'm from Kamenica near Aleksinac," He smiled and escorted me into an office where I presented my letter from Colonel Cortner.

"I know you, at least I know who you are! How is your father, Sretein Cedic?"

I stared at him, amazed to see a Yugoslavian before me. I said, "My father was killed in the War."

Oh, I'm so sorry to hear that. He was a good man. I often sang in concerts with him in our younger years. I also knew Budimir Jovanovic, your uncle, the Senator and I know he was murdered. We also thought you were dead for a long time. We discovered you quite by accident through Colonel Cortner."

I felt more comfortable with such a personal welcome and didn't feel too uncomfortable when he interrogated me. Later he escorted me to introduce me to the President Stephan Trifunac, agent of the King. I wasn't sure what he was president of in this new government but knew I'd eventually find out. He also was an older man with a worn, sagging face and skimpy gray hair. I don't believe he ever smiled.

Strictly business. I was glad I didn't have to work with him directly; I only had to do the legwork for his Yugoslavian refugee agency. He did reveal in the course of my interview that Sir Winston Churchill was financing this section. I'd understood Churchill had helped King Petar all along.

As I walked out, I couldn't believe my eyes. There stood Dihan in civilian clothes staring back with a widening grin. At the same instant, we yelled out greetings and started pounding on each other, laughing loudly. He immediately took my arm and led me into a private salon.

"Who is this boy in the fancy suit? We thought you were dead. You've been gone nearly a year!" He grabbed my shoulders at arms length and stared at me with a wide smile.

"I'm twenty years old so don't call me a boy anymore, Dihan," pretending to be insulted. "I don't believe it. Last time I saw you, you and the General were about to run for it."

Dihan let go of me and motioned us to sit down. "The old man did run with a broken heart, I'm afraid, even though we all think he is a hero and did his best to fight off the Germans and the Communists. He thought you'd been killed, Mila, when you just disappeared. No one had any information but he did try every channel to locate you." His smile turned serious.

"Mila, from the beginning, he resented having to try to manage the peasant guerrillas when he felt he should be running the regular army. Of course, the pitiful Army we had then had to surrender to the Germans. So he had to go underground trying to manage the peasant Chetniks, brave as they were. He's hiding in Ravna Gora, now. Poor guy, he's afraid Tito's new regime will come after him anytime.

"You wait. Stalin might still be in with the Allies but when that madman gets his own territory in Germany and Berlin, he'll claim it for himself and shut it off. We're going to see great changes, God forbid."

I looked at him closely. Dihan was the same, a little older, even the few wrinkles on his forehead had become grooves of worry but he still held that even, deep ability to read emotions and foresee the near future.

As we walked across the street he said, "Your German seems quite correct to me, Mila and I hear you can speak some English, too."

"English with an American accent and slang. Believe me, it's a lot more difficult to learn than German.

In an old apartment building, Dihan unlocked the door to a small room. I looked around the plain space with one window, two narrow beds and a sink. Here's where he was staying and informed me I'd be staying there, too when I was in Salzburg.

"Here's your bed, Army made, of course. I wrote to your Mother and she answered the letters but her words were guarded. I'm convinced she thinks you are dead."

He looked to see how I was going to take that but I just shrugged my shoulders. The frustration of her sorrow would never go away. He took out a handful of letters, handed them to me, and then told me a most bizarre incident concerning my mother.

"A Partisan officer asked her to come to a place outside Aleksinac and presented her with a body to identify as yours, but the head had been chopped off. She went through the gory process and pretended to hold the hand in honor. Actually, she searched for the crooked finger you've had since birth but the fingers were all straight. She didn't reveal her knowledge that it couldn't be your body but gave her permission to bury the body to keep them off your trail. I believe she suspected you were dead anyway," his forehead squinted up even more and his eyes held such a sad expression.

"Six months later after you disappeared, I heard Tito's people were looking for you. They thought you'd gone over to the Nazis. You'd better change your name here, Mila."

"They aren't taking my name away from me. I am who I am." I pointed to the sky. "I only belong to God. But don't worry, Dihan. I will be careful, I promise. I made it this far, haven't I? Thanks for helping my mother and keeping the letters for me. You sure took a risk. We have a lot of catching up to do."

He looked at me with that crooked, gentle smile and nodded his head.

I had to move forward. I could not allow my past to haunt me. I'd lost much of my youth. Dihan, one of my few friends left in the world could help release my stress.

"It looks like I'm going to be traveling again and this time in first class, my friend."

The town drinking places appeared to be on his regular beat. We settled in his favorite, and he smiled up at a pretty blonde fraulein. After a few flirting words to her, he ordered a couple of tall steins and turned to me.

I started with the battle near Tuzla and the shrapnel wounds in the calf and thigh, ending up in that dreary prison, rescue and the lucky chance of finding the Pickler family. As the long story rolled out, while drinking a few beers that appeared like magic in front of me, my soft side reared up.

I'd been so involved in my own survival, I'd hardly even thought about the people who cared about me and had no idea of my whereabouts. I felt ashamed. So I had one more, big stein of beer and tried to enjoy the nostalgic music. It didn't help.

The next evening, I lay down on my narrow bed, pumped up the pillow and forced myself to read all my mother's letters. I believe she tried to bolster herself for all the past tragedies by writing to me, her lost son.

She wrote that my sister Drgica started to teach children after getting out of the hospital from her breakdown. Majka wrote she'd taken it upon herself to find Drgica a husband, a Communist with a powerful father hoping to save our property for us. Jelica also tried teaching but refused to be forced to teach communism and was about to join a nunnery to escape from the new regime. How I longed to see them.

Chapter 17

Just before my first trip, Dihan and I went out to our favorite beerhaus. He confirmed all three of Tito's imposters were dead.

"No trace appeared but the general consensus was that Tito had them killed as they knew too much. His inner group of men who had been close to him from the beginning stayed faithful. He's still very strong, and if no one assassinates him, he'll run the country now."

Then Dihan leaned towards me and said, " I know another secret, but you must swear you'll never tell until you are about to die of old age." In that noisy place, no one could hear us anyway.

"I was in Graz on business in the British section in General Patton's private dining room. I heard from his mouth in front of a lot of people that he thought Eleanor Roosevelt, wife of the United States President, was an 'international whore!' "

"Some time after that, while I was still there down the hall from General Patton's offices late one night; he was sitting at his desk, furiously doing paper work. I heard a strange commotion and a gun shot. By the time I ran out and stood in the shadows, his permanent driver was driving up half dressed like he'd been called out in an emergency. Two unfamiliar soldiers dragged Patton out to his waiting jeep.

"His face was covered with blood running down his forehead and over his uniform front. They positioned him upright in the back seat and I heard the soldier driver ask, 'What happened?'

" 'He's had a hemorrhage. Get him to the hospital, now!' The soldier yelled frantically and the driver stepped on the gas, the staff car kicking up dirt.

"Then the soldier I'd never seen before spotted me, grabbed my shirt, and snarled, 'Don't go near his office on pain of death! It's off limits. We'll take care of it. Don't tell anyone until we get more information.'

"They immediately left the scene. The minute they were out of sight, I sneaked in. Blood and pieces of flesh were all over the wall in back of his desk. My heart stopped. That was no hemorrhage. That had to be a gun with a silencer that shot General Patton right through the head and blew his brains out.

"I ducked out just as I heard the soldiers coming into the hall and hid around the corner. I hid in my dark office and heard them scrubbing the blood off the wall.

"In the early hours of the morning, we all were sadly informed General George Patton's vehicle had been accidentally blown by a hidden mine up on the road. The General and his driver were dead with little remains. Even the papers worldwide announced General Patton's death 'from a jeep accident' or a 'traffic accident.' That's all as far as I know. The subject was never mentioned again."

Dihan paused and said quietly, "I didn't know what to do. You are the first person to hear this from me. I'm telling you Mila; it was an assassination! I believe it was Tito's work, don't you?

I sat there with my mouth open. "General Patton? One of the major American Generals of the war, the hero in Africa? Who would do that? Surely not just because he had called Mrs. Roosevelt 'an international whore,' or maybe so."

I bent even closer to Dihan and whispered in shock. "I wouldn't be surprised if it was Tito's assassins dressed in stolen uniforms. But you're right, Dihan. We can never tell anyone about this in our whole lives."

Best thing to do right then was to get really drunk.

In all we'd heard, seen and been through, we proclaimed our friendship to each other in the future. The more we drank, the braver we became. As we staggered back to our room, we decided we would represent every man who showed courage to care for his fellow man, no matter what his race or religion.

We meant well but felt sick.

⌐

In the first days of training in Salzburg, I walked around Salzburg, the spectacular snowy mountains shining down on the town. I noticed a building named after the Russian leader, Lenin and discovered he'd been born here. Someone told me they pronounced his name Lenion. He too, probably intended to change the world, to make things better. Where does it go so wrong? Is it just greed and power?

The Alpine features seemed to comfort me. Such bizarre behavior in this world especially against such beautiful, peaceful settings just boggles the mind.

My life style continued to change. I was able to wear good clothes with white gloves, have my long, curly hair styled down, and my nails manicured. Dressing well helped, but I still looked younger than my twenty years and hoped people would take me seriously.

My new look gave me the confidence to attempt flirting with a pretty blonde girl I had seen from a distance in the park. I walked up and down past where she was sitting on the bench to assure myself she was following me with her eyes. On the next walk-by, she smiled at me and lowered her head.

"Hello, nice day isn't it?" Ouch. I sounded so pitiful.

"May I sit here?"

I motioned to the bench, she nodded with a little smile, we sat down, and started up a conversation. Her name was Christl. We discovered we were both single, about the same age, living in Salzburg temporarily. We talked small talk and agreed to meet here the next day. I could hardly wait.

The next day, there she sat on our bench, her golden hair gleaming in the sun. Talking to her came easily and, after she accepted my invitation to lunch, I ended up telling about my family and just a little of the years since I left home. Eventually, her pretty mouth and sad, blue eyes told me her touching story. Her voice sounded so sweet.

"I married a boy from my hometown who became a Nazi. I'd known him all my life and we were all in the Hitler Youth Corps together. We had a few joyful weeks in our little apartment before he left to go to the French front. Soon after, my husband was killed in Brittany.

"Don't be upset at what I'm about to say. I discovered I was going to have a baby and I moved back in with my parents. I was out standing in line to buy food one day with my baby boy, when we heard the drone of planes sending us scurrying to the shelter. Later, when I could go home, I saw flames. A bomb hit directly on our house and my parents were both killed. A girlfriend ask me to come to Salzburg with her so I moved here with my little boy now two years old."

I sat taking in her story and the strangest emotion came over me. I stared at her full lips, her sad eyes and my heart pumped in a different way than even battle had produced but just as hard. Was this love?

Christl joined me for dinner in a good restaurant with a violin player, all on my expense account. We laughed and talked like old friends. Then she invited me to come to her room she shared with her girlfriend and her little boy. For the first time watching him play with his little toy on the floor, I felt real love, I was sure. I stared at the boy and stared at her and imagined what it would be like to have my own family.

Christl and I became close friends and the precious experience as lovers when we could be alone. Her soft voice and her way of trying to please me brought a new maturity to me and soon I planned in my mind how I would ask her to marry me at a future date. But as much as I thought I loved her, I couldn't carry it off.

I kept thinking of Baba's words and knew it would be unfair to encourage her. She was Austrian, not a drop of Serbian blood. My family would never approve.

Painfully, I told her how I felt and she started to cry. I tried to console her when suddenly she blurted out that she had deceived me. Her husband was actually in jail in France as a war criminal, not dead. She lied to me. The news hurt nearly as much as a bullet, I swear.

Leaving her, I was a broken man for a while. My determination to marry only a Serbian woman was set in stone.

⌒

My job involved finding and counseling former Yugoslavians to help decide choices on where to go to start a new life. When the Red Army left Yugoslavia and continued into Hungary last fall, they left the Partisans and Western Allies to try to drive out the remaining Germans, Ustashe, and Cetnici. I learned some of the bloodiest battles were fought then internally.

Many men fled to Austria. Many others who'd returned to Yugoslavia recognized and refused Communism and came back to Austria just as I'd predicted. Maybe we could help these displaced people including the hated Ustashe followers caught up in the postwar frenzy. Even many Partisans really didn't want the blossoming Communist government and came to Austria for protection.

I talked to desperate men from the Balkans who had joined the Wehrmacht, wore the uniforms but couldn't speak a word of German. What would happen to them? Would they dare go back? Many thousands had given up their birthright; displaced persons who belonged nowhere.

I heard the same tale time and time again in my job. Now a man like so many others faced me. He couldn't stay here and needed new papers to enter Bosnia to find his family. Because he was a native, we managed to get him back in. How does any man prove who he is? His actions alone should speak for him. Everyone was watching everyone with little trust.

Austria was still being partitioned and a large chunk was given to the feared Russians, so these people and even many natives wanted to find new homes in a hurry. Even more gruesome was hearing of a Swiss rescue mission. People who had entered the Polish prison camps like Maidanek at Lublin, a huge murder complex, found crematoriums where a half million people at been poisoned with chlorine gas.

Many were burned before the American or English soldiers or helpers could get in. The rescue missions were often too late. They found only human bones in barrels of lime, chlorine gas pipes, and piles of clothes to be rescued.

Would this devastation never end? Our information showed twelve million people died in camps. Many were just barely surviving in the rubble of the aftermath.

We searched all other countries that might be willing to take them and many were generous opening their doors to the refugees.

The next few months, I traveled all over Italy, Germany, Belgium, France, and England, to help refugees find new homes. Many of our people migrated to Brazil, Canada, America, Argentina, or Australia with the Colonel's help.

I could not go back to Yugoslavia myself. I learned Tito had confiscated my father's property, our livestock, and our houses despite my Majka's ruse demanding Drgica marry the Communist to try to prevent it. That property would have been mine. That bastard Tito.

I often rode on trains and sometimes in my own compartment, listened and learned to speak more English, trying to pronounce it very carefully.

By chance, I found myself speaking French with Charles de Gaulle. He knew my Uncle Budimir and had fond memories of General Mihailovic whom he greatly honored and respected for all his war efforts. From his words, it was obvious he was trying to bring some sign of semblance of order to his own bombed and burned country. He impressed me as the most imposing, wisest man I'd ever met.

I only saw the older but not wiser King Petar once. I talked to him but he did not remember me, my family, or our childhood outing with the goats. In fact, I thought he was still a boring, dumb coot and agreed with my fellow Serbs. He'd never make a real king. Too bad his younger brother is dead. Later, he left Salzburg. I never heard another word about him.

One of the men, whom I had tried to talk out of going home, just returned from Yugoslavia and came to talk to me. He told me the war had not ended there and probably never would.

Formerly a soldier, he said they were still usually in favor in Yugoslavia but most had shaved off their beards and acted as part-time, underground guerrillas only. He confirmed the fighting still went on.

I felt sad and started to hate this job.

As bonus, I was given cases of Chesterfield cigarettes from the PX, courtesy of Colonel Cortner. They were stacked in our little room. I exchanged them on the black market for shoes, socks, medicine, chocolate, thread, and cod liver oil. Dihan helped himself to all the cigarettes he wanted.

Linz was my next destination with the opportunity to visit old friends. In town, I visited Herr Atzmuller. His short, thin body was dressed perfectly, his tape measure still around his neck. He took pins in his mouth out when he spotted me coming through the door. He greeted me with open arms.

"My Mila, my boy, how we've missed you, you know. Oh, my wife will be so happy to see you. Where have you been? We have so much to tell you."

His wife immediately fixed a light meal for me, complete with wine. Around the table, he couldn't stop talking. My attention wandered somewhat as I stared at his wife, still beautiful with her hair longer and fixed up so pretty.

Herr Atzmuller didn't seem to notice my staring. "I don't know how you stay looking so young, Mila. Well, things are getting better, you know business has picked up, but we miss you around here. You must tell us all about your travels."

We sat down to a steaming dinner but before I could answer, he continued.

"I need to tell you. Some rather devious men were here looking for you but we told them nothing. And Mr. Pickler stops by now and then. He appreciates your letters to him so much. They've moved, you know. They re-assigned that area and gave it to the Russians. He's slowing down and they have a smaller place now in the American zone. I'll draw you a map. Not far from his old place. His daughter is married, you know. He still has no taste for clothes."

He finally paused to take a few bites of food. "I have a favor to ask you, my friend. I must tell you in total confidence that Adolph Hitler is living near here."

"He's what?" I nearly dropped my fork. Has the old man gone crazy?

"Yes, he sneaked back to his home town completely defeated but alive. He's seriously ill, you know."

"Not just ill," his wife looked me right in the face, "Adolph Hitler is crazy, loony, I went there in the beginning to see him with Herr Atzmuller but he rants and raves, still angry at being shunned and abused as a child. He's angry at his treatment even as Furher, and ends up screaming against his officers. Then he will calm down and stroll out to pick a flower for you. I just can't bear it."

"Anyway, my friend," Atzmuller turning back to me. "I know you have a good position now and I need you to do a great favor for me."

I hated to ask, "What is it?"

"I want you to carry some papers out of the country for me. These papers will prove Hitler is alive but no one must know, yet. There have been too many rumors and too many lies because along with friends, he has many enemies. His own officers tried to kill him, you know. We don't believe he ever knew about the murders. These documents are very valuable, Mila and contain evidence like receipts with his signature, his writing to prove he's still alive and living here. Many people in town know about their hero but no one speaks outside Linz. The papers must be hidden for a few years until he dies."

Stunned, I sat staring at him in silence. "I can't help him, Mr. Atzmuller. Out of respect for you, I would, but I cannot risk my life. Now, I'm searched at every border and have to use false papers many times just for myself. I could be killed for those documents from many sources. Don't try to move them. You must hide them here in a secure, safe place."

The excitement in his eyes faded to sorrow. "You are right, of course. They must stay with me. I would not jeopardize you, my friend. But Adolph is very ill in a good asylum where he is safe across in the Russian zone. You know he did not give the orders to kill all those people in the concentrations camps. Himmler, the beast, was in charge. SS guards killed the prisoners, you know. Adolph did not know until the war was over and he tried to poison himself when he learned of it. His new wife, Eva Braun did die, but he lives."

His wife looked at me to see if I believed him. I didn't know what to believe. Then Herr Atzmuller asked me, "My friend, you have all those cigarettes you offered me. Do you suppose I could send them out to the asylum for Adolph? That's what he smokes. Chesterfield cigarettes. He'd be so grateful."

I'd always heard Hitler was quite fastidious and didn't smoke but I promised to keep him in cigarettes. Herr Atzmuller never brought up the documents again.

After dinner we got down to the business of being measured for some new clothes in exchange for the cigarettes, plus I paid him money I'd accumulated from my travels.

When I departed, he held my shoulders, looked me right in the eye and smiled. "Mila, you must know I respect you and your character. Never let that go, and we will always remain friends."

He and his lovely wife did remain friends. On a later visit after his friend Adolph had supposedly received the cigarettes, he surprised me by asking me if I'd like to visit Hitler. I rolled my eyes and tried to imagine it. I turned him down. I may always be sorry but I just couldn't face that maniac. His wife heaved a sigh of relief.

⌐

Back in Salzburg one very cold day, I visited the library, roaming the aisles until my eyes fell on a book called History of Yugoslavia. I drew it out of its musty shelve, sat down and started to read. The words leaped out at me. This Balkans history in German mirrored the same words my Baba told me as a child. I read on in awe.

Here was the truth, the family and my teachers were right. Still, the amazement struck me again. How could that woman without any education teach me this history without written words, only word of mouth?

I stared into space. These were the very words she'd said, I swear. People from the beginning of time must have told the stories over and over, long before writing them down. My throat closed up. I shut the book and left it lying on the table, and I ran out of front door, down the long, wide flight of stairs, across the busy street through traffic, into a snow-covered park. I ran to a bench in a quiet area, sat down and cried my eyes out.

Oh, Baba, I miss you deep into my soul. You are always with me, to guide me and now after this vicious war, your very words come to me through these volumes.

I must do the same. I must pass on our history, people who lost their land, their families, everything dear to them. People who could not understand and love their neighbor must learn never, never to allow such a massive war with nothing good coming out of it. Just destruction of everything we built, everything all our families worked for, our very lives.

Scenes of my Tata's death, the courageous wounded soldiers, the death camps, and now orphaned children selling themselves for food, people starving, unemployment and starvation, the whole destruction of Europe jumped out at me. Relying on the Americans to save us. My sorrow went to the depths of my heart. I felt I could never recover.

I dragged myself up slowly but knew I'd lost some of the bravado of ignorance of that jolly little boy I used to be.

↜

I got the shocking word that one of General Mihailovic's senior commanders had been lured to Belgrade, arrested, recruited by the secret police and sent back to Ravna Gora. Colonel Cortner dug out the facts.

Draza Mihailovic had been lured into a trap. He was falsely accused of collaboration with the Germans as Tito dared not accuse him on his opposition to Communism.

Although the General was subjected to imprisonment, Colonel Cortner assured me was not tortured or drugged. He also gave me the details of his court proceedings, and how he gave his evidence honestly with a clean conscience.

According to the Colonel, the General's last words in court were, "Destiny was merciless towards me when I threw many men into the most difficult whirlwinds. I wanted much, I began much, but internal confusion carried me and my work away."

My heart felt like thousands of pounds of rubble had been laid on it. He didn't deserve that. He was a brave man, although sometimes overcome and unstable in his decision-making from the stormy times, he was not a fanatic.

General Draza Mihailovic, hero of two World Wars, was executed by a firing squad on July 17, bringing sorrow to many sympathetic, long-suffering people and condemnation from Churchill, de Gaulle, Truman, and many others. The only people who could voice their feelings were the Serbs in exile like myself.

I needed to talk to Dihan and tried to find him, calling and asking all over. Dihan, my "big brother" and best friend had disappeared, never to be heard of again. He knew too much. I fell into despair. Why me, God? Why am I left?

What is the point of my existence? I tried to listen to my Baba through my deep sorrow. "When you want to cry; sing, look up to your God and sing."

The rest of my life loomed before me. I would follow her loving advice and live it for all of us.

The End

World War II claimed 1.7 million Yugoslav lives, 11 percent of the prewar population, a mortality second only to that of Poland. About one million of those were killed by other Yugoslavs. The average age of the dead was twenty-two years. The country's major cities, production centers, and communications systems were in ruins, and starvation was widespread.

EPILOGUE

At age 26 in 1951, Mila felt he must leave Europe and going home to Serbia was still not an option. Out of several countries, he chose America. Using his contacts as an ex-patriot, an arrangement was made for Serbian family in Akron, Ohio to sponsor him.

In Linz, Mila met a young Russian Jewish man, Captain Mikowski, who had married a Jewish girl in a prison camp. He was training POW's to fight for the New Kingdom of Israel. Mila argued almost into a fight, that Israel shouldn't be divided and would be gone in 50 years, but they became friends anyway. The Russian wanted to take his father and his pregnant wife with him to America. It turned out his father chose to immigrate to Israel. Mila arranged to leave on the same ship as his new friends.

A group of about 46 displaced persons, mostly families, all traveled on a military ship to New York, U.S. Mila, the youngest of seven single Serbian men, bunked together. After speaking with the Russian captain of the military ship, Mila was assigned as entertainment assistant for the passengers for the duration of the voyage. He loved his assignment providing games and entertainment. Mila offered to become the unofficial interpreter for all the passengers. He hung out with Captain Mikowski and learned about the war from a different perspective.

The voyage, usually taking six or seven days to cross the Atlantic turned into 11 days, as the crew had to stop and help repair a stranded military ship.

Mila discovered the Jews would be the first to disembark at Ellis Island. So anxious to see his new home, he pretended he was Jewish also and got off with Mikowski and his wife. A Rabbi greeted them and asked Mila where his Star of David was.

He used his few new Yiddish words when once more he talked his way out of a situation.

Finally in Akron in April, Mila and the seven single men were housed in a big room with one bathroom in a junky old industrial building. From the first day, the sponsoring families active in the Serbian church, took turns bringing food to them and helped the newcomers find jobs and relocate. Mila soon started working as a "bag boy" in the A&P grocery store struggling with his awful English but talking with everyone.

One day, his sponsor, Mrs. Sivchev came with other ladies bringing food. She wanted to talk to them about joining the choir. She pointed out and invited three young men to dinner at her house nearby on a hill. Mila was not invited. Another lady also bringing food said, "Zorka, what about this handsome young man?" pointing to Mila standing there with a silly grin on his face running his fingers nervously through his curly hair.

"Got damn it, shut up. You pick who you want and I'll pick who I want to come to my house." They argued and Mrs. Sivchev said, "I don't want him there!"

At 5 P.M., one of the other shy guys begged Mila to come with them anyway.

Mila only had an hour to decide and embarrassed, went into the small bathroom The guys finally convinced him to come out and come along. He did.

Mrs. Sivchev opened the door, and gave him a dirty look as he said, "Good evening, Mrs. Sivchev." The daughters and father came right behind to greet the men. Mrs. Sivchev glared at him but invited him in at her husband's request. The other men pushed Mila into the living room.

He learned Mr. and Mrs. Sivchev were both born in Yugoslavia in 1910. They had lived in, then fled to Austria just before WWI broke out.

Their pretty, petite daughter, Dorothy caught Mila's eye immediately. She shyly told him she was the secretary of the church choir.

After a wonderful "Old World dinner," Dorothy asked, "Who can sing? We'd like to have you in the church choir. One of the men said teasingly, "Oh, yes, Mila can sing, he sings on the radio." Another said, "He sings day and night singing all over the place."

"No," Mila said in Serbian, "I said I sang *by* the radio!" He was so nervous, he started joking around in French. He did, however, end up singing off-key in the church choir just to start a romance with Dorothy, much to the dismay of her mother. Soon Dorothy married Mila, becoming the Serbian wife both had always dreamed of.

He learned his sponsors believed in the American Constitution, a concept new to Mila, now called Mike. He might have migrated anywhere but became very happy because he recognized America as the last country on Earth where people can talk openly, express their politics, and argue without fear.

The young determined Mike Cedic, learning English, moved quickly up through the ranks at the grocery business becoming a manager. He earned his citizenship, attended college, and saved his money successfully investing in real estate and the building business, finally earning approval from his mother-in-law. The lifetime marriage of Mike and Dorothy brought success and two boys, now businessmen themselves in Sedona.

In our interviews, now at age 75, Mike told me, "I chose to come to America in 1951 and became a citizen. I was stuck in Austria. I couldn't go back to Yugoslavia because I knew too much, or was presumed dead. I love this country as my home but I care strongly about my homeland, too.

"I can't believe what's happening all over the Balkans. The people including my Serbians are still murdering each other. Killing should never be repeated anywhere on Earth. How could this still be happening? When will my people learn to understand and forgive one another? Unless Americans find a way to teach the people of the Balkans, Afghanistan and other political enemies how to trust and cooperate with each other, they have no business being there!

"Americans are the most misled people around the globe. People born here believe everything they hear and don't even truly appreciate our freedom. You trust other people who hate you and just bumble around as if peace could last forever. Do you know that? And what's more, only two weeks after I arrived in America, the government had the nerve to try to draft me into the Army to go to Korea, a war invented by your own heroes, Henry Kissinger and Richard Nixon!

"I said, 'No! I want nothing to do with your phony wars,' and I nearly got arrested but I wasn't drafted, either! Yet, I love this country as the best place on Earth. No one in America should run for office unless parents and grandparents were born here. This is the only way we'll all survive." His voice became mellow; "Even today most of the Balkan states people never travel away from their villages and don't trust anyone they don't know. As Mike spoke, he heard himself repeating his grandmother's words, "The Germans still think the Balkan people are the most dangerous people on Earth."

Mike slid down in his chair, head bowed, feeling strength ebbing out his body. The old shrapnel wounds in his leg throbbed. Waves of fatigue rolled over him. He looked down at his wrinkled, spotted hands. "Why am I still here when so many are dead?" His nightmares tortured him and his heart felt sick. "Where did that boy they called Mila go?"

This is a true story —Jeanie Colp